# Modern Slavery Survivor Pathways

This book presents a critical chronology of the modern slavery survivor journey in the UK, from intervention by the authorities to long-term recovery. The work examines the modern slavery survivor pathway and assesses the support systems available to survivors throughout this process. It also explores links to other traumatic crimes and investigates how the role of 'witness' in the criminal justice system impacts survivors' experiences. The work showcases findings from interviews with frontline practitioners alongside analysis of government publications and independent reports. It emphasises the importance of holistic care pathways with a consistent, benchmark standard of support across all services, including advocacy for each individual. It further argues that the UK government needs to extend its anti-slavery efforts towards long-term support and understanding of survivor needs, which should include a focus on survivor narratives and input. It is argued that this would not only improve recovery outcomes but would advance the criminal justice process in this area through witness retention and stronger evidence. The book will be of interest to academics, researchers and policy-makers in the areas of human rights, criminal justice, social justice and victimology. Based on international legal instruments, the work will appeal to an international readership.

**Anne-Marie Greenslade** is a senior lecturer in law at Leeds Beckett University, UK.

## Routledge Studies in Law, Rights and Justice

Series Editor: Chris Monaghan

*He is the Head of Law and a Principal Lecturer in Law at the University of Worcester, and holds a PhD from the Dickson Poon School of Law at King's College London. He has published widely on aspects of public law.*

*Routledge Studies in Law, Rights and Justice* seeks to publish leading monographs and edited collections that explore the interplay between rights and justice across different areas of law and legal practice. The series serves as a home for scholars working in areas such as human rights, social justice, constitutional justice, business and human rights, equality rights and civil justice. It encourages authors to address the theoretical and practical aspects of the application of rights, the achievability of justice in these uncertain times, and the methods available to individuals, organisations, and states to achieve justice. *Routledge Studies in Law, Rights and Justice* embraces both scholarship from a national and international viewpoint and encourages authors to explore rights and justice from a global perspective. It strives to break down existing disciplinary silos and encourage collaboration, which offers the opportunity to publish thought provoking, original and cutting-edge work. The aim is to foster debates, build bridges between different areas of scholarship, and encourage a wider perspective on the underlying issues that might limit the applicability of rights, or render justice difficult to achieve.

*Routledge Studies in Law, Rights and Justice* primarily consider rights and justice from a legal perspective, but does however, welcome submissions that take a broader view and engage with the wider socio-economic, political, and social context. The series editor is very keen to consider works by established and early-career academics, and submissions are encouraged from scholars based all around the world.

Titles in this series:

**The Evolution of International Criminal Procedure**
From Nuremberg and Tokyo to the International Criminal Court
*Giovanni Chiarini*

**Modern Slavery Survivor Pathways**
Policy, Legislation and Practice in the UK
*Anne-Marie Greenslade*

# Modern Slavery Survivor Pathways

## Policy, Legislation and Practice in the UK

**Anne-Marie Greenslade**

Routledge
Taylor & Francis Group
LONDON AND NEW YORK

First published 2025
by Routledge
4 Park Square, Milton Park, Abingdon, Oxon OX14 4RN

and by Routledge
605 Third Avenue, New York, NY 10158

*Routledge is an imprint of the Taylor & Francis Group, an informa business*



*British Library Cataloguing-in-Publication Data*
A catalogue record for this book is available from the British Library

ISBN: 978-1-032-62243-9 (hbk)
ISBN: 978-1-032-63980-2 (pbk)
ISBN: 978-1-032-63989-5 (ebk)

DOI: 10.4324/9781032639895

Typeset in Galliard
by Apex CoVantage, LLC

# Contents

# Figures

# Tables

# 1 Introduction

The enactment of the Modern Slavery Act[1] (MSA) in 2015 initiated something of a sea change in public awareness of modern slavery and human trafficking. Craig et al. highlight early awareness of the phenomenon, stating that at the turn of the 21st century, most of the British public's connotations of 'slavery' were either:

- William Wilberforce;
- The historic transatlantic slave trade;
- The Fairtrade movement/poor labour conditions in developing nations;
- Child sexual exploitation/sex tourism in South East Asia.[2]

Even in the early days of the MSA, however, there were already several statutory and independent organisations across the UK that had been either designated or created to provide support to survivors of this trauma.[3] Around the same time, it appeared that law enforcement for modern slavery was in the same place that child sexual exploitation (CSE) policy had been fifteen years before. The parallels of exploitative, abusive relationships in domestic abuse, sexual violence, CSE and modern slavery have been extensively flagged,[4] and although there are more specific needs within each area, the foundations are remarkably similar.

Victims of any trauma are usually juggling multiple issues concerning their health, family, finances and accommodation. For modern slavery survivors, it

1 Modern Slavery Act 2015.

2 Gary Craig and others (eds), *The Modern Slavery Agenda: Policy, Politics and Practice in the UK* (Policy Press 2019).

3 The Salvation Army currently holds the largest government contract in this respect, taking referrals from across the whole of England and Wales. The majority of charities, for example, Hope for Justice, Unseen and Snowdrop, are regionally based.

4 Susan SM Edwards, 'Coercion and Compulsion – Re-Imagining Crimes and Defences' (2016) *Criminal Law Review* 876; Paola Michelle Contreras, Diya Kallivayalil and Judith Lewis Herman, 'Psychotherapy in the Aftermath of Human Trafficking: Working through the Consequences of Psychological Coercion' (2017) 40 *Women & Therapy* 31.

DOI: 10.4324/9781032639895-1

is also crucial to identify their additional needs and how they are addressed within the wider system. With the nascent but growing organisational support networks across the UK, this book examines what levels of support are offered and how consistent these are from region to region. A 2014 UN report stated that globally, 30% of *detected* victims were men and boys,[5] while UK figures for the first three quarters of 2019 consistently indicate that male victims make up approximately two-thirds of referred potential victims.[6] This creates a new dimension to the nature of support given, as most adult services for trauma support have grown up around feminist models, based on the traditionally gendered nature of domestic and sexual violence.[7] Additionally, as modern slavery often involves trafficking across international borders, language barriers and precarious immigration statuses[8] are added to support needs, creating another layer of complexity. The aim of this work, therefore, is to examine the modern slavery survivor pathway from intervention to recovery. By evaluating key aspects of policy and assessing the successes and limitations of these areas in practice, it is anticipated that best practice initiatives can be implemented as a nationwide standard for all survivors who access these services.

Throughout, this book refers to 'victims' and 'survivors' simultaneously; for clarification, 'victim' is used to represent someone currently experiencing enslavement and exploitation or to indicate their status within the criminal justice system, whereas 'survivor' denotes those who are no longer under control in captivity. For this reason, the use of 'survivor' in the book's title demonstrates the focus on post-intervention pathways.

## 1.1 Background: insights from practitioner experience

I became interested this subject when I was a frontline practitioner for the survivor-supporting charity Rape Crisis in the north west of England. As an

5 United Nations Office on Drugs and Crime, *Global Report on Trafficking in Persons* (United Nations 2014).

6 National Crime Agency, *National Referral Mechanism Statistics Quarter 1 2019 – January to March* (National Crime Agency 2019); Home Office, *National Referral Mechanism Statistics Quarter 2 2019 – April to June* (Home Office 2019); Home Office, *National Referral Mechanism Statistics Quarter 3 2019 – July to September* (Home Office 2019).

7 Kathleen E Krieger and others, 'Evaluating Human Trafficking Service Programs: What Can Be Learned from Domestic Violence Service Program Evaluations' (2020) 8(5) *Journal of Human Trafficking* 157–183 <https://doi.org/10.1080/23322705.2020.1784686>; Shanti Joy Kulkarni and others, 'Successful Rules Reduction Implementation Process in Domestic Violence Shelters: From Vision to Practice' (2019) 64(2) *Social Work* 147; Rebecca J Macy and Natalie Johns, 'Aftercare Services for International Sex Trafficking Survivors: Informing US Service and Program Development in an Emerging Practice Area' (2011) 12(2) *Trauma, Violence & Abuse* 87.

8 Independent Chief Inspector of Borders and Immigration, *An Inspection of Border Force's Identification and Treatment of Potential Victims of Modern Slavery: July to October 2016* (Williams Lea Group on behalf of the Controller of Her Majesty's Stationery Office 2017).

independent sexual violence adviser (ISVA) for victims of violent and traumatic sexual crimes, I had a first-hand view of their experiences in the criminal justice system (CJS): reporting to the police, finding out if and when their perpetrator was arrested, the long, drawn-out wait for a Crown Prosecution Service (CPS) decision, and finally – if it ever got that far – the fear and distress of providing witness evidence to the courts. The service was provided at a local level for clients based in that community, regardless of where the crime occurred (and consequently which Constabulary and Crown Court would process the case). We were available through professional contacts or self-referral to anyone, male or female, over the age of thirteen who had experienced rape or sexual abuse at any point in their lives. This meant that many service users were survivors of CSE or domestic abuse and in some cases both, reflecting the crossover element to these crimes. The client caseload was therefore diverse, often with nuanced and complex needs. They were frequently grappling with myriad other issues, such as mental and physical health problems, changing family dynamics and financial difficulties, sometimes as a result of the abuse. A small but significant proportion of clients had also developed unhelpful coping strategies which had led to further problems of addiction or other long-term issues. Almost all of them felt that their life was on hold until the case was resolved either way, although the majority were seeking justice, which for them meant seeing their perpetrator behind bars. For a few, simply speaking out to the authorities and being believed provided catharsis, especially in historical abuse cases.

The fact was, a disproportionate number of survivors failed to even make it to court. This reflected the national picture,[9] with statistics showing a steady decline in rape and sexual assault prosecution figures over the past few years.[10] Some clients made the decision to withdraw their police complaint early on; recovery does not necessarily begin and end with a jury verdict. Where the case continued, the majority of assigned police officers were professional, empathic and seemed genuinely motivated to pursue a thorough investigation. There were of course time constraints: even before years of austerity measures that led to a 13% drop in officers,[11] the police were burdened with heavy workloads and, where the case concerned historical abuse, the amount of available evidence was severely limited. Nonetheless, the working relationship between my organisation and the local constabularies ensured that there was enough communication to keep clients informed as to the progress of their complaint and when the case was likely to be passed to the CPS for a decision on charging. This communication, and the general advocacy of the ISVA role, proved to be vital for both the wellbeing of the client and the potential outcome of the case, a factor

9 Ministry of Justice, Home Office and the Office for National Statistics, *An Overview of Sexual Offending in England and Wales: Statistics Bulletin* (Ministry of Justice 2013).

10 Home Office, *Crime Outcomes in England and Wales: Year Ending March 2019: Statistical Bulletin HOSB 12/19* (Home Office 2019).

11 Jodie Hargreaves and others, *Police Workforce, England and Wales, 30 September 2016 Statistical Bulletin 02/17* (Home Office 2017).

that was reiterated in an independent review in 2010.[12] Client expectations were frequently much higher than the reality: many assumed that the case would automatically culminate in a trial and that the court date would follow their complaint in a matter of weeks. On average, my cases took nine months from the initial police complaint to providing evidence in court.[13] One historical case took over two years to investigate, ultimately resulting in a CPS decision not to charge the perpetrator. Part of the ISVA role, therefore, was to manage those expectations and support clients emotionally throughout the process.

Frequently, the CPS made their decision without explaining their reasoning to the victim concerned. Where information was provided, responsibility for No Further Action (NFA) appeared to revert to the victim; the CPS would proffer their opinion that the victim was not up to acting as witness or that the victim's 'credibility' would be questionable in court. These observations have been borne out in a 2013 study, which described this approach as a 'focus on victims,' where 'belief in the victim's account is central and is at issue.'[14] The findings provided examples of cases where CPS concerns about not achieving conviction had led to NFA, resulting in those rape victims experiencing a negative perspective of the CJS. One relatively mainstream illustration of this is in the BBC miniseries 'Three Girls,'[15] which dramatised the events surrounding the Rochdale child sexual trafficking case. In one scene, a CPS lawyer asks, 'What is the point in subjecting a girl like Holly to a trial if a jury is not going to believe she's telling the truth?'[16] Later, a heated debate between two police officers casts further light on the criminal justice system concept of witness credibility:

| | |
|---|---|
| *Police Officer 1:* | 'Look, I'm sorry, but we cannot put her in a witness box.' |
| *Police Officer 2:* | 'No. I don't believe it. No' |
| *PO 1:* | 'She's just too volatile.' |
| *PO 2:* | 'What she's been through and what the other girls have gone through, and more . . .' |
| *PO 1:* | 'I know, but a jury-' |
| *PO 2:* | 'A jury can see a damaged person when there's one in front of them.' |
| *PO 1:* | 'But she will not go down well with a jury. . . . It's just a statement of fact about what the legal system demands'[17] |

12 Baroness Vivien Stern, *The Stern Review: A Report by Baroness Vivien Stern CBE of an Independent Review into How Rape Complaints Are Handled by Public Authorities in England and Wales* (Government Equalities Office and Home Office 2010).

13 Based on quarterly statistical reports which the organisation was required to draft and submit as part of our funding contracts.

14 Marianne Hester, *From Report to Court: Rape Cases and the Criminal Justice System in the North East* (Report of a research project, University of Bristol in association with the Northern Rock Foundation 2013) 16.

15 Philippa Lowthorpe, 'Three Girls' [Television broadcast] (Drama, BBC, 1 May 2017).

16 ibid.

17 ibid.

In fact, the Rochdale case was initially dropped due to concerns over the chief witness's credibility[18] despite the CPS representative never meeting the victim. Further evidence also shows that the CPS figures for rape charges fell by 23% from 2016/17 to 2017/18, despite incidences of reporting rising exponentially each year.[19]

Like rape, CSE and domestic abuse survivors, victims of modern slavery frequently exhibit vulnerability and post-trauma,[20] and these parallels are discussed throughout this book, particularly in Chapters 4, 6 and 8, which address short-term support, therapeutic intervention and long-term support, respectively. Chapter 7 examines the criminal justice system and discusses the transition from 'victim' to 'witness.' Despite the similarities to other traumatic crimes, modern slavery survivors often have additional needs that require specific support provisions. For example, a significant majority of potential victims are not UK nationals; consequently, a pertinent issue for many victims concerns immigration, which is explored in Chapter 5.

Overall, the phenomenon of slavery within legal and academic discourse has evolved to produce a body of legislation and commentary that draw in part from other phenomena while incorporating features that are unique to the survivor experience. The following section thus charts the legal and political background to the UK's modern slavery approach, showing how various historical factors continue to resonate in current policy decisions and awareness.

## 1.2 Legal development and definition of modern slavery

Slave trade thrived in Africa between the 16th and 18th centuries,[21] but by the end of the latter, an abolitionist movement had gained momentum.[22] Following the Somerset case in 1772,[23] which held that slavery was unsupported by English law, the slave trade was eventually abolished in Great Britain in 1807.[24] This was followed by the 13th Amendment to the US constitution,[25] with the

18 Anonymous (Girl A), *Girl A: The Truth about the Rochdale Sex Ring by the Victim Who Stopped Them* (Ebury Press 2013).

19 EVAW, 'Collapse in Number of Rape Cases Charged by CPS Despite Huge Rise in Reports' (*End Violence against Women*) <www.endviolenceagainstwomen.org.uk/collapse-in-number-of-rape-cases-charged-by-cps-despite-huge-rise-in-reports/> accessed 13 March 2020.

20 Edwards (n 4) 876; Contreras and others (n 4) 31.

21 Nlerum S Okugbule, 'Combating the "New Slavery" in Nigeria: An Appraisal of Legal and Policy Responses to Human Trafficking' (2013) 57(1) *Journal of African Law* 57.

22 Jean Allain and Robin Hickey, 'Property and the Definition of Slavery' (2012) *International and Comparative Law Quarterly* 915.

23 *Somerset v Stewart* [1772] 98 ER 499.

24 EachOther, 'Article 4 – Prohibition of Slavery and Forced Labour' (*EachOther*) <https://eachother.org.uk/article-4-prohibition-of-slavery-and-forced-labour/> accessed 12 November 2020.

25 Constitution of the United States (passed by Congress 31 January 1865, ratified 6 December 1865) Amendment XIII <www.archives.gov/exhibits/charters/constitution_amendments_11-27.html> accessed 10 January 2019.

whole of Europe making a commitment to end African slavery by 1885.[26] By the inter-war period of the 20th century, the modern international community dawned with the formation of the League of Nations, and with it came the development of modern international law. Reinforcing and enhancing domestic abolition laws, the League adopted the 1926 Slavery Convention,[27] which states: 'slavery is the status or condition of a person over whom any or all of the powers attaching to the right of ownership are exercised.'[28] This was followed by the International Labour Organisation's (ILO) 1930 Convention on Forced Labour[29] prohibiting 'all work or service which is exacted from any person under the menace of any penalty and for which the said person has not offered himself voluntarily.'[30] Following the atrocities of World War II, the United Nations' (UN) Universal Declaration of Human Rights included Article 4, providing that 'No one shall be held in slavery or servitude; slavery and the slave trade shall be prohibited in all their forms.'[31] In 1953, the UN's Protocol[32] further increased the 1926 Convention's remit 'to involve international cooperation in addressing the economic and social factors that supported the existence of contemporary slavery'[33] with a Supplementary Convention three years later to 'intensify national as well as international efforts'[34] in the abolition of slavery. It also expanded the definition of contemporary slavery to include debt bondage, serfdom, the selling of women by their families for marriage, certain forms of abuse of women and the buying and selling of children for labour or prostitution,[35] while the UN's International Covenant on Civil and Political Rights (ICCPR) later precluded all 'forced or compulsory labour.'[36] Regional systems have also incorporated the message, including the

26 EachOther (n 24).
27 Convention to Suppress the Slave Trade and Slavery (adopted 25 September 1926, entered into force 9 March 1927) 60 LNTS 253 (Slavery Convention).
28 ibid art 1(1).
29 International Labour Organisation (ILO) Forced Labour Convention (adopted 28 June 1930, entered into force 1 May 1932) C29.
30 ibid art 2(1).
31 Universal Declaration of Human Rights (adopted 10 December 1948) UNGA Res 217 A(III) (UDHR) art 4.
32 Protocol amending the Slavery Convention (adopted 7 December 1953, entered into force 7 July 1955) 212 UNTS 17.
33 Jessica Bell, 'Contemporary Slavery and International Law' (2008) *Human Rights and Human Welfare* 35, 36 <www.du.edu/korbel/hrhw/researchdigest/slavery/index.html> accessed 10 January 2017.
34 Supplementary Convention on the Abolition of Slavery, the Slave Trade, and Institutions and Practices Similar to Slavery (adopted 30 April 1956, entered into force 30 April 1957) 266 UNTS 3, preamble.
35 Bell (n 33) 35.
36 International Covenant on Civil and Political Rights (adopted 16 December 1966, entered into force 23 March 1976) 999 UNTS 171 (ICCPR) art 8.

European Convention on Human Rights[37] (ECHR) and the African Charter.[38] Responding to new international challenges at the end of the century, the UN established the Convention against Transnational Organized Crime[39] with a supplementary Protocol to Prevent, Suppress and Punish Trafficking in Persons, Especially Women and Children[40] (the Palermo Protocol) to 'fill the gaps.'[41] Additionally, the ILO's 1999 Convention Concerning the Prohibition and Immediate Action for the Elimination of the Worst Forms of Child Labour[42] demands 'protection against the sale and trafficking of children, the use, procuring or offering of a child for prostitution, for the production of pornography or for pornographic performances.'[43]

It is worth remarking that many of these instruments place an emphasis on sexual exploitation, with particular regard to women and girls. This is largely a continuum of concerns over 'white slavery,'[44] born of a moral panic at the turn of the 20th century in which it was believed that white girls in Europe and the United States were being kidnapped and sold into prostitution.[45] Although the practice of trafficking young women for sexual exploitation was a real problem at the time, around 99% of victims were not white.[46] Current feminist theory suggests that the panic arose amidst '"anxieties about changing gender, sex, class and race relations at the turn of the century"'[47] and 'concern for the virtue of white women';[48] however, it is notable that similar fears were not raised with regard to women of colour. One hundred years later, the 'new challenges' that led to the drafting of the Palermo Protocol were centred around the flow

37 Convention for the Protection of Human Rights and Fundamental Freedoms (European Convention on Human Rights, as amended) (adopted 4 November 1950, entered into force 3 September 1953) ETS 5 (ECHR) art 4.

38 African Charter on Human and Peoples' Rights (adopted 27 June 1981, entered into force 21 October 1986) (1982) 21 ILM 58 (African Charter).

39 United Nations General Assembly Convention against Transnational Organised Crime (adopted 15 November 2000, entered into force 29 September 2003) UN Doc. A/55/383.

40 United Nations General Assembly Protocol to Prevent, Suppress and Punish Trafficking in Persons, especially Women and Children (adopted 15 November 2000, entered into force 25 December 2003) 2237 UNTS 319 (Palermo Protocol).

41 Harmen van der Wilt, 'Trafficking in Human Beings, Enslavement, Crimes Against Humanity: Unravelling the Concepts' (2014) 13(2) *Chinese Journal of International Law* 297, 301.

42 International Labour Organization (ILO) Worst Forms of Child Labour Convention (adopted 17 June 1999, entered into force 19 November 2000) C182.

43 Kadriye Bakirci, 'Human Trafficking and Forced Labour: A Criticism of the International Labour Organisation' (2009) 16(2) *JFC* 160, 164.

44 Kevin Bales and Becky Cornell, 'The Next Step in the Fight against Human Trafficking: Outlawing the Trade in Slave-made Goods' (2006) 1 *Intercultural Human Rights Law Review* 211.

45 Jennifer K Lobasz, 'Beyond Border Security: Feminist Approaches to Human Trafficking' (2009) 18 *Security Studies* 319.

46 ibid.

47 Wendy Chapkis, *Live Sex Acts: Women Performing Erotic Labour* (Routledge 1997), cited in Lobasz (n 45) 319, 342.

48 Lobasz (n 45) 319, 342.

of trafficked sex workers from the former USSR, where newly independent states struggled to quickly transition their socio-political economies from the Soviet regime to a more globalised, liberal model.[49] Most of these victims were also white and female,[50] and 'Natashas' euphemistically became shorthand for any young woman caught up in this type of exploitation.[51] Again, modern discourse suggests that the connection between this phenomenon and the creation of new anti-trafficking laws betrays a hierarchical agenda:

> Until it became possible to present the victims as like 'one of our own,' trafficking was a low priority. Unlike the women from Asia and Africa, who were women of color, the new trafficking victims were more likely to be recognized as just like 'girls next door.' The old image of white slaves was invoked, and this resonated with the developed countries of the West.[52]

It should also be considered that, despite a plethora of international legal instruments, a major issue appears to be a lack of legal clarity on the terms 'slavery,' 'servitude,' 'forced labour' or 'trafficking.' 'Modern slavery' is usually labelled thus simply due to the fact it is universally prohibited and therefore legally differentiated from the property law-based slavery of previous centuries[53]. The Palermo Protocol itself provides this definition of 'trafficking' as:

> the recruitment, transportation, transfer, harbouring or receipt of persons, by means of the threat or use of force or other forms of coercion, of abduction, of fraud, of deception, of the abuse of power or of a position of vulnerability or of the giving or receiving of payments or benefits to achieve the consent of a person having control over another person, for the purpose of exploitation. Exploitation shall include, at a minimum, the exploitation of the prostitution of others or other forms of sexual exploitation, forced labour or services, slavery or practices similar to slavery, servitude or the removal of organs.[54]

Trafficking does not even require movement; put in the context of the illegal drug trade, this means it is the selling or transfer of ownership that constitutes the act of trafficking.[55]

49 Donna Hughes, 'The Natasha Trade: The Transnational Shadow Market of Trafficking in Women' (2000) 53(2) *Journal of International Affairs* 625.

50 Lobasz (n 45) 319.

51 Victor Malarek, *The Natashas: Inside the New Global Sex Trade* (Arcade Publishing 2004).

52 Galma Jahic and James O Finckenauer, 'Representations and Misrepresentations of Human Trafficking' (2005) 8(3) *Trends in Organised Crime* 24, 26.

53 Jean Allain, '*Rantsev v Cyprus and Russia*: The European Court of Human Rights and Trafficking as Slavery' (2010) 10(3) *Human Rights Law Review* 546.

54 (n 40) art 3(a).

55 Bakirci (n 43) 160.

Under this umbrella there also exists a multitude of industries into which people can be trafficked, including: 'agriculture/farm labour, factory work/"sweat shops", domestic servitude/housekeeping/nannies, construction, food service, entertainment/modelling [sic], peddling.'[56] Additionally, activities such as begging and drug transporting, although not strictly 'work,' have been included in ILO Convention No. 182,[57] acknowledging the forms of forced labour that children can be trafficked into.[58] In 2012 the UN Special Rapporteur for contemporary forms of slavery, including its causes and its consequences, added forced marriage as a thematic concern,[59] and this category is now included in estimated global slavery figures.[60] As the definitions and theoretical principles have expanded, so the 'conceptual borders between enslavement and trafficking in human beings'[61] have increasingly blurred. This could be a double-edged sword. Potentially, concepts of trafficking and slavery 'cover such a wide range of practices as to be virtually meaningless,'[62] but this also means that a 'wide range of exploitative practices'[63] are now included, which will allow greater scope for legal interpretation.

This can be witnessed through key international case law, which has further refined and clarified the legal definition of 'slavery' in human rights terms. *Kunarac*[64] defined enslavement as a crime against humanity, adding it to the realms of humanitarian law. *Siliadin*[65] required the European Court of Human Rights (ECtHR) to address Article 4 in terms of its horizontal effect[66] (the capacity for individuals to enforce their rights against the state) and was unanimous in its verdict that France's failure to provide suitable protection against servitude and forced labour violated the Applicant's Article 4 rights.[67] However, the Court found that the 'classic' meaning of slavery was 'only applicable where there was a *de jure* right of ownership over a person.'[68] As proprietary rights to ownership of people have been abolished, this is a 'legal

56 ibid 160, 163.
57 (n 42) C182.
58 Bakirci (n 43) 160.
59 United Nations General Assembly (UNGA), 'Report of the Special Rapporteur on Contemporary Forms of Slavery, Including Its Causes and Consequences' (10 July 2012) UN Human Rights Council 21st Session Agenda item 3 UN Doc A/HRC/21/41.
60 Walk Free Foundation, *Global Slavery Index* (Walk Free Foundation 2018) <www.globalslaveryindex.org/resources/downloads/> accessed 16 June 2021.
61 van der Wilt (n 41) 297, 305.
62 Suzanne Miers, *Slavery in the Twentieth Century* (AltaMira Press 2003) 453, quoted in Allain and Hickey (n 22) 915, 918.
63 ibid.
64 *Prosecutor v Kunarac et al.* (Judgment) ICTY-96–23&23/1 (12 June 2002).
65 *Siliadin v. France* (Application no. 73316/01) ECHR 2005-VII.
66 Virginia Mantouvalou, 'Servitude and Forced Labour in the 21st Century: The Human Rights of Domestic Workers' (2006) 35(4) *Industrial Law Journal* 395.
67 (n 37) art 4.
68 Allain and Hickey (n 22) 915, 921.

impossibility,'[69] the logical conclusion being that no incidents of slavery can ever be claimed in Europe. However, the facts of *Mani*,[70] heard by the Community Court of Justice of the Economic Community of West African States (ECOWAS), were so compelling that 'it was submitted on her behalf that a clearer case of slavery would be difficult to envisage.'[71] Crucially though, the ECOWAS Court reaffirmed the *de facto* definition of slavery by validating the interpretations regarding powers of ownership and control as appropriate indicia of enslavement.[72] Most recently, the ECtHR in *Rantsev*[73] attempted to reconcile 'trafficking,' a term not specifically outlined in the ECHR, with concepts of enslavement. Unfortunately, the Court did not elucidate on whether trafficking, in this instance, could be categorised as 'slavery,' 'servitude' or 'forced labour.'[74] Nonetheless, it 'made a determination that trafficking is based on slavery,'[75] widening both the definition of slavery and the jurisprudence of the ECtHR. Significantly, *Rantsev* demanded further positive obligations from states to protect victims of trafficking and extended these obligations beyond criminal law, building on the recommendations from *Siliadin*.[76]

These rulings 'highlighted the need to address the most severe instances of labour exploitation,'[77] and the European Union (EU) took steps to tackle the issue. The Convention on Action Against Trafficking in Human Beings[78] was entered into force in 2008, and in 2011, a directive on preventing and combating trafficking in human beings and protecting its victims[79] was introduced. The UK followed suit in 2009, setting up the National Referral Mechanism (NRM) to identify victims of modern slavery and later creating a Victim Care Contract (VCC) to support and assist their recovery. Although human trafficking had been criminalised in the UK under the Coroners and Justice Act,[80] the government fulfilled its commitment to the EU directive by drafting a new

69 Allain (n 53) 546, 557.

70 *Hadijatou Mani Koraou v The Republic of Niger* (Judgment) ECW/CCJ/JUD/06/08 (27 October 2008).

71 Helen Duffy, 'Hadijatou Mani Koroua v Niger: Slavery Unveiled by the ECOWAS Court' (2009) 9(1) *Human Rights Law Review* 151, 160.

72 ibid 151.

73 *Rantsev v Cyprus and Russia* (Application no. 25965/04) ECHR, 7 January 2010.

74 van der Wilt (n 41) 297.

75 Allain (n 53) 546, 553.

76 Ryszard Piotrowicz, 'States' Obligations under Human Rights Law towards Victims of Trafficking in Human Beings: Positive Developments in Positive Obligations' (2012) 24(2) *International Journal of Refugee Law* 181.

77 Virginia Mantouvalou, 'The UK Modern Slavery Act 2015 Three Years On' (2018) 81(6) Modern Law Review 1017, 1020.

78 Council of Europe Convention on Action against Trafficking in Human Beings (adopted 16 May 2005, entered into force 1 February 2008) CETS 197.

79 Directive 2011/36/EU of the European Parliament and of the Council of Europe on preventing and combating trafficking in human beings and protecting its victims (replacing Council Framework Decision 2002/629/JHA) (5 April 2011).

80 Coroners and Justice Act 2009 s71.

piece of legislation that specifically made provisions for the offences of slavery and human trafficking. Thus, in 2015, the Modern Slavery Act was born. The statute consequently sits within the continuum of the criminal approach to modern slavery and human trafficking,[81] with a greater focus on perpetrators and organised criminal networks than labour law or human rights.[82]

In order to bring about any justice, trafficking has to be detected, which is extremely problematic, due to the very nature of the 'powers of ownership' exercised by traffickers.[83] Given the necessary covertness of trafficking, there is consequently an 'absence of hard data,'[84] and any available statistics are so varied as to be virtually useless. Most recent estimates suggest that there are 40.3 million victims worldwide,[85] while a previous estimate of approximately 10–13,000[86] victims in the UK alone was indicated to be 'the tip of the iceberg.'[87] In July 2020, the UK estimate rose to 100,000 victims,[88] although this figure was extrapolated from the data of one police force (West Midlands). During the same period, a total of 7,779 modern slavery crimes were recorded by the police across the whole of the UK.[89] Therefore, the 'dark figure' of slavery is as hard to detect as it is to calculate.

A small but significant number of academics have been reviewing the MSA and NRM since their inceptions, and this work was instructive as a foundation for my own study: Craig,[90] Elliott[91] and Mantouvalou,[92] for example, have

81 Idil Atak and James C Simeon, 'Human Trafficking: Mapping the Legal Boundaries of International Refugee Law and Criminal Justice' (2014) 12(5) *Journal of International Criminal Justice* 1019.

82 Ruth van Dyke, 'The UK's Response to Modern Slavery: Law, Policy and Politics' in Gary Craig and others (eds), *The Modern Slavery Agenda: Policy, Politics and Practice in the UK* (Policy Press 2019).

83 Suzanne Egan, 'Tackling the Rise of Child Labour in Europe: Homework for the European Court of Human Rights' (2015) 64(3) *International and Comparative Law Quarterly* 601.

84 Anne Gallagher, 'The Global Slavery Index: Seduction and Obfuscation' (4 December 2014) 50(50) *Inclusive Democracy* 2.

85 Walk Free Foundation, *Global Slavery Index* (Walk Free Foundation 2018) <www.globalslaveryindex.org/resources/downloads/> accessed 16 June 2021.

86 Independent Anti-Slavery Commissioner, *Independent Anti-Slavery Commissioner Strategic Plan 2015–17* (Independent Anti-Slavery Commissioner 2017).

87 BBC News, 'Modern Slavery and Trafficking 'in Every UK Town and City' *BBC News* (10 August 2017) <www.bbc.co.uk/news/uk-40885353> accessed 14 November 2017.

88 The Centre for Social Justice and Justice and Care, *It Still Happens Here: Fighting UK Slavery in the 2020s* (CSJ/Justice and Care 2020) <www.centreforsocialjustice.org.uk/wp-content/uploads/2020/07/It-Still-Happens-Here.pdf> accessed 16 June 2021.

89 HM Government, *2020 UK Annual Report on Modern Slavery* (HM Government 2020).

90 Gary Craig, 'The UK's Modern Slavery Legislation: An Early Assessment of Progress' (2017) 5(2) *Social Inclusion* 16.

91 Jess Elliott, 'The National Referral Mechanism: Querying the Response of "First Responders" and the Competence of "Competent Authorities"' (2016) 30(1) *Journal of Immigration, Asylum and Nationality Law* 9.

92 Virginia Mantouvalou, 'Modern Slavery: The UK Response' (2010) 39(4) *Industrial Law Journal* 425; Mantouvalou (n 77) 1017.

produced several critiques on the UK's anti-slavery approach. Much of their research was doctrinal in nature, although some scholars, including Mantouvalou, have worked in partnership with some of the organisations that provide frontline services to modern slavery survivors. Their findings and recommendations identified some of the issues that currently exist, such as the change in UK visa rules for Overseas Domestic Workers and how this has negatively impacted their rights and immigration statuses, ultimately putting them at higher risk of domestic servitude and abuse[93] (see Chapters 2 and 5). Wider searches produced literature relating to the structural causes of modern slavery,[94] while there is a plethora of research on human trafficking and modern slavery in the international sphere from authors such as Bales,[95] alongside a substantial amount of US-based research. Much of this is couched in the procurement and exploitation process rather than post-intervention pathways, and a majority of the available literature on aftercare – in keeping with the previously mentioned themes – focuses on survivors of sex trafficking.[96] This showed that there is currently scant academic understanding of the survivor experience beyond slavery, confirming the gap in literature that this book aims to fill.

## 1.3 Methodology

Although we are beginning to establish some statistical knowledge of the UK's modern slavery support networks through official government records, the lived reality for survivors within the system is still largely unknown. Drawing on the experiences of those at the heart of the subject can result in information that challenges established views.[97] Therefore, this book draws on qualitative data to gauge real, lived experiences from those who were best placed to see the direct outcomes of the UK's modern slavery policies: practitioners from frontline agencies and support services. There is no substitute for being

93 Amy Weatherburn, 'The Impact of the 2012 Domestic Workers in a Private Household Visa on Human Trafficking for Domestic Servitude' (2016) 30(3) *Journal of Immigration Asylum and Nationality Law* 204.

94 Hannah Lewis and Louise Waite, 'Migrant Illegality, Slavery and Exploitative Work' in G Craig and others (eds), *The Modern Slavery Agenda: Policy, Politics and Practice in the UK* (Policy Press 2019); Steve French, 'Between Globalisation and Brexit: Migration, Ppay and the Road to Modern Slavery in the UK Hospitality Industry' (2018) 8(1) *Research in Hospitality Management* 23.

95 Kevin Bales, *Disposable People: New Slavery in the Modern Economy* (University of California Press 2000); Kevin Bales, *Blood and Earth: Modern Slavery, Ecocide, and the Secret to Saving the World* (Random House 2016).

96 Alexandra C Duncan and Dana DeHart, 'Provider Perspectives on Sex Trafficking: Victim Pathways, Service Needs, & Blurred Boundaries' (2019) 14(4) *Victims & Offenders* 510; Macy and Johns (n 7) 87; April Rieger, 'Missing the Mark: Why the Trafficking Victims Protection Act Fails to Protect Sex Trafficking Victims in the United States' (2007) 30 *Harvard Journal of Law & Gender* 231.

97 Martyn Hammersley, 'On Feminist Methodology' (1992) *Sociology* 28(2).

engaged every day, over a period of years, in direct contact with both the system and the people it aims to assist. Frontline practitioners are situated within a field where their experience gives them a huge insight into the realities of human lives, and they often intuitively develop an awareness of patterns and flaws in the process.[98] Key support workers will use this to make decisions about the care pathways of their clients and to develop the provisions of their organisation.

Participants have been pseudonymised and details anonymised to ensure confidentiality, although they were given the opportunity to grant permission for specific mention of areas of good practice. Only one participant requested complete anonymisation. The interview data included throughout this book is always referenced as such, using pseudonyms 'David,' 'Ayesha,' 'Caroline' and so on throughout, with towns and cities also attributed. Quotes are generally inserted ad verbatim; however, where they have been edited to delete superfluous detail (for instance, context that has already been established) this is indicated with . . . . Edits to the actual language, for example, place or organisation names, are for anonymisation purposes only.

Two underlying feelings came out of every interview: all participants clearly felt passionately about the work they were doing and cared deeply about the welfare of survivors, but each one also expressed a level of frustration about aspects of the system. These aspects differed depending on the nature of their individual roles, but all participants gave views on the changes they would like to make. Most commonly, these issues concerned funding and overall resources. Some made recommendations which reflected inferences already made from the literature review, suggesting that there is an element of universality to the general desired goals of those within the field.

The Human Trafficking Foundation has created a UK service map of anti-modern slavery organisations[99] which augments the information already collated for this book. There is a point to be made about the lack of official knowledge regarding the number and nature of independent organisations who support modern slavery survivors. This parallels a rather relaxed governmental approach to monitoring that appears as a recurring theme throughout this book.

Given that the UK's approach to combatting modern slavery is heavily underpinned by the criminal justice model, it was prudent to investigate how modern slavery prosecution rates compared to other data. The strong

98 Kathleen Gerson and Ruth Horowitz, 'Observation and Interviewing: Options and Choices in Qualitative Research' in Tim May (ed), *Qualitative Research: An International Guide to Issues in Practice* (Sage 2002).

99 Human Trafficking Foundation, 'Mapping Trafficking Support Services' (*Human Trafficking Foundation)* <>www.humantraffickingfoundation.org/support-services> accessed 20 May 2020.

reliance on witness evidence can cause long delays in police investigations,[100] and survivors of this crime do not always place a priority on seeing their perpetrators brought to justice (see Chapter 7). However, none of the key UK agencies (Independent Anti-Slavery Commissioner (IASC), National Crime Agency (NCA) or Crown Prosecution Service) currently collate or hold this information centrally. Caroline, who is instrumental in campaigning for better long-term support, commented that 'one of the biggest criticisms of the field is that there's very little intelligent data of survivor outcomes.'[101] Thus, it is difficult to establish a clear outline of justice pathways for victims from the NRM stage through to police investigation and CPS intervention, which diminishes our understanding of what is working well. Returning victim figures are not formally recorded either, further skewing intelligence:

> We've still got this problem where we anecdotally understand that this is happening, but it's then never recorded. So where on the NRM form is there a place where it records that this person was a victim of human trafficking or this person has come out of the NRM prior to being identified? There isn't, it isn't, so that piece of work needs to be done.[102]

This all signifies a substantial gap in understanding how effectively the MSA and wider policy are being implemented (see Section 8.3).

Unfortunately, even where frontline practitioners are forthcoming in sharing information and opinions, they are more reluctant to introduce researchers to survivors. For some, this is based on concerns about re-traumatisation. Others state that they receive multiple requests for research participation and are unwilling to repeatedly ask survivors to talk to strangers. The former IASC, Dame Sara Thornton, confirmed that organisations are inundated with research requests, and other academics have described the 'research fatigue' they encounter when asking for access.[103] Although these reasons are understandable, it is a shame that this has effectively led to a blanket ban on opportunities for independent researchers to approach survivors for their narrative. It is impossible to say how many survivors would be happy to share their stories in the knowledge that they are potentially contributing to improving services for others in similar situations. One of the central aims of research in this field is to empower those at the heart of modern slavery by giving them an opportunity to have their voices heard and 'lift the veil of invisibility.'[104]

100 The Human Trafficking Foundation and others, *Supporting Adult Survivors of Slavery to Facilitate Recovery and Reintegration and Prevent Re-Exploitation* (Human Trafficking Foundation 2017).

101 Caroline, Nottingham, UK, 22 November 2019.

102 Diana, Bristol, UK, 22 February 2019.

103 Dame Sara Thornton, in conversation at a report launch, Sheffield, 20 January 2020.

104 Anne Opie, 'Qualitative Research, Appropriation of the "Other" and Empowerment' (1992) *Feminist Review* 20, 66.

Consequently, senior representatives at these services have been appointed as 'gatekeepers' to the wider organisation and, as such, make executive decisions on behalf of their service users and even staff members.[105] There is something paternalistic about believing that you are *protecting* people, thereby not giving them the option to decide for themselves. Interestingly, this was a point that was raised by one research participant, the only practitioner who had been a survivor, and this is further explored in Section 8.4. In terms of this overall book, it also means that voices of survivors themselves remain virtually silent, something that almost all other stakeholders claim needs to be addressed.

## 1.4 Structure of book

This book contains seven substantive chapters, each of which focuses on an element of the survivor pathway. These chapters can be read in order to understand the pathway from intervention to recovery and rehabilitation, or they can be read as standalone pieces if the reader wishes to concentrate on a specific area of survivor support.

### *Policy and legislation*

This chapter presents a critical analysis of the development and current status of the UK's modern slavery legislation and policies as written and as operating in practice. It addresses how effective the UK's current approach is and, in particular, examines the successes and limitations of the UK's legislation, policies and practices in supporting survivors. This includes a critique of the National Referral Mechanism (NRM) and the Modern Slavery Act before looking at possible developments for the future of the UK's anti-slavery approach.

### *Voluntary sector organisations*

This chapter provides a detailed examination of the voluntary sector's role and highlights service differences in survivor support across the UK. It evaluates the level of consistencies and disparities in service delivery across the UK and demonstrates how austerity, combined with growing reliance by the government on charities, has impacted anti-modern slavery organisations in the longer term. Finally, there is an analysis of the charitable organisations that offer services for survivors of modern slavery.

### *Short-term support*

This chapter discusses the evidence of good practice and barriers to success in the immediate support needs of survivors and evaluates how government

105 Alan Bryman, *Social Research Methods* (3rd edn, Oxford University Press 2008).

guidelines and policies work in practice across the UK's service delivery systems. It provides a deeper examination as to the effectiveness of these policies, particularly in relation to the National Referral Mechanism. The theme of multi-agency partnerships straddles both of these discussions, and there is a final, separate section dedicated to this topic.

### *Immigration*

This chapter offers a critical analysis of the UK's immigration policies and their impact on survivor pathways and the anti-modern slavery system. It aims to understand the avenues a survivor pathway can take when their immigration status is uncertain and includes commentary on the Rwanda policy and the UK government's endeavours to stop small, refugee-carrying boats from landing on British shores.

### *Trauma and therapeutic intervention*

This chapter focuses on the appropriate management of post-trauma in survivors and identifies further examples of good practice in this area. It discusses trauma in survivors and how the manifestation of post-trauma symptoms can affect recovery before considering the therapeutic intervention that survivors are currently able to access. The chapter then examines whether current legislative and policy approaches in this area are fit for purpose.

### *Criminal justice*

This chapter presents a critical analysis of the UK's criminal justice system in relation to the 'victim' and 'offender' status of survivors. It presents an overview of key relevant organisations, identifying some positive early developments and barriers to success, and critiques the traditional criminal justice approach as a means of combatting modern slavery. The overall modern slavery legal framework pertaining to criminal justice is explored, and alternative means of empowering and supporting survivors throughout the criminal justice process are offered.

### *Long-term support*

This chapter discusses the evidence of good practice and barriers to success in the long-term recovery needs of survivors, with more in-depth focus on accommodation, education and employment. It also addresses the issue of aftercare monitoring and what is being done to develop understanding of long-term survivor outcomes. The chapter then explores the survivor voice within frontline organisational policy and in government-level decision making and how this could contribute towards future best practice.

This book attempts, as a whole, to chart the UK's modern slavery survivor pathways, from policy decisions and legislation drafting through to the possible outcomes via support and therapeutic intervention from the voluntary sector, immigration control and the criminal justice system. The aim of this is to provide a chronological narrative of the potential survivor journey from intervention (removal from slavery) to independence (when reliance on support services is minimal to none) and thereby demonstrate the strengths and limitations of the current national modern slavery support network. By presenting the book in this order, it shows recurring themes and patterns that exist across the network of services, some of which repeat the dynamics of survivor relationships during, and even before, their lives in confinement.

# 2 Policy and legislation

## 2.1 Introduction

This chapter focuses on the development of modern slavery statute and policy over the past two decades, following the UK's signing of the Palermo Protocol[1] in December 2000 and ratification in February 2006. Taking the lead from the international approach, the UK has adopted a criminal justice model in its legislative efforts to combat slavery. While there is some mention of survivor support in the law, the majority of aftercare provisions take the form of guidance and are aimed at non-governmental organisations. The survivor pathway, therefore, traverses both the statutory and non-statutory sectors. This chapter addresses how effective the UK's current approach is and, in particular, examines the successes and limitations of the UK's legislation, policies and practices in supporting survivors. It outlines the policies that were implemented prior to the Modern Slavery Act[2] and discusses the outcomes of early attempts to combat human trafficking and support survivors. This includes a critique of the National Referral Mechanism and how successive UK governments, statutory agencies and relevant independent organisations have managed the identification and protection of victims of modern slavery. There is then an overview of the drafting of the Modern Slavery Bill and its eventual enactment before addressing some initial issues arising from the implementation of the Act. Finally, this chapter looks at possible developments for the future of the UK's anti-slavery approach and discusses how other factors such as Brexit and a change in government may affect UK strategies to tackle modern slavery.

## 2.2 Pre–Modern Slavery Act developments in the UK

Although national policy makers have erred towards replicating the international approach to human trafficking and slavery by maintaining a criminal

1 United Nations General Assembly Protocol to Prevent, Suppress and Punish Trafficking in Persons, especially Women and Children (adopted 15 November 2000, entered into force 25 December 2003) 2237 UNTS 319 (Palermo Protocol).

2 Modern Slavery Act 2015.

DOI: 10.4324/9781032639895-2

model, the UK was an early adopter of more holistic methods. At the turn of the 21st century, it was recognised that a victim-centric approach would actually benefit the criminal justice process in combating human trafficking and modern slavery, and in 2003, the Poppy Project – established through the charity Eaves – became the first government-funded project with the specific aims of protecting and supporting survivors of trafficking.[3] International law has recognised trafficking and slavery as a human rights abuse since the adoption of the League of Nations' Slavery Convention in 1926,[4] and subsequent Conventions have included the absolute prohibition of all forms of slavery and servitude amongst their articles. Despite its ratification of many major treaties, however, the UK has historically taken its time to implement its international human rights obligations into domestic law. The Human Rights Act 1998, created to 'bring rights home,'[5] was enacted five decades after the European Convention on Human Rights was adopted. Although Article 4 of the ECHR distinctly prohibits slavery and servitude,[6] the UK government waited another decade before criminalising the practices in the Coroners and Justice Act 2009.[7] In the same year, and in keeping with the criminal justice approach, the Sexual Offences Act 2003 was also amended with the addition of a new offence under section 14 of the Policing and Crime Act 2009. This criminalised payment for sex with individuals forced to provide sexual services but resulted in few charges, primarily attributable to lack of police understanding about the offence.[8] Recent European human rights instruments[9] have provided for more detailed stipulations in the assistance and support of survivors (see also Chapter 6). While the UK was quicker to sign up to both the 2005 Convention and 2011 EU Directive, neither action was achieved without public and political pressure.[10] Ratification of the 2005 Convention, however, led

3 Ruth van Dyke, 'The UK's Response to Modern Slavery: Law, Policy and Politics' in Gary Craig and others (eds), *The Modern Slavery Agenda: Policy, Politics and Practice in the UK* (Policy Press 2019).
4 League of Nations Convention to Suppress the Slave Trade and Slavery (adopted 25 September 1926, entered into force 9 March 1927) 60 LNTS 253 (Slavery Convention).
5 Secretary of State for the Home Department, *Rights Brought Home: The Human Rights Bill* (White Paper, Cm 3782, 1997).
6 Convention for the Protection of Human Rights and Fundamental Freedoms (European Convention on Human Rights, as amended) (adopted 4 November 1950, entered into force 3 September 1953) ETS 5 (ECHR) art 4.
7 Coroners and Justice Act 2009 s71.
8 van Dyke (n 3).
9 Council of Europe Convention on Action Against Trafficking in Human Beings (adopted 16 May 2005, entered into force 1 February 2008) CETS 197; Directive 2011/36/EU of the European Parliament and of the Council of Europe on preventing and combating trafficking in human beings and protecting its victims (replacing Council Framework Decision 2002/629/JHA) (5 April 2011).
10 van Dyke (n 3).

to the 2009 introduction of the National Referral Mechanism,[11] the administrative mechanism by which victims of modern slavery and human trafficking are formally identified. The policy updates also included a forty-five-day 'reflection and recovery' period for victims following intervention. This period exceeded the minimum thirty days endorsed in the Convention and, alongside the potential offer of a one-year residence permit (twice the Convention's recommended six months)[12], the government believed that their 'commitment to putting victim care and protection at the heart of our human trafficking strategy'[13] was more than adequately demonstrated.

Meanwhile, UK policy and legislation for migrant domestic workers has fluctuated in recent years. Recognising their often precarious immigration status, a 2011 Council of Europe resolution[14] urged member states to 'develop independent visa schemes for migrant domestic workers and care workers which would allow legal entry, provide a standardized working contract, allow for a change of employer . . . and ensure that visas are not tied to particular employers.'[15] At this point, the UK was a step ahead, having amended its Immigration Rules in 1998 to provide for an Overseas Domestic Worker (ODW) visa for those working in private households. The visa period could last up to twelve months, allowing for extensions of a further twelve months at a time.[16] Significantly, ODWs were entitled to change employers with the proviso that they stayed within the domestic work sector.[17] However, in 2012, despite 'recommendations of the House of Commons Select Committee and the UN Special Rapporteur,'[18] the coalition government restricted newly admitted ODW visas to a maximum of six months, after which time they were required to leave the UK.[19] Additionally, ODWs were no longer permitted to extend their visa or change employers, and while those working for diplomatic employers were entitled to a stay of up to five years, they were exempt from applying for permanent residence, 'despite the policy that allows those on work visas (Tier 2 visa) to apply for permanent residence after a continuous period of five years

11 Alex Balch and Andrew Geddes, 'Opportunity from Crisis? Organisational Responses to Human Trafficking in the UK' (2011) 13 BJPIR 26.

12 ibid.

13 Home Office and Scottish Executive, *Update to the UK Action Plan on Tackling Human Trafficking* (Home Office 2008) 3.

14 Parliamentary Assembly of the Council of Europe, 'Protecting Migrant Women in the Labour Market: Report of the Committee on Migration, Refugees and Population' (15 April 2011) Parliamentary Assembly 18th Sitting Resolution 1811 (2011).

15 ibid.

16 Cliodhna Murphy, 'The Enduring Vulnerability of Migrant Domestic Workers in Europe' (2013) 62(3) *The International and Comparative Law Quarterly* 599.

17 ibid.

18 ibid 599, 619.

19 Home Office, 'Immigration Rules Part 5: Working in the UK' (*UK Government*, updated 5 October 2020) <www.gov.uk/guidance/immigration-rules/immigration-rules-part-5-working-in-the-uk> accessed 4 November 2020.

in the UK.'[20] By way of justification, the government submitted that 'existing visa arrangements for domestic workers were more generous than in other EU countries,'[21] implying that lower standards should be the benchmark. 2011 also saw the adoption of the International Labour Organisation Domestic Workers Convention[22] (DWC), which set out clear regulations to member states ensuring that domestic workers receive fair terms and conditions; a minimum wage; regular rest periods; and protection against abuse, harassment and violence, as well as calling for regulation of private employment agencies, notably requiring that 'fees charged by private employment agencies are not deducted from the remuneration of domestic workers.'[23] The DWC currently has thirty-six ratifications,[24] although the UK is notable by its absence. The UK government justified its inaction by highlighting 'the irreconcilable differences between the Convention and the UK health and safety law.'[25] While household inspections by health and safety executives may appear to contravene privacy rights,[26] this ignores the fact that private childminders are subject to Ofsted inspections in their own homes.[27] A trend in European immigration rules 'towards restricting access to the labour market and a secure legal status for migrant domestic workers,'[28] reflecting policies of '"less migrants" *and* "less rights"'[29] has also been noted. This observation is almost certainly confirmed by the UK's increasingly aggressive stance towards migrant workers, particularly those classed as 'low skilled.' By the late 2010s, the UK government had adopted a post-Brexit policy that intended to 'shift the focus of our economy away from a reliance on cheap labour from Europe,'[30] adding that

20 Ismail Idowu Salih, 'Viewing Domestic Workers Problems through a Human Rights Lens' (2015) 34(7) *Equality, Diversity and Inclusion: An International Journal* 622, 623.

21 Cliodhna Murphy, 'Enforcing Employment Standards for Undocumented Domestic Workers in the UK and Ireland: Rethinking Illegality in Zones of Invisibility' (2015) 29(4) *Immigration, Asylum and Nationality Law* 349, 355.

22 International Labour Organisation (ILO) Domestic Workers Convention (adopted 16 June 2011, entered into force 5 September 2013) C189.

23 ibid art 15.

24 International Labour Organisation, 'Ratifications of C189 – Domestic Workers Convention, 2011 (No. 189)' (*Ratifications of ILO Conventions*) <www.ilo.org/dyn/normlex/en/f?p=NORMLEXPUB:11300:0::NO:11300:P11300_INSTRUMENT_ID:2551460:NO> accessed 14 March 2024.

25 Salih (n 20) 622, 629.

26 ibid.

27 UK Government, 'Being Inspected as a Childminder or Childcare Provider' (*UK Government*) <www.gov.uk/ofsted-inspection-childcare-provider> accessed 15 August 2016.

28 Murphy, 'The Enduring Vulnerability of Migrant Domestic Workers in Europe' (n 16) 599, 602.

29 Murphy, 'Enforcing Employment Standards for Undocumented Domestic Workers in the UK and Ireland' (n 21) 349, 356.

30 Home Office/UK Visas and Immigration, 'The UK's Points-based Immigration System: Policy Statement' (*UK Government*, 19 February 2020) <www.gov.uk/

employers 'will need to adjust'[31] (see Chapter 5). The outcome of the 2012 regulation changes, however, mean that ODWs are legally unable to move on if their employer becomes abusive; should they take the chance and try to leave their employer, they will automatically be in violation of their visa regulations and potentially face detention and deportation. Early reports from Kalayaan, a charity that supports and campaigns on behalf of migrant domestic workers, strongly suggested that mistreatment of this demographic group increased under the restrictions.[32]

## 2.3 National Referral Mechanism

The NRM process involves a number of steps before an individual is formally identified as a victim of trafficking or slavery. A primary assessment is conducted by a first responder, who decides whether the individual is a *potential victim.*[33] First responders are based in designated organisations; these include statutory agencies such as the police, the Gangmasters and Labour Abuse Authority (GLAA), as well as third-sector agencies like the Salvation Army and Barnardo's.[34] The GLAA conducts its own regular checks and investigations on licenced premises, which enables them to directly identify potential victims, whereas the police are more reliant on intelligence that can lead to the apprehension of traffickers and consequently the identification of victims. Additionally, members of the public are encouraged to provide information that may assist with the identification of victims via the modern slavery helpline or online.[35] Home Office records, however, demonstrate that UK Visas and Immigration (UKVI) have provided the highest proportion of referrals year on year.[36] From there, first responders refer the potential victim on to a competent authority (CA) by completing a form which provides the necessary

government/publications/the-uks-points-based-immigration-system-policy-statement/the-uks-points-based-immigration-system-policy-statement> accessed 8 August 2020.

31 ibid.

32 Virginia Mantouvalou, 'What Is to Be Done for Migrant Domestic Workers?' in Bernard Ryan (ed), *Labour Migration in Hard Times: Reforming Labour Market Regulation* (Institute of Employment Rights 2013).

33 Home Office, 'Report Modern Slavery as a First Responder' (*UK Government*) <www.gov.uk/guidance/report-modern-slavery-as-a-first-responder> accessed 13 March 2020.

34 Home Office/UK Visas and Immigration, 'National Referral Mechanism Guidance: Adult (England and Wales)' (*UK Government*, updated 28 November 2019) <www.gov.uk/government/publications/human-trafficking-victims-referral-and-assessment-forms/guidance-on-the-national-referral-mechanism-for-potential-adult-victims-of-modern-slavery-england-and-wales> accessed 16 January 2020.

35 Home Office, 'Report Modern Slavery as a First Responder' (n 33).

36 Home Office, 'Modern Slavery: National Referral Mechanism and Duty to Notify Statistics UK, End of Year Summary 2023' (*HM Government*, 7 March 2024) <www.gov.uk/government/statistics/modern-slavery-nrm-and-dtn-statistics-end-of-year-summary-2023/modern-slavery-national-referral-mechanism-and-duty-to-notify-statistics-uk-end-of-year-summary-2023> accessed 14 March 2024.

information. Initially, CA status was granted to the NCA's Modern Slavery and Human Trafficking Unit (MSHTU) and UK Borders Agency[37] (later UKVI) but, following several changes, is now primarily the domain of caseworkers under a single competent authority (SCA).[38] From November 2021, referrals could also be made to the Immigration Enforcement Competent Authority (IECA), introduced to process referrals for foreign nationals who are in prison or immigration detention, who are in the process of being deported or individuals whose asylum claims have been deemed inadmissible.[39] The IECA currently account for around one-fifth of referrals.[40] The respective authorities are responsible for formally identifying whether an individual has been subjected to trafficking or slavery. This process begins with a ***reasonable grounds*** (RG) decision: where the authority 'suspects but cannot prove' that slavery has occurred, a positive reasonable grounds decision is granted, entitling the individual to state-funded support, including housing.[41] At this point, the 'reflection and recovery' period begins. Additional evidence is then collated to assess 'whether on the balance of probabilities "it is more likely than not" that the person is a victim of modern slavery.'[42] A positive decision at this stage provides the individual with ***conclusive grounds*** (CG). Guidance for these decisions has been issued by the government and is regularly updated.[43]

The government has also issued guidance for frontline staff outlining the indicators of modern slavery or trafficking, including physical, sexual health, psychological and situational/environmental signs;[44] however, a 2017 report carried out by the charity Unseen suggested that this guidance was not reaching all stakeholders. An assessment of calls made to the service by health professionals found that 50% of all callers were inquiring about indicators of slavery.[45] This is likely due to the fact that health professionals are not currently designated first responders. Nonetheless, one in eight practitioners state

37 Jessica Elliott, 'The National Referral Mechanism: Querying the Response of "First Responders" and the Competence of "Competent Authorities"' (2016) 30(1) *Journal of Immigration, Asylum and Nationality Law* 9.

38 Department of Justice, *The Scottish Government and the Welsh Government, '2019 UK Annual Report on Modern Slavery'* (HM Government 2019).

39 Home Office, 'Modern Slavery: Statutory Guidance for England and Wales (under s49 of the Modern Slavery Act 2015) and Non-statutory Guidance for Scotland and Northern Ireland v2.5' (Home Office, 8 November 2021).

40 Home Office, 'Modern Slavery: National Referral Mechanism and Duty to Notify Statistics UK, End of Year Summary 2023' (n 36).

41 Department of Justice (n 38).

42 ibid 8.

43 Home Office, 'Modern Slavery: Statutory Guidance for England and Wales (under s49 of the Modern Slavery Act 2015) and Non-statutory Guidance for Scotland and Northern Ireland v3.8' (Home Office, updated 22 February 2024).

44 Home Office, *Victims of Modern Slavery: Frontline Staff Guidance v3.0* (Home Office 2016).

45 Unseen, *Identification of Modern Slavery Victims by Health Professionals* (Modern Slavery Helpline and Resource Centre 2017).

that they have witnessed signs of slavery in a patient,[46] while one in five victims report having had contact with a health professional during their time in captivity;[47] thus these statistics could be even higher in reality. Health visitors, for example, are privy to some of the most intimate details of people's lives, including access to their homes. This level of proximity facilitates not just the identification of warning signs but also creates an atmosphere of confidence in which a victim may alert their health visitor to the situation.[48] Campaign group Stop the Traffik have collated information that illustrates the trend:

> In one case, an unregistered male came into a GPs surgery suffering from back pain. He explained that it was due to lifting paving slabs all day whilst working on a local traveller site. The GP suspected he was being exploited and, by asking the right questions, found out that the patient was not in possession of his passport and was living in a caravan on the site. The patient revealed that he planned to escape as he had managed to obtain a mobile phone. Unfortunately, as the doctor did not know how to report his concerns without endangering the patient *the case was never followed-up.*[49]

Caroline, who provides training in this area, also identified this as a problem:

> The feedback from pretty much every single person in the field has said certain health professionals should be First Responders because we've got evidence, researched and evidenced to show that the places that victims of trafficking turn up are A&E, midwifery services, GP services and in some instances, you might get it in infectious diseases, there are a few other random places, but generally speaking, we know where they turn up.[50]

She added that too many local authority staff were not even aware of their status as first responders and that training was lacking for all frontline workers in the public sector. In response to this gap, Lara Bundock (former CEO of Snowdrop) and Dr Kathryn Hodges created training standards with the aim of rolling out a national training programme for all relevant stakeholders.[51]

46 Helen Bird, 'Out of the Shadows' (March 2017) *Community Practitioner* 37.

47 Ruth Dearnley, 'Preventing Modern Slavery: The Role of the NHS' (NHS *England*, 22 February 2019) <www.england.nhs.uk/blog/preventing-modern-slavery-the-role-of-the-nhs/> accessed 15 March 2020.

48 Bird (n 46) 37.

49 Dearnley (n 47) (italics added).

50 Caroline, Nottingham, UK, 22 November 2019.

51 Lara Bundock and Kathryn Hodges, 'Training Framework: Identification, Care and Support of Victims and Survivors of Modern Slavery and Human Trafficking' (Skills for Care, 2020) <www.skillsforcare.org.uk/Documents/Topics/Modern-Slavery/Training-Framework-

*Table 2.1* Number of NRM referrals by year

| *Year* | *2014* | *2015* | *2016* | *2017* | *2018* | *2019* | *2020* | *2021* | *2022* | *2023* |
|---|---|---|---|---|---|---|---|---|---|---|
| **NRM referrals** | 2337 | 3263 | 3805 | 5136 | 6974 | 10606 | 10582 | 12400 | 16921 | 17004 |

The government has also sought to improve training and awareness for health professionals, including a thirty-minute e-learning session,[52] a pocket guide for nurses and midwives and access to a range of other online sources. NHS England additionally pledged to build on this by incorporating modern slavery awareness into safeguarding training and ensuring that all staff have access to training and support in the identification and reporting of potential modern slavery and human trafficking incidents.[53]

Nonetheless, NRM referrals have steadily increased year on year at an average annual increase of just over 1600 referrals.[54]

2020 was the only year that saw a slight decrease in referrals, attributable to the COVID pandemic, which the Home Office acknowledges.[55] From 2021, however, the numbers continued to climb again, with a record high increase of 4211 in 2022.

A fundamental feature of the NRM is that individuals over the age of 18 must give their informed consent to be referred. First responders are thus required to explain to potential victims: 'what the NRM is; what support is available through it; and what the possible outcomes are for an individual being referred.'[56] Where a victim declines to be referred into the NRM, first responders must instead complete a Duty to Notify form online, which anonymises the victim and is 'used to build a better picture of modern slavery in England and Wales, and to improve law enforcement response.'[57] One of the flaws in this system is that individuals

Identification-Care-and-Support-of-Victims-and-Survivors-of-Modern-Slavery-and-Human-Trafficking.pdf> accessed 10 November 2020.

52 Home Office, 'Modern Slavery Training: Resource Page' (*UK Government*, updated 2 April 2020) <www.gov.uk/government/publications/modern-slavery-training-resource-page/modern-slavery-training-resource-page> accessed 15 April 2020.

53 Simon Stevens, 'NHS England Slavery and Human Trafficking Statement' (*NHS England*, March 2019) <www.england.nhs.uk/safeguarding/slavery-human-trafficking-statement/> accessed 15 March 2020.

54 Home Office, *National Referral Mechanism and Duty to Notify Statistics – End of Year Summary 2023* (Home Office 2023).

55 Home Office, *National Referral Mechanism and Duty to Notify Statistics – End of Year Summary 2020* (Home Office 2020).

56 Home Office/UK Visas and Immigration, 'National Referral Mechanism Guidance: Adult (England and Wales)' (*UK Government*, updated 22 January 2020) <www.gov.uk/government/publications/human-trafficking-victims-referral-and-assessment-forms/guidance-on-the-national-referral-mechanism-for-potential-adult-victims-of-modern-slavery-england-and-wales> accessed 13 March 2020.

57 Home Office, *Modern Slavery Act 2015: Statutory Guidance for England and Wales* (Home Office 2020) 45.

may have a number of reasons they do not wish to provide their consent. Dame Sara Thornton, former IASC, found that 4107 potential victims appeared to have declined the NRM over a three-year period, according to the Home Office's own figures.[58] In 2023, that figure was overtaken in just twelve months, with a record 4929 people reported under the Duty to Notify.[59] Research by the by the British Institute for International and Comparative Law and the Human Trafficking Foundation found that reasons for refusing consent included the individual denying the exploitation experience or victim status and/or stating that the NRM didn't apply to them, a desire to put the experience behind them and move on or fear of their traffickers.[60] Furthermore, the vast majority of victims just want to work,[61] and, having left their country of origin and very often their families, the desire to create a better life is paramount. Under the NRM, however, survivors are prohibited from undertaking new employment during the mandatory 'recovery and reflection' period. This leaves many survivors with a difficult choice; even where they have previously been subjected to terrible conditions and abuse, they were at least eking out an existence:

> At the moment we've got a situation where they're like 'You're offering me this NRM, I've got to sign this piece of paper, you're telling me I'll be somewhere safe for 45 days and after that you're promising me nothing, so maybe it's better to stay with the devil I know, and even though it's really hard, I am still able to send some money home,' so you're probably telling yourself it's only for a short period of time and that the debt you have will start diminishing because those are the survival techniques you need to use in those situations.[62]

For some, the fear of arrest and deportation overrides any desire to accept offers of assistance.[63] Attention from the authorities can also result in altogether new financial problems:

> If somebody gets a negative conclusive grounds decision . . . and the debts suddenly start coming through the door because they've surfaced and National Insurance numbers have been registered for benefits or

58 Dame Sara Thornton, *Independent Anti-Slavery Commissioner Strategic Plan 2019–2021* (Independent Anti-Slavery Commissioner 2019).

59 Home Office, *National Referral Mechanism and Duty to Notify Statistics* (n 54).

60 Modern Slavery and Human Rights Policy and Evidence Centre, 'Thousands of Potential Survivors Decline Formal Identification and Support' (*Modern Slavery and Human Rights Policy and Evidence Centre*, 7 February 2024) <https://modernslaverypec.org/latest/report-thousands-of-potential-survivors-of-modern-slavery-choose-not-to-be-considered-for-formal-identification-and-support> accessed 22 March 2024.

61 Kendra Strauss, 'Sorting Victims from Workers: Forced Labour, Trafficking, and the Process of Jurisdiction' (2016) 41(2) *Progress in Human Geography* 140.

62 Ayesha, Portsmouth, UK, 30 October 2018.

63 Virginia Mantouvalou, 'Modern Slavery: The UK Response' (2010) 39(4) *Industrial Law Journal* 425.

> whatever that those problems start pretty much as soon as they surface on the radar.[64]

A respondent to one academic study even indicated that the NRM form 'has been used for the capture of data about the victim's traffickers,'[65] which reinforces the suggestion that authorities still defer to their crime targets rather than focusing resources on more complex and lengthy survivor support. This issue does appear to be a problem, as further discussed in Chapter 7.

In 2013, the Anti-Trafficking Monitoring Group (ATMG) reviewed the UK's progress so far and found the system lacking. The group noted that, while the number of referrals into the NRM was steadily growing, the assistance provided to victims was not improving.[66] The ATMG also described delays in the identification process, the effects of which have been highlighted by Survivor Alliance UK:

> Waiting for a decision following the interview is retraumatising, and is a re-trafficking process. Like a trafficker, the Home Office promises you care and quality support. Like your trafficking experience, you feel that you cannot run away from the Home Office, because they know all your details and everything about you.[67]

> The wait is re-traumatising. I am still waiting. . . . I have been for more than 900 days. This has caused serious consequences and delays to my asylum claim. I have been diagnosed with post-traumatic stress disorder, anxiety with panic attacks, and low mood by my psychotherapist, in the context of this traumatic experience and the uncertainty of whether I will reunite with my children.[68]

Note that both quotes describe the waiting period as retraumatising. Diana was also critical of the long delays, stating that survivors in the NRM were often given extension after extension only to end up homeless and, in some cases, re-trafficked.[69] Even when a survivor is in the NRM, communication problems can disrupt the support and justice pathways:

> Once they're in the NRM, obviously everything goes quiet, that victim is moved and so to try and catch up with that victim is very difficult and the Home Office have just made the process a whole lot harder. The

64 Donna, Nottingham, UK, 10 May 2019.

65 Elliott (n 37) 9, 17.

66 The Anti-Trafficking Monitoring Group, 'Hidden in Plain Sight – Three Years on: Updated Analysis of UK Measures to Protect Trafficked Persons' (Executive Summary) (ATMG 2013).

67 Hannah Browne and others, *The Journey of our UK Survivor Network: Challenges and Successes* (Survivor Alliance UK 2019) 6.

68 ibid.

69 Diana, Bristol, UK, 22 February 2019.

> National Crime Agency used to be able to respond to subject access requests really quickly. The Home Office process requires pretty much that the survivor remembers stuff . . . remembers all of their family details, if they were to communicate with you, it's much more long-winded to get the subject access request through to you. And I can see the value in that, in terms of protecting people's information, however, when you're trying to advocate for them and you need their file, it's you know . . . it's very frustrating.[70]

Diana, a frontline investigator, raised the conflict between confidentiality and information gathering:

> I've found with the process that victims that I've been dealing with, gained their confidence with and they've gone into the NRM, that the NRM wouldn't let me speak to them because it was victim-centric, but we were losing time waiting for somebody somewhere to get their permission.[71]

Several participants mirrored these views and an overarching theme is that communication between all agencies needs drastic improvement in order to fully protect and support survivors (see also Chapters 4 and 8).

The NRM has also been criticised for its rigidity and failure to take into account the reality of survivors' lives, particularly when they display behaviours that are not in line with traditional perceptions of the 'ideal victim.'[72]

> One of the hardest lessons I learned is that victims don't always behave like victims. You expect them to want help and be . . . I don't know . . . I don't mean 'grateful' but recognise they've been given an opportunity to make amends and I've (laughs) I've had quite a few victims who have just – through their lifestyle and that's the reason why they were chosen in the first place – who would naturally progress to drink, and drink whenever they could, who would naturally progress to violence, because that's the environment they've come from, who would naturally progress to drugs, and understanding that if you get very well-meaning people involved, that sometimes these potential victims don't always behave and so will beat people up and wreck places.[73]

70 Donna, Nottingham, UK, 10 May 2019.
71 Diana, Bristol, UK, 22 February 2019.
72 Alexandra Louise Anderson Baxter, 'When the Line between Victimization and Criminalization Blurs: The Victim-Offender Overlap Observed in Female Offenders in Cases of Trafficking in Persons for Sexual Exploitation in Australia' (2019) 6(3) *Journal of Human Trafficking* 327–338 <https://doi.org/10.1080/23322705.2019.1578579>.
73 Diana, Bristol, UK, 22 February 2019.

Thus, decision-makers often struggle to personally connect with them and establish their needs, resulting in highly traumatised individuals missing out on the support they are entitled to. Elliott notes that

> [i]f putative victims are not identified in a timely fashion, or are misidentified entirely, then they have no access to the bespoke system of rights and assistance which is applicable to those who are formally identified as conclusively having been 'trafficked'.[74]

Taking this into account, Figure 2.1 collates the National Crime Agency's and Home Office's own figures[75] to illustrate the breakdown of Reasonable and Conclusive Grounds decisions since 2014.

The chart shows that while RG decisions are increasing, largely in tandem with the amount of NRM referrals, CG decisions reached something of a plateau during the lockdown years of 2020 and 2021, with a trend towards decline since then. In fact, CG decisions appear to have experienced a proportional decrease from 82% of all referrals in 2014 to just 9% in 2023. The decline is partially explained by a rising number of pending cases: 46% of 2023 referrals are still awaiting either RG or CG decisions. While guidance states that RG decisions should be made within five working days of referral, the average waiting time leapt to twenty-six days in 2023. It confirms the lengthy waits that survivors say they have been subjected to and suggests that the CAs are unable to cope with either the level or complexity of the referrals they receive. Even the Home Office conceded that 'this is a result of the current length of time taken to make conclusive grounds decisions,'[76] while 2020 published guidance stated that there was 'no target to make a Conclusive Grounds decision within a specific timeframe.'[77] A 2019 job advert for national referral mechanism decision maker was criticised in *The Independent* by several Labour MPs, who noted that the position was 'marked as temporary and appears to require no previous experience,'[78] offering *up to* £9.08 per hour (only 33p more than the national minimum wage at the time). It was stated that the role required a high level of experience and knowledge which should be reflected in both the job description and salary in order to attract a 'superior operator.' The advert also stipulated that 'Successful candidates will

74 Elliott (n 37) 9.

75 Home Office, *National Referral Mechanism Statistics – End of Year Summary 2023* (Home Office 2023).

76 Home Office, *National Referral Mechanism Statistics – End of Year Summary 2019* (Home Office 2019) 5.

77 Home Office, *Modern Slavery Act 2015* (n 57) 110.

78 May Bulman, 'Home Office Using Low-paid Temporary Workers to Make 'Life-or-death' Decisions on Human Trafficking' *The Independent* (London, 13 February 2019) <www.independent.co.uk/news/uk/home-news/modern-slavery-human-trafficking-home-office-job-description-nrm-decision-maker-a8777331.html> accessed 22 April 2020.

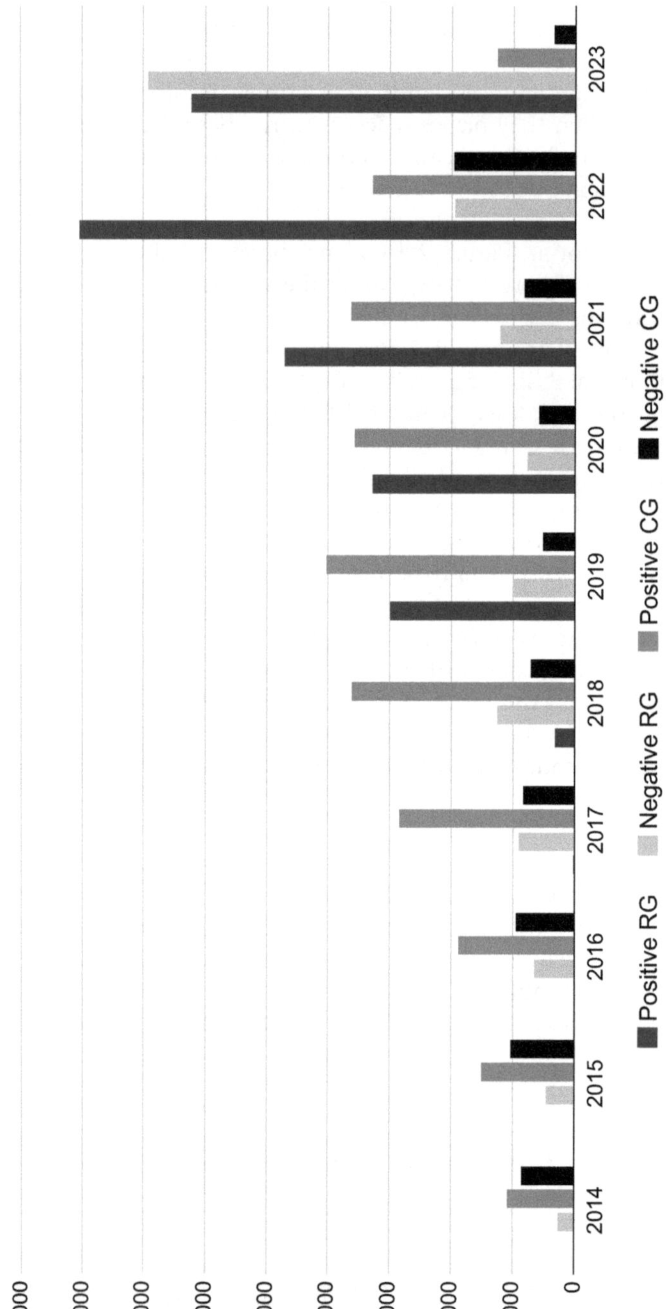


*Figure 2.1* NRM decisions 2014–2023

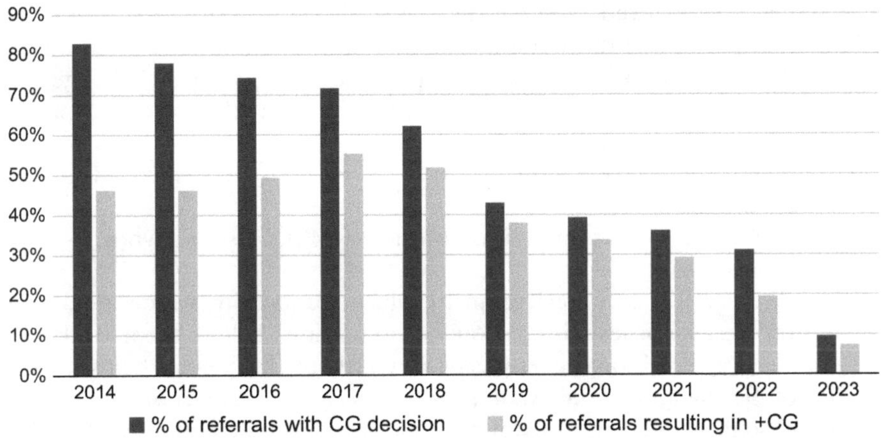


*Figure 2.2* Conclusive grounds as a % of NRM referrals

be provided with full training and be supported through close mentoring by experienced members of the team'[79] but made no mention of career progression or qualifying wage increases. In 2021, alongside the introduction of the IECA, the Home Office employed 200 more staff at the SCA in an attempt to reduce waiting times.[80]

One point of interest is that where a CG decision is made, the comparative number of positive decisions are actually rising, relatively speaking.

Reading these figures in conjunction with Figure 2.1, however, the sharp increase in negative RG decisions will almost certainly have contributed to this. In 2023, only 55% of referrals received a positive RG decision, compared to 88% the year before. This is most likely a direct result of the 'objective' evidence rules introduced in the Modern Slavery Statutory Guidance in January 2023, which created a higher threshold of proof; fundamentally, 'a victim's own account, by itself, would not be sufficient absent objective factors to have real suspicion.'[81] However, this was swiftly subject to a legal challenge,[82] and the day before the case was heard in the High Court, the Home Secretary deferred, publishing amended guidance on 10 July 2023.

79 Brook Street, 'National Referral Mechanism Decision Maker (Home Office)' (*Brook Street*) <www.brookstreet.co.uk/job/national-referral-mechanism-decision-maker-home-office-1/?fbclid=IwAR3IDv1baTKeSi_bT42KDWWo2qASMJA0huXf7sT260Lw-iY0Fw1QYbz l9x4> accessed 22 April 2020.

80 Home Office, *2021 UK Annual Report on Modern Slavery* (HM Government October 2021).

81 Home Office, 'Modern Slavery: Statutory Guidance for England and Wales (under s49 of the Modern Slavery Act 2015) and Non-Statutory Guidance for Scotland and Northern Ireland v3.1' (Home Office updated 3 March 2023).

82 Matrix Chambers, 'SSHD Withdraws New Evidential Test for "Reasonable Grounds" Decisions in Modern Slavery Statutory Guidance' (*Matrix Law*, 27 June 2023) www.matrixlaw.co.uk/

The similarly short-lived Public Order Disqualification policy took a further 331 individuals out of the system, although most of these took place during the first half of 2023 prior to the policy pause following a legal challenge.[83]

Reconsideration requests are also on the rise, with 888 of these applications made to CAs in 2023; 60% ($n = 400$) of reconsidered RG decisions later received a positive decision, and 64% ($n = 89$) of reconsidered CG decisions were overturned.

Many frontline workers are critical of the NRM process as a whole:

> I think the NRM is a mechanism by which we identify, we decide as a country 'yes, we believe this person' or 'no we don't believe them' or they don't fit our definition, but it means very little to the person themselves. One of the changes I would want to bring about is what *conclusive grounds* means, so if the NRM remains and we still have this system of research and assessment of that person at the point at which someone is given a positive conclusive grounds decision, it should mean something.[84]

Jenni voiced similar scepticism: 'It's not clear what having a positive conclusive grounds and negative grounds actually does for people. It's not linked into immigration status or anything.'[85] Ayesha felt that the goalposts had shifted from the initial aim, 'which in my understanding was meant to be an administrative process and now it's become an access to support mechanism.'[86] For that reason, 'consent' may not always be as freely given as anticipated:

> Survivors have said . . . 'sure we consent but basically because people are saying that if you don't go into the NRM you are going to be homeless' or you don't have access to anything, so . . . it's consent with very constrained options so I fear that what people think is consent to enter the NRM is not full consent, or fully aware consent.[87]

> I think of course there are people who are choosing not to go into NRM because the only reason you would choose to go into the NRM, if you're

news/sshd-withdraws-new-evidential-test-for-reasonable-grounds-decisions-in-modern-slavery-statutory-guidance/ accessed 26 March 2024.

83 Matrix Chambers, 'High Court Orders No Public Order Disqualifications of Slavery Victims May Take Place without a Risk Assessment Pending Trial' (*Matrix Law*, 27 July 2023) <www.matrixlaw.co.uk/news/high-courts-orders-no-public-order-disqualifications-of-slavery-victims-may-take-place-without-a-risk-assessment-pending-trial/> accessed 22 March 2024.

84 Caroline, Nottingham, UK, 22 November 2019.

85 Jenni, Manchester, UK, 13 August 2019.

86 Ayesha, Portsmouth, UK, 30 October 2018.

87 Jenni, Manchester, UK, 13 August 2019.

an adult, is if you're absolutely destitute and at risk, that's the only safeguarding route we have for adults at the moment.[88]

Jenni even stated that she had never yet heard of anyone who said they were glad they entered the NRM. Indeed, the NRM received widespread criticism from the start,[89] and, following the Home Office review in 2014,[90] the coalition government consequently made a number of changes which they then piloted in two regions: West Yorkshire and the South West.[91] This culminated in the digitalisation of the NRM, which aimed to streamline the referral process and give frontline workers 'all the information they need to provide good quality, tailored support.'[92] In February 2019 the forty-five-day reflection period was also doubled to ninety days[93].

These amendments were already being mooted several years prior to the changes, and participants expressed positive opinions regarding the proposed NRM updates but felt there was room for even more comprehensive structural change:

> I'm glad we're digitalising the NRM. I would be interested to see how that works with First Responders so, again, in my mind, this is perfect timing to rehash First Responders and how they operate.[94]

> I think there's something about understanding what support is needed at the moment of referral and that mixture of administrative process versus support process and they seem to sometimes to be at odds with each other and then how someone in the system might decide that that individual isn't a victim of trafficking but that isn't saying they're not somewhere on the exploitative spectrum and then what do we do with that individual?[95]

> I think, some of the reforms to the NRM are very positive, but I think also it's going to come down to how they're not just developed but implemented as well and is there a robust enough mechanism in place

88 Caroline, Nottingham, UK, 22 November 2019.
89 Elliott (n 37) 9.
90 Home Office, *Review of the National Referral Mechanism for Victims of Human Trafficking* (Home Office 2014).
91 Nicola Ellis and others, *An Evaluation of the National Referral Mechanism Pilot* (Research Report 94, Home Office 2017).
92 Victoria Atkins/Home Office, 'New System to Simplify and Speed Up Modern Slavery Referrals' (*UK Government*, 3 September 2019) <www.gov.uk/government/news/new-system-to-simplify-and-speed-up-modern-slavery-referrals> accessed 13 March 2020.
93 ibid.
94 Caroline, Nottingham, UK, 22 November 2019.
95 Ayesha, Portsmouth, UK, 30 October 2018.

to deal with every eventuality, because supporting victims of modern slavery is extremely complex.[96]

Fundamentally, the NRM still appears to be in a fluid state of progress, with a lot of trial and error – whether important lessons are learned and acted upon remains to be seen. One of the main ongoing difficulties is the lack of joined-up monitoring (see Sections 4.3 and 8.3). Even ninety days is very little time for a traumatised individual to turn their life around and begin independent living, and it is still not evident that post-NRM survivors are getting the support they need, particularly as the UK has yet to provide clear statutory standards for long-term care (see Chapter 8).

## 2.4 The Modern Slavery Act 2015

Further to ratification of the 2005 Convention and 2011 EU Anti-Trafficking Directive, the UK enacted the MSA in 2015, incorporating s4 of the Immigration and Asylum Act 2004 and s71 of the Coroners and Justice Act 2009 and six sections of the Sexual Offences Act 2003. In keeping with international approaches and legislation, the UK has adopted a criminal model approach to tackling modern slavery; notably, the Act extended the maximum prison sentence from fourteen years to life imprisonment for those convicted. Consequently, law enforcement and the judiciary are key actors in the field, taking on responsibility for a complex new offence during a prolonged period of austerity and government cuts (see Section 7.2). The complexity of the offence is reflected in the fact that it is also a human rights abuse[97] and a labour law issue,[98] with features that frequently connect it to the corporate retail sector. This is abetted by the fact that many businesses, in a fiercely competitive market, are pushing down the prices of their products in response to consumer demands. The clothing industry, for instance, has seen a relentless drive towards 'fast fashion' in the past few decades. While allegations that Nike were running sweatshops in the 1990s caused enduring financial and reputational damage,[99] and numerous studies indicate that customers would be prepared to pay more for products that have come from ethical supply chains,[100] 'there is no decisive conclusion that consumers in fact act differently based

96 Puja, Leeds, UK, 8 January 2019.

97 Notably an *absolute* human rights abuse, prohibited by multiple international and regional legal instruments.

98 van Dyke (n 3).

99 Debra Cohen Maryanov, 'Sweatshop Liability: Corporate Codes of Conduct and the Governance of Labor Standards in the International Supply Chain' (2010) 14 *Lewis & Clark Law Review* 397.

100 E Christopher Johnson, 'The Corporate Lawyer, Human Trafficking and Child Labor: Who's in Your Supply Chain?' (2013) 30 *T.M. Cooley Law Review* 27.

on particular knowledge of a corporation's business practices.'[101] This knowledge may not even be fully informed; although the public is by now mostly aware of poor labour practices in supply chains originating in developing countries, buying British will not guarantee an ethical product. Investigations into Leicester's garment manufacturing industry uncovered 'dark factories' in which workers were paid an average of £4.25 an hour,[102] less than half the current over-25's then minimum wage of £8.72.[103] This should have placed these factories under the radar of the authorities, but many avoid scrutiny by under-recording workers' hours, meaning that 'people's payslips look as if they have been paid the minimum wage.'[104] In a move to combat such practices, the MSA also contains a Transparency in Supply Chains Provision,[105] which requires companies with a turnover of at least £36 million to report on what steps they are taking to monitor and eliminate labour abuses in their supply chains by way of a published Modern Slavery Statement. Unfortunately, the clause has been heavily criticised as weak and ineffective, given that there are no repercussions for non-compliance.[106] A survey from the Chartered Institute of Procurement and Supply (CIPS) reinforces this, finding that over a third of qualifying businesses had failed to provide a statement even two years after the MSA was enacted.[107] More worryingly, the minimum wage requirement for all UK workers in supply chains has been largely ignored, as the percentage of supply managers meeting this obligation has actually fallen since the commencement of the MSA.[108] Given the traditional view that business is amoral,[109] calls for companies to transcend their responsibilities beyond commercial interest are frequently ignored in the absence of a strong incentive.

101 Kemi Mustapha, 'Taste of Child Labor Not So Sweet: A Critique of Regulatory Approaches to Combating Child Labor Abuses by the U.S. Chocolate Industry' (2010) 87 *Washington University Law Review* 1163, 1776–77.

102 Sarah O'Connor, 'Dark Factories: Labour Exploitation in Britain's Garment Industry' *Financial Times* (London, 17 May 2018) <www.ft.com/content/e427327e-5892-11e8-b8b2-d6ceb45fa9d0> accessed 1 July 2020.

103 UK Government, 'National Minimum Wage and National Living Wage Rates' (*UK Government*) <www.gov.uk/national-minimum-wage-rates> accessed 1 July 2020.

104 Sarah O'Connor, 'Dark Factories: Labour Exploitation in Britain's Garment Industry' *Financial Times* (London, 17 May 2018) <www.ft.com/content/e427327e-5892-11e8-b8b2-d6ceb45fa9d0> accessed 1 July 2020.

105 Modern Slavery Act 2015, s54.

106 Gary Craig 'The UK's Modern Slavery Legislation: An Early Assessment of Progress' (2017) 5(2) *Social Inclusion* 16.

107 Chartered Institute of Procurement and Supply (CIPS), 'One in Three Businesses Are Flouting Modern Slavery Legislation – and Getting Away with It' *CIPS News* (6 September 2017) <www.cips.org/en-gb/news/news/one-in-three-businesses-are-flouting-modern-slavery-legislation-and-getting-away-with-it/> accessed 14 October 2017.

108 ibid.

109 Elizabeth Tuttle, 'Made in Violation: Non-legal Solutions to Labor Abuses Perpetrated by American Multinational Corporations in Foreign Sweatshops' (2015) 17 *Duquesne Business Law Journal* 101.

Most evidence suggests that only profit truly motivates businesses to adopt corporate social responsibility (CSR) and ethical practices,[110] and profit comes from the consumer. Unfortunately, as one participant observed, 'if you're not showing us as consumers where the slavery may be, we don't then have a choice, we can't choose company A, B and C because you're not all producing reports.'[111] While high-profile cases can produce a boycott of a particular brand,[112] perhaps the public is content enough with superficial CSR images as long as prices remain low. The reality is, most consumers are constantly 'demanding cheap goods and services but failing to question how these goods and services can be sold so inexpensively.'[113] In other words, while the public will freely support moves to punish perpetrators of such a universally abhorrent act, convincing them to vote with their own money is a harder sell:

> [M]ost middle-class people now will not buy unfairly traded coffee, bananas and chocolate and yet the late 1990s everyone was like 'it's expensive, we're not doing it'. We've changed the culture around that and we need to start looking at how we change the culture around the car washes, nail bars etc. Ten years ago no one was having their car washed, all of a sudden everyone gets their car washed for a fiver. Painting nails . . . since when did . . . ? All these things are indicative of our fast living immediate gratification culture, actually link in to some pretty dark stuff where you can see the impact of what we're doing and how do you raise awareness in a community to let people know that?[114]

This dichotomy, and other challenges, can erode the best of corporate intentions if not backed up by robust legislation and enforcement.

One significant feature of the MSA is that, where sexual exploitation has been the focus of legislation in many other countries, the UK has widened the remit to cover all aspects of labour exploitation. Although sex trafficking, and the wider issue of sex work, were debated during the passage of the Modern Slavery Bill,[115] the legislation acknowledges the increasing number of male victims and incidences of slavery within other industrial sectors. As progressive as this appears, *prima facie*, the practicalities of passing the Bill illustrate a less laudable set of circumstances. Theresa May, the then home secretary, opted to set up an evidence review rather than asking the Home Office to produce

110 Kevin Bales, *Disposable People: New Slavery in the Modern Economy* (University of California Press 2000).

111 Ayesha, Portsmouth, UK, 30 October 2018.

112 Dana C Nicholas, 'China's Labor Enforcement Crisis: International Intervention and Corporate Social Responsibility' (2009) 11 *SCHOLAR* 155.

113 E Christopher Johnson, 'The Corporate Lawyer, Human Trafficking and Child Labor: Who's in Your Supply Chain?' (2013) 30 *T.M. Cooley Law Review* 27, 30.

114 Ayesha, Portsmouth, UK, 30 October 2018.

115 HC Deb, 4 November 2014, vol 587, cols 769–76.

a white paper outlining the government's plans.[116] The stakeholders who presented to the review indicated that the Bill should prioritise protecting victims of slavery,[117] with the Joint Committee on the Draft Modern Slavery Bill subsequently making significant recommendations to this effect, including to:

> put victim support and assistance on a statutory footing; create separate offences of exploiting and trafficking a child; ensure victims were not prosecuted for crimes that they were forced to commit while enslaved; strengthen the asset recovery regime to seize illicit gains made from modern slavery; ensure the independence of the Anti-Slavery Commissioner and broaden its functions to include victim protection and partnerships; and make it obligatory that businesses above a certain size audit modern slavery in their supply chains.[118]

At the time of the Bill's introduction to Parliament, the Conservative Party also had an eye towards the upcoming general election in May 2015. Dogged by net migration figures that heavily belied their 2010 election pledge to reduce immigration and threatened by the rising popularity of the UK Independence Party, the Conservatives were keenly aware of the need to placate the anti-immigration demographic of the electorate.[119] This resulted in the introduction of a new Immigration Bill, created to 'make the UK the least attractive destination for illegal immigrants.'[120] Conversely, the Anglican and Catholic Churches – another core group of voters – were conciliated by the more humanitarian aims of a pro-migrant MSA. In short, Theresa May's 'personal priority'[121] was winning the general election. Time was therefore of the essence, and the Modern Slavery Bill was ultimately pushed through Parliament hastily, with requests from government that further proposed amendments be kept to a minimum. Despite the issue of sexual trafficking and exploitation being introduced at the debating stage, the MSA does not specifically address it. Moreover, the inclusion of specific support provisions was dismissed on the basis that the NRM was 'not fit for purpose and therefore should not be set

116 van Dyke (n 3).

117 Baroness Butler-Sloss and others, 'Establishing Britain as a World Leader in the Fight against Modern Slavery: Report of the Modern Slavery Bill Evidence Review' (2013) Presented to the Home Secretary on 16 December 2013.

118 van Dyke (n 3).

119 Caroline Robinson, 'Claiming Space for Labour Rights within the United Kingdom Modern Slavery Crusade' (2015) 5 *Anti-Trafficking Review* 129.

120 Home Office, *Immigration Bill Factsheet: Overview of the Bill* (Home Office 2013) 3 <www.gov.uk/government/uploads/system/uploads/attachment_data/file/249251/Overview_Immigration_Bill_Factsheet.pdf> accessed 4 December 2017.

121 Press Association, 'Theresa May Makes Modern Slavery Her "Personal Priority"' *The Guardian* (London, 24 November 2013) <www.theguardian.com/world/2013/nov/24/theresa-may-modern-slavery-priority> accessed 14 March 2020.

out in inflexible legislation.'[122] This is hardly an endorsement of the UK's official anti-slavery administrative mechanism. More pressingly, the repercussions of the Immigration Act 2016 conflicted with the aims of the MSA. By making it an offence for people to work if they have a precarious immigration status, the government in fact made certain groups even more vulnerable to human trafficking and labour exploitation – fear of deportation is a major coercion tool utilised by traffickers.[123] Chapter 5 provides a comprehensive analysis of this issue.

The MSA did, however, adopt core provisions from the Anti-Trafficking Directive and additionally established the post of IASC. The 'independence' of the role was debated and campaigned for at the Committee stages of the Modern Slavery Bill, as some Members raised concerns about the potential for corporate intervention.[124] In any event, the commissioner's autonomy is open to challenge: the IASC reports to the government, rather than Parliament, and the executive has the authority to 'redact elements of any report produced by the IASC.'[125] Kevin Hyland, the UK's first IASC, resigned from the post in May 2018, citing government interference as a partial factor.[126] He had also repeatedly expressed frustration at what he perceived to be the failings of the police[127] and the UK's anti-slavery system in general; since then, he has continued to be critical of the UK's approach to modern slavery, noting the potential for conflict as the Home Office – primarily responsible for immigration – is also now responsible for the NRM[128] (see Chapter 5). One participant was similarly unimpressed with the departmental change: 'I wish they'd left it with the National Crime Agency though, not the Home Office, because the Home Office are buggers! They're a law unto themselves! They have no accountability so they can do what they like!'[129]

One year on from its enactment, Theresa May commissioned an independent review of the MSA, which was undertaken by Caroline Haughey.[130]

122 Vicky Brotherton, 'Class Acts? A Comparative Analysis of Modern Slavery Legislation across the UK' in Gary Craig and others (eds), *The Modern Slavery Agenda: Policy, Politics and Practice in the UK* (Policy Press 2019) 107.

123 van Dyke (n 3).

124 Modern Slavery Bill HC Bill (2014–15) [8].

125 Gary Craig and others (eds), *The Modern Slavery Agenda: Policy, Politics and Practice in the UK* (Policy Press 2019) 5.

126 ibid.

127 Daniel Silverstone and Claire Brickell, *Combating Modern Slavery Experienced by Vietnamese Nationals En Route to, and within, the UK* (Office of the Independent Anti-Slavery Commissioner 2017).

128 Amelia Gentleman, 'Ex-commissioner Condemns "Failing" UK Approach to Human Trafficking' *The Guardian* (London, 28 October 2019) <www.theguardian.com/law/2019/oct/28/ex-commissioner-condemns-failing-uk-approach-to-human-trafficking> accessed 16 April 2020.

129 Donna, Nottingham, UK, 10 May 2019.

130 Caroline Haughey, *The Modern Slavery Act Review: One Year on* (Home Office 2016).

The review flagged a 'lack of consistency'[131] across the criminal justice system and noted the need for a structured approach that evidenced best practice and revised procedures that were not working well. Haughey also found that some survivors were not offered vulnerable witness protections such as special measures in Court. The report recommended training for all criminal justice professionals, placing emphasis on the need for victim awareness and vulnerable witness training. Multi-partnership working was strongly encouraged, an issue that is discussed more fully in Chapter 4, stating that police training should include awareness of 'trusted and credible'[132] charities. The parallels between human trafficking and other forms of abuse are discussed throughout this book, and they are further reflected by how recorded rape and conviction rates remarkably diverge between police forces; coupled with 'different attitudes and beliefs regarding the appropriate methods and practices for policing,'[133] it is clear that national guidelines and training are not delivering the uniformity of standards expected for vulnerable victims. Haughey, however, acknowledged this paradigm by recommending the creation of a list of advocates, drawn from the rape list, who have the appropriate skills to prosecute offences under the MSA. Reaffirming the EU Anti-Trafficking Directive, which 'imposes a duty to investigate human trafficking, and to do so irrespective of any report by the victim,'[134] the report also urges police to 'consider investigating and prosecution in all cases, even where the victim has decided not to engage with the criminal justice system.'[135] This would not only reduce the pressure on survivors to provide a witness statement but would place less of a burden on law enforcement agencies to obtain the statement and maintain witness engagement to the point of possible trial. Indeed, Diana remarked that often, many hours of work are undertaken during an investigation only to culminate in a survivor withdrawing from the CJS.[136] These issues and potential outcomes are discussed further in Chapters 6 and 7.

## 2.5 The future of modern slavery policy and legislation in the UK

The UK government can indulge in some hubris towards its modern slavery approach. UK police have presented more intelligence and information and initiated more joint investigation teams (JITs) than any other EU member state.[137] One characteristic of trafficking is that 'victims are moved from place

131 ibid 3.
132 ibid 5.
133 Balch and Geddes (n 11) 26, 38.
134 Steven Bird and Philippa Southwell, 'Does the New "Slavery" Defence Offer Victims of Trafficking Any Greater Protection?' (2015) 9 *Archbold Review* 7.
135 Haughey (n 130) 8.
136 Diana, Bristol, UK, 22 February 2019.
137 van Dyke (n 3).

to place, so that they are kept in disorientation,'[138] making it much harder to trace their whereabouts.[139] The casual nature of the work, high turnover and lack of record-keeping create further difficulties for intelligence gathering agencies;[140] when slavery crosses borders, interstate co-operation is required, which only adds to the burden of efficient law enforcement.[141] Many states are still catching up and their domestic legislation is in its nascent stages.[142] Diana, whose job remit involves interstate-partnership working, indicated that no other European country has established the level of structured investigation as the UK. At the time of the interview, she was developing strong partnerships with her European counterparts to enhance investigation operations and co-ordinate better care pathways for survivors. David, based in strategic law enforcement, also commented on this:

> I think some of the law enforcement in some of the countries in Europe have really appreciated the learning and the way we've gone about some of the joint investigations and that's where the Europol involvement is important as well because they, clearly it's part of their role to help co-ordinated and support, and fund actually, some of those investigations, so I think that's where it really comes into its own, regarding that European co-operation.[143]

For this reason, several participants expressed their reservations over the potential impact of Brexit on countering modern slavery and human trafficking. Concerns ranged from the reduced capacity for cross-border investigations and arrests to how the change in immigration status for EU nationals will affect their ability to work in the UK, leading to a possible rise in supply and demand for traffickers: 'with Brexit, we are going to have a massive hole in the job market, absolutely massive,'[144] and, consequently:

> if you need a supply of labour and you've got a contract that's got to be fulfilled, or you might be responsible for financial penalties if that contract's not fulfilled, where are you going to go? Are you gonna go to the guy that says, 'yeah I can get you twenty guys in the morning'? You're

138 Stephanie Hepburn and Rita J Simon, 'Hidden in Plain Sight: Human Trafficking in the United States' (2010) 27(1) *Gender Issues* 6, 26.
139 Ryszard Piotrowicz, 'States' Obligations under Human Rights Law towards Victims of Trafficking in Human Beings: Positive Developments in Positive Obligations' (2012) 24(2) *International Journal of Refugee Law* 181.
140 Haughey (n 130).
141 Piotrowicz (n 139) 181.
142 Ruth Farrugia, 'State Responsibility for Human Trafficking: Perspectives from Malta' (2012) 15(2) *JMLC* 142.
143 David, Birmingham, UK, 20 October 2018.
144 Ayesha, Portsmouth, UK, 30 October 2018.

> not going to ask any questions. So this whole arena of exploitation can grow exponentially.[145]

The potential uncertainty also raises serious threats that undermine much of the progress so far:

> I think it's just it's hard-won processes that have been put in place over the years, so Europol. We've had a presentation from them at some of our regional events through the Transformation Programme, again, funding that we secured, £8million worth of funding to roll out the programme, again to raise awareness of some of the tools around joint investigation teams, obviously European Arrest Warrants are crucial and actually the UK is the biggest user of European Arrest Warrants because of our proactive, because of work that we undertake in this area and there's a whole thing around Schengen information sharing agreements, so it is quite complex but the bottom line is without a proper agreement, then some of that is potentially at risk, which will make things a lot harder, basically.[146]

The Anti-Trafficking Monitoring Group has also raised concerns about the effects of Brexit, which largely reflected these fears. They suggested that collaborative efforts with Europe may suffer as 'the current standing that the UK enjoys as an EU Member State i.e. having a strategic role in Europol's management and in the setting of its organisational priorities, is likely to be lost.'[147] The ATMG further iterates how the problematic offence of illegal working under the Immigration Act 2016 is likely to put large numbers of EU citizens at risk of becoming victims of modern slavery, citing the vulnerability issues identified since the regulation changes for ODW visas.[148] The possible impact on the UK's labour market will place even greater strain on the already-stretched GLAA (see Section 7.2.1). Boris Johnson, in his period as prime minister overseeing the Brexit process, was unhelpfully ambiguous about the future status of workers' rights in general, although his enthusiasm for liberating the UK from EU employment regulations was more clearly enunciated.[149] The ATMG warned that risks of exploitation 'are exacerbated when coupled with a labour market that favours deregulation and flexibility; in practice, this has resulted in an erosion of workers' rights.'[150]

145 Diana, Bristol, UK, 22 February 2019.
146 David, Birmingham, UK, 20 October 2018.
147 Anti-Trafficking Monitoring Group, *Brexit & the UK's Fight against Modern Slavery* (ATMG July 2017) 6.
148 ibid.
149 Michael Ford QC, 'The Effect of Brexit on Workers' Rights' (2017) 27 *King's Law Journal* 3, 398.
150 Anti-Trafficking Monitoring Group (n 147) 2.

One of the other concerns is the rapid erosion of established EU law in the UK. Under Prime Minister Theresa May, the EU Withdrawal Act 2018 ensured that EU laws were to be converted into domestic law or, where this had already taken place, retained.[151] However, the UK was 'specifically not retaining'[152] EU Directives themselves, although any domestic legislation that already implemented the rights and obligations contained within Directives was to remain the same. Since then, however, the Retained EU Law (Revocation and Reform) Act 2023 has revoked almost 600 pieces of EU law; while the majority of these were mostly defunct and related to food, tax, agriculture and the environment, it also repealed the part of the EU Withdrawal Act 2018, stipulating that this will render some retained EU law unrecognised or unavailable in domestic law and, 'accordingly, is not to be enforced, allowed or followed.' This creates a legal vacuum; the Act does not specify the laws to be revoked and does not require the government to identify them. Once again, the lack of legal certainty will only leave frontline practitioners and campaigners scratching their heads in dismay.

Along the same parameters, it is crucial to remember that the UK has not made survivor support a part of modern slavery legislation. Where lawyers have been instructed to hold the government to account in this area, they have instead relied on the EU Anti-Trafficking Directive, meaning that victims will have even less legal backing post-Brexit. The UK-ratified Convention against Trafficking also emphasises the importance of post-trauma support:

> [It] includes legally binding obligations on States to assist victims in their physical, psychological and social recovery. These include obligations to provide appropriate and secure accommodation, psychological and material assistance, counselling and information, and access to education for children.[153]

It is not clear why, despite leading the charge in identifying and investigating cases of modern slavery, the UK has been slow to legislate a comprehensive support system for the actual survivors. A previous commitment to provide a guaranteed twelve months of support following a positive Conclusive Grounds decision was scrapped in December 2023; this was on the premise that support decisions would instead be made by the Home Office on individual cases.[154] Way back in June 2017, Lord McColl introduced the Modern Slavery (Victim Support) Bill that aims to '[m]ake provision about identifying and

151 Graeme Cowie, *The Status of "Retained EU Law"* (Commons Library Briefing 08375, 2019).
152 ibid 4.
153 Suzanne Egan, 'Tackling the Rise of Child Labour in Europe: Homework for the European Court of Human Rights' (2015) 64(3) *International and Comparative Law Quarterly* 601, 612.
154 Modern Slavery Unit, 'NRM Reform Newsletter' (Home Office mailing list) (1 December 2023).

supporting victims of modern slavery,'[155] stating his concern that this aspect of the EU Anti-Trafficking Directive has not been enshrined in domestic law.[156] The Bill, if passed, would ensure that survivors are provided with accommodation, material assistance, medical treatment, translation services, legal assistance, counselling and a support worker, as well as twelve months' leave to remain in the UK. The Bill took the entirety of the 2017–2019 Parliament to makes its way through the early reading stages of debate but was discontinued as a result of the dissolution of Parliament in October 2019 prior to the general election. Undeterred, Lord McColl reintroduced the Bill soon after the new Parliamentary session began in December 2019. The Bill continues to progress at a glacial pace, despite strong support from some prominent Parliamentarians.[157] The Bill has also been largely well received by stakeholders and NGOs, as expressed by some research participants, for example:

> What [Lord McColl's Bill] means is they would get twelve months discretionary leave, which basically entitles them to the same entitlements as a British person – for twelve months – but that would also come with twelve months of support that goes along with that because the stability that we see that both discretionary leave combined with the support brings, and somebody's ability to process what's happened to them and start to recover and move forwards is hugely different to a person who is still in a state of uncertainty and insecurity.[158]

The Bill, or rather, its long-term implications, are nonetheless open to challenge as 'whilst in principle, great, in practice, if it's a year to remain but they've still got no job or access to education and we've still got a housing crisis, actually what are they doing in that year other than prolonging the inevitable?'[159] In fact, long-term support and more pertinently, long-term residence in the UK for foreign nationals, is an area that has received relatively little attention in the law and is discussed in more detail in Chapters 6 and 8.

## 2.6 Conclusion

This chapter aimed to evaluate the successes and limitations of the UK's legislation, policies and practices in supporting survivors. The difficulty for any government in tackling modern slavery and human trafficking is that the issue does not fit neatly into one clear policy area. There is no argument that it is a serious crime and should therefore be treated as such in law. Nonetheless,

155 Modern Slavery (Victim Support) HL Bill (2017–2019) 4.
156 HL Deb, 8 September 2017, vol 783, col 2213.
157 Free for Good, 'UK's Campaign for The Modern Slavery (Victim Support) Bill 2019–2020' (*Free for Good*) <https://freeforgood.org.uk/about-the-bill/> accessed 15 March 2020.
158 Caroline, Nottingham, UK, 22 November 2019.
159 Ayesha, Portsmouth, UK, 30 October 2018.

a purely criminal approach does not take into account the human needs that emerge as a result of the crime. These needs are complex and often deep-seated, meaning that a forty-five-day or even ninety-day turnaround may look impressive on paper but does not offer much to survivors in the long term. Even legislative efforts to increase this time and provide greater support for victims may serve only to postpone the problem rather than address it. The crime also overlaps with labour laws, and while the MSA acknowledges this with its Transparency in Supply Chains Provision, it fundamentally pays lip service to the idea rather than offering a tangible means of enforcement.

Overall, rather than implementing a multiple streams approach, which 'can help in recognizing the wide spectrum of problem interpretations and corresponding solutions that these different manifestations inspire,'[160] the government appears to be compartmentalising its responsibilities. Where these responsibilities merge or conflict, the priority does not appear to be the wellbeing of the survivors themselves, as demonstrated by the backlog of individuals awaiting Conclusive Grounds decisions. Frontline practitioners, particularly those from law enforcement, clearly extoll the benefits of joint initiatives and strong communication; yet many of these individuals and the organisations they represent find that they are precluded from doing their job when an NRM 'gatekeeper' stands between them and the survivor. This fragmented approach is not only inefficient, it undermines the UK's aims and commitments to a survivor-centred system. Perhaps the most indicative measure of government attitudes to survivors, however, is the way in which responsibility for their support has been franchised wholesale to the voluntary sector. The next chapter addresses this decision and evaluates the effectiveness of the system as it currently operates.

160 Alison Gardner, 'An Idea Whose Time Has Come? Modern Slavery, Multiple Streams Approach and Multilayer Policy Implementation' (2018) 10 *Journal of Human Rights Practice* 461, 464.

# 3 Voluntary sector organisations

## 3.1 Introduction

While the government is swift to herald any move it makes to advance anti-slavery initiatives, it is fair to say that without charitable organisations, many of these initiatives would not exist. As the phenomenon of modern slavery became increasingly apparent in the UK, the voluntary sector swiftly rose to the challenge of providing the requisite support and assistance to victims. Several existing UK charities expanded their services (including the Salvation Army, Barnardo's and the Helen Bamber Foundation), while others were established with the express intent to do so (for example, Hope for Justice, Unseen and the Medaille Trust)[1]. Shortly after the enactment of the Modern Slavery Act, a survey counted 71 independent UK charities that provided assistance to modern slavery survivors;[2] in European countries, the average number of organisations is twelve.[3] These changes coincided with a steady public policy move towards reliance on the voluntary sector to strengthen or even fill voids in governmental support, from David Cameron's 'Big Society' to more government funding of charitable organisations.[4] Meanwhile, smaller, independently funded organisations are 'said to have a comparative advantage in terms of their ability to personalise and adjust services to the needs of users compared to public providers'[5] but are usually compelled to achieve this on a much tighter budget. Either way, although charities are not aiming to create financial profit, they are still obligated to raise the necessary funds to operate, and to create a social benefit, as well as engaging with a broad range of

1 Ruth van Dyke, 'The UK's Response to Modern Slavery: Law, Policy and Politics' in Gary Craig and others (eds), *The Modern Slavery Agenda: Policy, Politics and Practice in the UK* (Policy Press 2019).

2 Stephanie A Limoncelli, 'What in the World Are Anti-Trafficking NGOs Doing? Findings from a Global Study' (2016) 2(4) *Journal of Human Trafficking* 316.

3 David Gadd and Rose Broad, 'Troubling Recognitions in British Responses to Modern Slavery' (2018) 58 *British Journal of Criminology* 1440.

4 David Clifford and John Mohan, 'The Sources of Income of English and Welsh Charities: An Organisation-Level Perspective' (2016) 27 *Voluntas* 487.

5 ibid 487, 493.

DOI: 10.4324/9781032639895-3

stakeholders, such as funders, community partnerships and, of course, their beneficiaries and service users.[6]

This chapter provides an overview of the current landscape of the voluntary sector in the UK to further examine the UK's legislation and policies in practice and the support systems currently in place. In particular, this chapter evaluates the level of consistencies and disparities in service delivery across the UK. It also demonstrates how austerity, combined with growing reliance by the government on charities, has impacted anti-modern slavery organisations in the longer term. This is pertinent due to the nascency of many organisations, who are still developing and expanding their support services amidst a rapidly changing area of policy. Fundraising efforts, particularly applications for government grants, are taking place in an increasingly competitive and saturated market, which has led to challenges as to the quality of support that is being provided by some organisations. The chapter also discusses the transparency and accountability of the charity sector, including funding, and how disparities in reporting standards lead to potential differences in the care and support of survivors. This segues, ultimately, into an analysis of the charitable organisations that offer services for survivors of modern slavery.

## 3.2 Pre-National Referral Mechanism service developments

The first single-issue service for survivors of human trafficking to be granted government funding was in 2003, when the Poppy Project was established as part of Eaves Housing for Women.[7] The project continued operating until 2011 when the decision was made by the Ministry of Justice to award the renewed £4million[8] contract to the Salvation Army, a move which would reduce the Poppy Project's income by around 60% per victim.[9] The funding change – under the twelve-month-old coalition government – appeared to be a controversial move, given the Salvation Army's evangelist underpinning. Labour MP Vera Baird expressed her disgust via Twitter, with the post 'Abysmal decision to give Sally Army Eaves contract to help trafficked women. If u were sexually abused wld u go to male Christian in uniform?',[10] while immigration information service Free Movement called it 'a clear signal of a return to

6 J David Cabedo and others, 'Improving and Measuring Transparency in NGOs: A Disclosure Index for Activities and Projects' (2018) 28 *Nonprofit Management and Leadership* 329.

7 van Dyke (n 1).

8 The figure of £6million was cited by several publications at the time but was later cited as £4million – £2million per year over a two year period.

9 Patrick Butler and Alan Travis, 'Sex Trafficking Charity Loses Out to Salvation Army over £6m Contract' *The Guardian* (London, 11 April 2011) <www.theguardian.com/society/2011/apr/11/eaves-housing-trafficking-salvation-army> accessed 14 May 2020.

10 GA Ponsonby, 'Labour Candidate in Salvation Army "Male Christian" Insult' (*Newsnet Scotland*, 17 April 2011) <https://web.archive.org/web/20110418061038/www.newsnetscotland.com/scottish-politics/2122-labour-candidate-in-salvation-army-male-christian-insult.html> accessed 14 May 2020.

Victorian values of the undeserving poor and salvation through faith.'[11] Eaves Housing criticised the 'ideological decision,' stating that it 'marked a change in the way government supports care for victims of trafficking: 'They were after a bare minimum service, not a specialist service.'[12] Certainly, the economic viewpoint was that the Salvation Army's funding bid had requested significantly less income while offering a more diluted service.[13] The latter perspective may have been in response to the fact that the Salvation Army was to act as 'gatekeeper' of the new contract, subcontracting frontline services to other partnership organisations across the UK rather than providing the services directly. Eaves Housing additionally cited political motivation as a factor, given that Eaves was responsible for seventeen successful appeals against UK Border Agency decisions on identification of trafficking victims over the previous two years,[14] while in early 2011, then-CEO Denise Marshall had returned her MBE in protest at government cuts to charities and services.[15] Within a week of the funding withdrawal, the Poppy Project announced that it was under threat of closure; it needed to raise £450,000 by the end of June that year if it was to continue.[16] The project was sustained for a while, but on a significantly reduced budget, meaning that services were accordingly condensed. By June 2013, the Poppy Project had gone from providing fifty-six bed spaces across nine sites to a total of nine bed spaces.[17] Ultimately, however, the project's umbrella organisation, Eaves Housing for Women, was unable to continue operating under an overall increasing deficit and announced that the entire organisation would be closing on 30 October 2015. The announcement, issued on the charity's website, included a statement attacking the government's position on voluntary sector funding, in particular women's organisations:

> It is abysmal commissioning whereby commissioners either do not know or do not care what they should be looking for or how to assess a bid other than by lowest unit cost with no regard to quality. This is evidenced by the fact that large, generic, non-specialist organisations are winning tenders, expanding, accumulating vast reserves and specialist, smaller organisations with 40+ years of history with high levels of self referrals

11 Free Movement, 'Poppy Project to Close, Funding Going to Missionaries Instead' (*Free Movement*, 12 April 2011) <www.freemovement.org.uk/poppy-project-to-close-funding-going-to-missionaries-instead/> accessed 18 May 2020.

12 Butler and Travis (n 9).

13 Julie Bindel, 'The Demise of Women's Charity Eaves Should Worry Us All' *The Guardian* (London, 3 November 2015) <www.theguardian.com/lifeandstyle/womens-blog/2015/nov/03/the-demise-of-womens-charity-eaves-should-worry-us-all> accessed 18 May 2020.

14 Mark Townsend, 'Sex-trafficked Women's Charity Poppy Project in Danger as Funding Withdrawn' *The Guardian* (London, 17 April 2011) <www.theguardian.com/society/2011/apr/17/prostitution-human-trafficking> accessed 18 May 2020.

15 Butler and Travis (n 9).

16 Townsend (n 14).

17 Home Affairs Committee, *Human Trafficking* (HC 2013–14 72-i).

> from women (a sure sign of the value of the service to the women) – are shrinking and having to use their scarce reserves to survive.[18]

The reference to 'large, generic, non-specialist organisations' echoes the comments made by Eaves Housing representatives at the time of the funding shift and appears to also cast shade on the quality of support offered by The Salvation Army and similar charities. Elsewhere, a former service user and now ex-employee of Eaves reported that the repeated undercutting of grant bids by these organisations was offset by low staff salaries and poor support services.[19] While this tone may represent the embitterment of losing the service as well as their jobs, Eaves Housing's sentiments were reiterated by other organisations across the sector. Polly Neate, then CEO of Women's Aid, raised concerns about the motivations of large charities 'bidding competitively for someone else's existing work.'[20] In fact, many commentators felt that this competitive tendering was disproportionately detrimental to women's services: specialist women's refuges, for example, had decreased from 187 to 155 between 2010 and 2014.[21] Given that even larger specialist charities such as Women's Aid, Refuge and Rape Crisis cater for survivors of sexual exploitation and sex trafficking, this trend places many vulnerable women at risk of losing bespoke support that is unavailable elsewhere.

## 3.3 Funding and accountability

Fear of losing precious funds is, naturally, a major driver for organisations:

> I have learned that in pretty much all organisational cultures in NGOs across the board, NGOs' relationships with business, NGOs' relationship with government, that people really struggle to put their cards on the table. There's this constant game around 'let's not be fully transparent'. When you are funded by an organisation, you're worried about losing your funding and so how do you challenge your funder if you think

18 Eaves for Women, 'Closure of Eaves – Another Nail in the Coffin for the Women's Sector?' (*Eaves for Women*) <https://web.archive.org/web/20151102004206/www.eavesforwomen.org.uk/news-events/news/closure-of-eaves-another-nail-in-the-coffin-for-the-women-s-sector> accessed 18 May 2020.

19 Bindel (n 13).

20 Emily Corfe, 'Women's Charity Eaves Shuts Down, Blaming "Abysmal Commissioning"' (*Civil Society*, 2 November 2015) <www.civilsociety.co.uk/news/women-s-charity-eaves-shuts-down-blaming-abysmal-commissioning-.html> accessed 18 May 2020.

21 Rebecca Winson, 'The Closure of Eaves Charity Is the Tip of the Iceberg in the Crisis for Women's Services' (*Centre for Labour and Social Studies*, 19 November 2015) <http://classonline.org.uk/blog/item/the-closure-of-eaves-charity-is-the-tip-of-the-iceberg-in-the-crisis-for-wo> accessed 18 May 2020.

> they're doing things wrong? Mostly, you're trying to meet their expectations, not changing what those expectations should be.[22]

For this reason, some funding sources can also be more attractive than others. Some NGOs actually prefer *not* to receive government funding:

> One of the advantages I suppose, of not being funded by someone telling you that you're funding this, this and this but not that, that and that means we've had a lot of flexibility about who we work with and the way we work with people as well.[23]

While there is an acknowledgement that financial restrictions can be tighter without the bolster of a government contract, many charities feel that full independence is, on balance, the greater dividend. Part of the difficulty with statutory funding in the modern slavery sector is that it links specifically to the NRM. Given the strict time limitations of the 'recovery and reflection' period, this automatically narrows the scope of services that government-contracted organisations can provide (see also Chapter 8):

> The trouble is with the NRM providers and a lot of the other people who work in this field, they're not there for the long haul, they've then got six months funding, they've only got . . . you know they're restricted to what services they can provide.[24]

It is also a concern for best practice if funding restrictions prevent tangible reform efforts:

> I think that the NGOs that are not government-funded seem to have more capacity to hear, maybe address, but definitely to hear the challenges to their way of working. And maybe they can hear it because they feel as if they have more leeway to address them. And the government-contracted agencies here in the UK, what I've noticed is there is a difficulty, they can be hiding behind those contract negotiations and rather than saying 'We disagree with this as well, our hands are tied but can we do this or that?'[25]

Again, this supports the view that complete autonomy is preferable to a deeper pot of money for some organisations, which in turn facilitates better provisions for survivors. This issue was raised emphatically by the Poppy Project's

22 Jenni, Manchester, UK, 13 August 2019.
23 Becky, Sheffield, UK, 19 December 2018.
24 Donna, Nottingham, UK, 10 May 2019.
25 Jenni, Manchester, UK, 13 August 2019.

National Coordinator, Dorcas Erskine, in front of the Home Affairs Committee in June 2013, two years after her charity's funding had been lost to the Salvation Army. The hearing began with the following exchange:

*Chair:* I am going to start with a very quick question. Do you think that the issue of combating human trafficking is now better served because the Salvation Army is involved?

*Dorcas Erskine:* I come from the Poppy Project, as you know, and we used to hold the Government contracts before, so, of course, I have to declare that conflict of interest in my answer, and you can decide whether objectively what I say is right. No, I do not think, under the Salvation Army, that victims are better served. That is not because the Salvation Army is not a brilliant organisation; it is, and in a past life I have worked with them on different issues before I joined this. The Salvation Army is operating under a system that ties their hands. The Government only allows them to support victims of trafficking for 45 days. The Government has decided, around the identification of victims of trafficking who come from outside the European Union, that it is the UKBA[26] who decides whether they are a victim of trafficking. An agency charged with delivering the Government's challenging targets on immigration is not best served to identify victims of trafficking. All of these things make the Salvation Army unable to provide a good service.[27]

Additionally of note here are Erskine's criticisms regarding the identification of victims from outside the EU, which are echoed strongly by commentators from various sectors and addressed in Chapter 5. Interestingly, Ayesha – who represented a government-contracted organisation – felt that she *was* able to express the views of her organisation freely, albeit couched in diplomacy:

> I have been referred to as a 'critical friend' by the Home Office, which is a good thing I think, but very much our mode of operation is that if we find or see issues or see ways of improving things we would go and speak to the Home Office privately – we're not really going to bash them over the heads.[28]

26 UK Borders Agency.
27 Home Affairs Committee, *Human Trafficking* (HC 2013–14 72-i).
28 Ayesha, Portsmouth, UK, 30 October 2018.

It is fair to say that those on the ground are in the best position to identify issues that could be improved and, if the government is funding those operations, it should welcome suggestions that will provide greater value for money:

> I think it's important not to lose sight of the importance of frontline experience and making sure that it informs policy all the way through, so I think that kind of . . . I think there needs to be a bit more parity there[29].

In other words, the voluntary sector cannot be merely relegated to 'the position of a sub-contractor of state services.'[30]

Another issue for these voluntary organisations is that, where NRM referrals have steadily increased each year (see Section 2.3), so has the number of survivors requiring support, but government funding to anti-slavery charities has not reflected the rate of this growth. The Salvation Army, for example, was granted the Victim Care Contract (VCC) in 2013 with an annual support income of £4million; that year, the total number of identified victims receiving support in the UK was 550 . By 2015, the latter figure had doubled, but the Salvation Army's government funding remained static.[31] To give the government some credit, it simply could not have predicted the rapid increase in referrals, particularly as public awareness of modern slavery grew. Like domestic abuse and child sexual exploitation, there is a 'dark figure' behind official records and estimates,[32] and financial plans had to be based on the available information at the time. The VCC is also currently granted on a five-year tender. The 2015–2020 contract thus provided the Salvation Army with a larger fund worth £53.2 million over the five-year period,[33] while the 2020–2025 VCC was advertised at a total value of £160 – 305 million.[34] The substantial difference between the low and high figure allows for: 'a) the option to extend the contract from 5 to 8 years; b) volumetric variations and c) legislative or policy changes,'[35] but the advert stipulates that the grant award is expected to be at the lowest end of the scale. However, another more critical factor is the longer timeframes required to support survivors, and this is partly due to the

29 Puja, Leeds, UK, 8 January 2019.

30 Agatha Herman and Richard Yarwood, 'From Warfare to Welfare: Veterans, Military Charities and the Blurred Spatiality of Post-service Welfare in the United Kingdom' (2015) 47 *Environment and Planning A* 2628, 2631.

31 van Dyke (n 1).

32 Anne Gallagher, 'The Global Slavery Index: Seduction and Obfuscation' (4 December 2014) 50(50) *Inclusive Democracy.*

33 National Audit Office, *Home Office: Reducing Modern Slavery* (HC 2017–19 630).

34 Home Office, '2020 Modern Slavery Victim Care Procurement' (*UK Government,* 11 October 2019) <www.contractsfinder.service.gov.uk/Notice/d7f9cb92-f9f1-47dd-aced-89e996ab1855?origin=SearchResults&p=1> accessed 23 April 2020.

35 ibid.

increasingly extended NRM process. The House of Commons Committee of Public Accounts found that:

> Delays in NRM decision making have also increased the cost of the Department's victim care contract with the Salvation Army, because support is being provided for much longer than the Department assumed would be necessary when letting the contract. The Department now estimates that the cost of the five year contract to 2020 will be around £90 million, more than double its early estimates.[36]

This observation was made in May 2018; by the end of the year, a total of 6159 people were awaiting Reasonable Grounds or Conclusive Grounds decisions on their NRM status, with four cases from as far back as 2013.[37] At the end of 2023, there were 7880 decisions pending from that year alone.[38] Front-line practitioners are keenly aware of the resource deficits:

> If you look at over 5000[39] people, have the numbers of the charities of . . . that are involved in outsourcing, so the Salvation Army are used for outsourcing and providing accommodation or support, has that grown exponentially with that number? What we're finding practically is that a victim is identified, oftentimes 5 o'clock on a Friday afternoon, out of hours, that person has got to be looked after. If they want to go into the NRM or they want to be taken away, they will have to stay where they are until they can either be transported or taken to a known environment.[40]

> Given the context of austerity and cuts to services, that's my biggest worry, that the capacity for different organisations to really play their full role is quite diminished in a funding environment that is squeezed beyond anything that I've seen in thirty-odd years of involvement of public and private sector work.[41]

Participants also pointed to the unique characteristics of support for modern slavery survivors and the difficulties this can bring to service providers:

36 Committee of Public Accounts, *Reducing Modern Slavery* (HC 2017–19 886) 6–7.
37 National Crime Agency, *National Referral Mechanism Statistics – End of Year Summary 2018* (National Crime Agency 2018).
38 Home Office, *National Referral Mechanism Statistics – End of Year Summary 2023* (Home Office 2024).
39 This figure refers to the approximate number of referrals made to the NRM during 2018.
40 Diana, Bristol, UK, 22 February 2019.
41 David, Birmingham, UK, 20 October 2018.

> I think it's fair to say with the increase of complexities with clients that we've seen over the last few years the expectation on providers for adding extra services in has certainly increased.[42]

> There are other organisations as well who go over and above what's required in terms of statutory services because obviously we are talking about extremely vulnerable people who have been exploited, quite horrifically really, over long periods of time, so that ongoing training and getting the different agencies to understand their roles is so important.[43]

One conclusion taken from this is that 'the government is not bearing the full cost of provision, but relies on NGOs to meet the shortfall for both immediate needs and longer-term support to help in the reintegration process,'[44] while GRETA[45] stated that charities 'often had to use their own funds to provide these services.'[46]

Although annual government funding has stayed at roughly the same figure over the past decade (between £15.8 and £16.1 billion), as a proportion of voluntary sector income streams, it fell continuously from a high of 37% of the total income in 2009/10 to a low of 26% in 2019/20.[47] This rose slightly from 2020 onwards to 30%, possibly as a result of 'greater government activity during the covid-19 pandemic.'[48] However, a 2017 study by New Philanthropy Capital found that nearly two-thirds of charities reported using the money raised from public donations to bolster their government-contracted services,[49] highlighting 'concerns that public sector bodies are regularly requiring charities to agree to subsidise the cost of contracts with donor funds as a condition to being awarded them in the first place.'[50] Overall, public donations still make up around half of the voluntary sector's total income each year.[51] A Charity Finance Group survey suggested that government contracts were actually resulting in a loss for voluntary organisations, with some larger charities subsidising

42 Ayesha, Portsmouth, UK, 30 October 2018.
43 David, Birmingham, UK, 20 October 2018.
44 van Dyke (n 1) 57.
45 Council of Europe's Group of Experts on Action against Trafficking in Human Beings.
46 van Dyke (n 1) 57.
47 UK Civil Society Almanac 2023, 'What Are the Trends in Income from Government?' (*NCVO*) <www.ncvo.org.uk/news-and-insights/news-index/uk-civil-society-almanac-2023/financials/what-are-the-trends-in-income-from-government/#overview> accessed 22 March 2024.
48 ibid.
49 Patrick Butler, 'Two-thirds of Charities Subsidising Public Sector Contracts to Survive' *The Guardian* (London, 19 May 2017) <www.theguardian.com/society/2017/may/19/two-thirds-charities-subsidising-public-sector-contracts-survive> accessed 24 April 2020.
50 ibid.
51 UK Civil Society Almanac 2023 (n 47).

their services by up to 16% of the contract amount[52]. To illustrate, in addition to its statutory funding, the Salvation Army established an independent Victim Care Fund, later the Survivor Support Fund, drawn from the charity's resources through donations and regular giving initiatives; this amounted to £213,212.25 in 2022–23,[53] which was just 2% of its £10.6-m annual contract value. Charitable organisations have also learned the potential benefits of collaborating quid pro quo with for-profit companies, who are themselves keen to enhance their corporate social responsibility image. These collaborations can take the form of financial sponsorship from the company in exchange for product placement and positive PR from the charity.[54] The trade can also take the form of 'cashless transactions,' 'for example, when an organisation exchanges the use of premises for free accounting services from another organisation.'[55] This type of trade exchange cannot be catalogued in numerical terms but symbolises the creative nature of enterprising NGOs in a competitive market (see also Chapter 8 for specific examples).

## 3.4 Analysis of frontline organisations

To understand the landscape of the voluntary and non-profit sector within the anti-modern slavery arena, a mapping exercise was conducted of those organisations who are involved with supporting survivors in the UK. ninety-six organisations were identified in total, from well-funded UK-based agencies that operate as part of a larger international organisation to grassroots community groups run solely by volunteers. The vast majority of these were registered charities; only four organisations were solely registered as community interest companies (CICs), which means that although they work on a non-profit basis, they are not part of the charity sector. An individual may prefer to set up a CIC for several reasons: their financial reports do not require auditing, directors and trustees be paid, and they can self-fund through the sale of products and services, as well as receiving grants.[56] However, charitable organisations benefit from tax concessions and can register as a business interest alongside their Charity Commission registration, meaning that their trustees are not liable for financial loss or debt.[57] Approximately three-quarters of all identified organisations operated frontline services, with the remainder

52 Butler (n 49).

53 Salvation Army, *Behind the Shield: Protecting and Supporting Survivors of Modern Slavery* (2023) <https://indd.adobe.com/view/19577fb3-963f-4a97-aeea-32314d2ed7a7>.

54 Clifford and Mohan (n 4) 487.

55 ibid 487, 493.

56 TBL Accountants, 'Charity Setups: What Are the Differences between CIC and CIO?' (*TBL Accountants*, 21 June 2019) <https://tblaccountants.co.uk/news/charity-setups-cic-cio> accessed 2 June 2020.

57 ibid.

offering either signposting or referral support (helpline services) or providing indirect assistance through campaigning, research or fundraising for grants to other charities. This is represented in Figure 3.1.

Of the seventy-one frontline services, there was a relatively even split between single-issue support ($n$ = 30), in which the whole organisation is dedicated to providing services for modern slavery and human trafficking survivors, and multi-issue organisations ($n$ = 41), whose overall aims cover a wider client base, such as survivors of sexual abuse or homeless individuals. This is represented in Figure 3.2.

While many other multi-issue charities cater for the needs of modern slavery survivors – food banks, for example, provide practical support – the intention

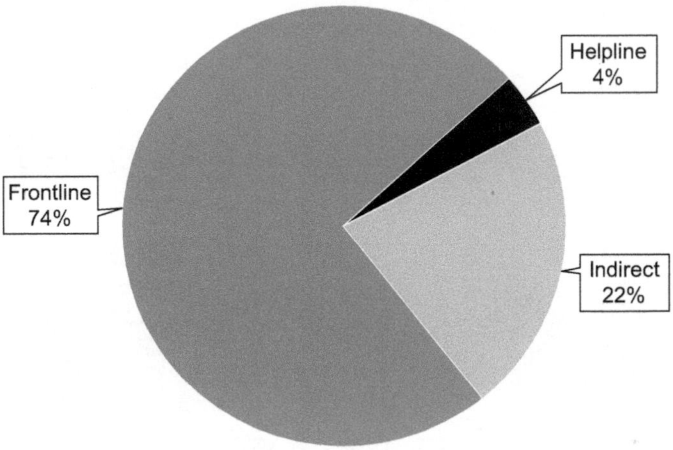


*Figure 3.1* Level of service engagement

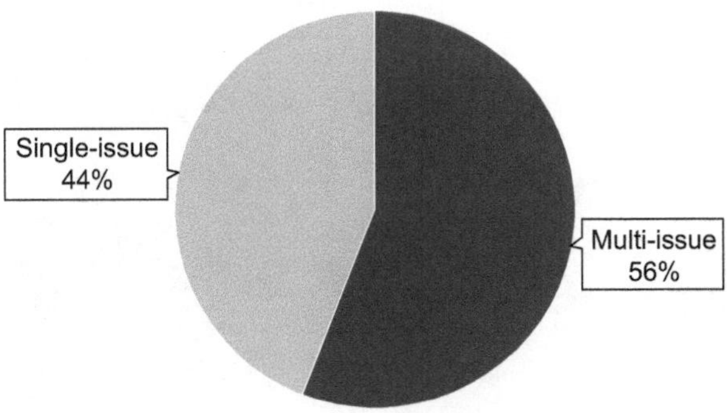


*Figure 3.2* Specialisation of frontline services

was to focus on those organisations that specifically make mention of modern slavery and human trafficking as part of either a specialist project or services that they offer. At first glance, this appears to be a fairly healthy number of service provisions for a demographic that has only been part of serious public discourse for five years. However, when the location of these services is addressed in more detail, the picture looks less balanced.

The numbers in Figure 3.3 also take into account organisations that cover the whole of the UK, meaning that regions such as the East of England, the

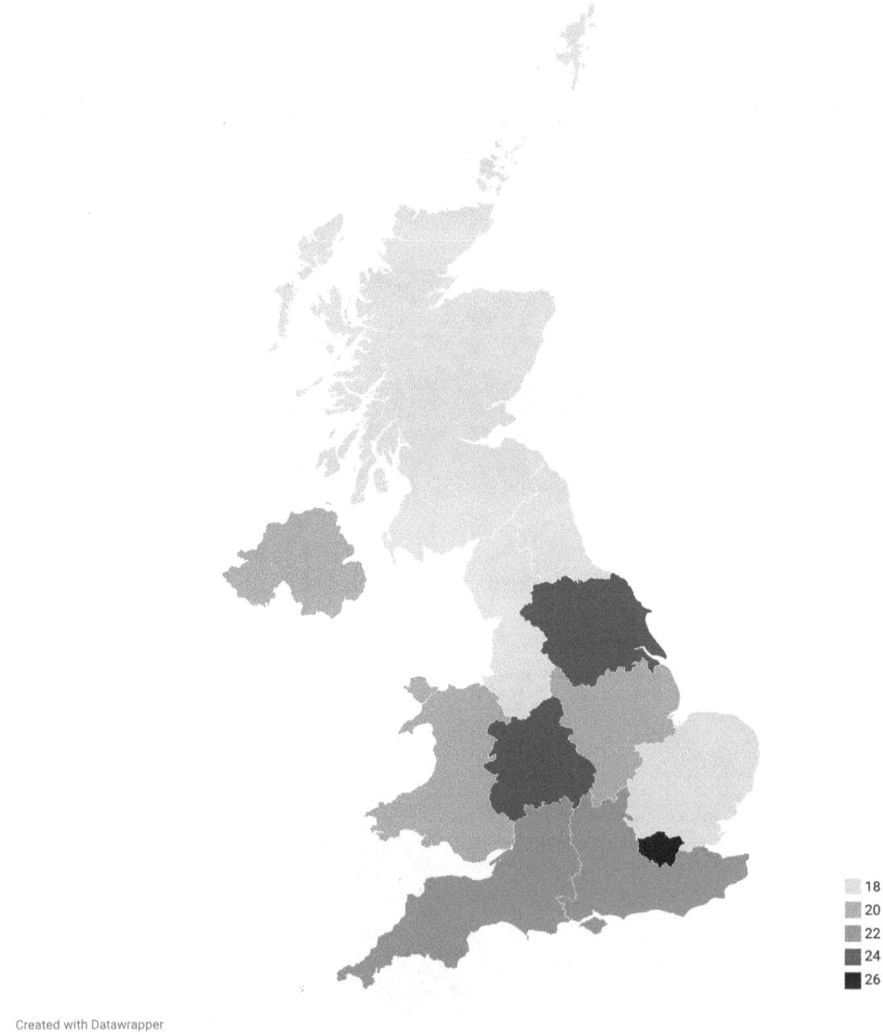


*Figure 3.3* Number of frontline support services by region

North West and the whole of Scotland have very little in the way of frontline support for survivors of modern slavery. This is even more starkly highlighted in the case of single-issue services.

Again, Figure 3.4 includes those organisations that cover the whole of the UK, meaning that only a small cluster of regions cater for the complex needs of survivors at a local/community level. Both charts, meanwhile, highlight a significant prevalence of support services in the London area. While some charity representatives argue that situating themselves in London allows them greater access to policy makers,[58] this places their operational running costs in the most expensive city in the UK. Furthermore, any survivors who require these services will also have to contend with the associated costs of travelling to or even living in the area, and these expenses are not automatically covered

*Figure 3.4* Number of single-issue frontline support services across the UK

58 Observational data from interactions in the field.

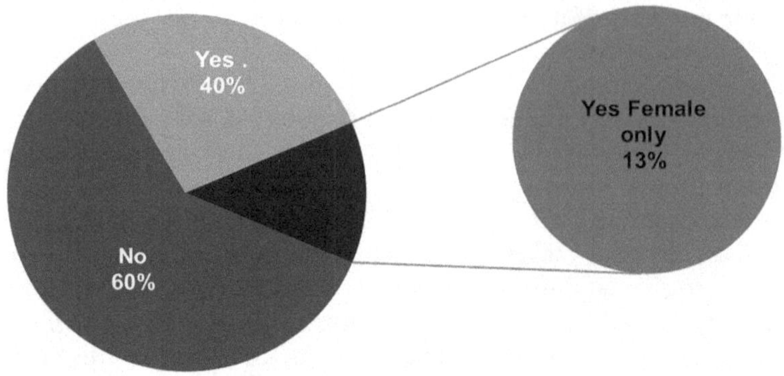


*Figure 3.5* Breakdown of accommodation offered

by their benefits[59] (see also Section 8.2). Survivors who refuse or fail to get referred into the NRM face even higher restrictions on their ability to physically access appropriate support, none more so than basic housing. In fact, accommodation, one of the key needs of service users leaving enslavement, is offered by only 40% $(n = 28)$ of all frontline services, although this figure rises slightly to 43% $(n = 13)$ among single-issue organisations. Considering the concerns raised previously regarding specialist support for women, it is notable that that only 13% $(n = 9)$ of all frontline services offer female-only support *plus* accommodation:

Female-only safehouses provide greater security for traumatised women and girls, particularly those who have been subjected to sexual abuse and other gender-based violence. Furthermore, women who come from cultural backgrounds that traditionally facilitate female-only spaces are often reluctant to share accommodation with men. In fact, women may refuse housing altogether if they do not feel safe there,[60] highlighting the importance of ensuring that this fundamental need is met in order to fulfil the UK's obligations to modern slavery survivors. Additionally, the regional overview of accommodation mirrors that of frontline services in general.

This data does not tell us how many spaces are available within each service, but even taking into account the higher population density of London as compared to the whole of Scotland, the information shows how few regions fully provide for the essential needs of modern slavery survivors. Alternatively, it tells us that many survivors are given very little choice in where they can go to access support, a point that one participant identified during the course of our interview:

59 Home Affairs Committee, *Modern Slavery* (HC 2017–19 1460).
60 Frontline practitioner, in conversation.

*Table 3.1* Accommodation services by region

| *Region* | *No. of accommodation services* |
|---|---|
| East Midlands | 1 |
| East of England | 0 |
| London | 9 |
| North East | 1 |
| South East | 1 |
| South West | 2 |
| West Midlands | 2 |
| Yorkshire and the Humber | 5 |
| Northern Ireland | 2 |
| Scotland | 1 |
| Wales | 1 |
| Grand Total | 25 |

> So [my organisation] does a rescue, in West Yorkshire, that person is then put into City Hearts in Sheffield and then they're referred into Rebuild in Derby and then they go to Jericho [in Birmingham] as an employee and then they're in Spring Housing and they then go to mainstream employment. That's a perfect journey for a survivor because they've got accommodation throughout, they've got to a safehouse, wherever that might be. . . . I mean the ideal for me would be that they have a job for two years in the same place because if you think about what I've just said, *how many moves*? And what are we doing for a trafficking victim? We're trafficking them for employment, although not exploitative. That's exactly what's going on in that victim's head[61].

In 2019, Survivor Alliance published a report to illustrate survivor experiences of the UK system and found that multiple moves across the country were common. One survivor was initially moved from the South East to Yorkshire, then transferred a further three times within the region over a period of less than eighteen months; another was moved seven times in three-and-a-half years, including a two-day stay in London that was sandwiched between placements in the north of England.[62] This also impacts the criminal justice process (see Chapter 7), as investigators lose face-to-face access to key witnesses:

> Whilst it's a good idea to remove a victim geographically a long way away from where the alleged exploitation has happened, that actually can have a detrimental effect on the wider investigation because that officer or

61 Donna, Nottingham, UK, 10 May 2019.

62 Hannah Browne, Nancy Esiovwa and Minh Dang, *The Journey of Our UK Survivor Network: Challenges and Successes* (Survivor Alliance UK October 2019).

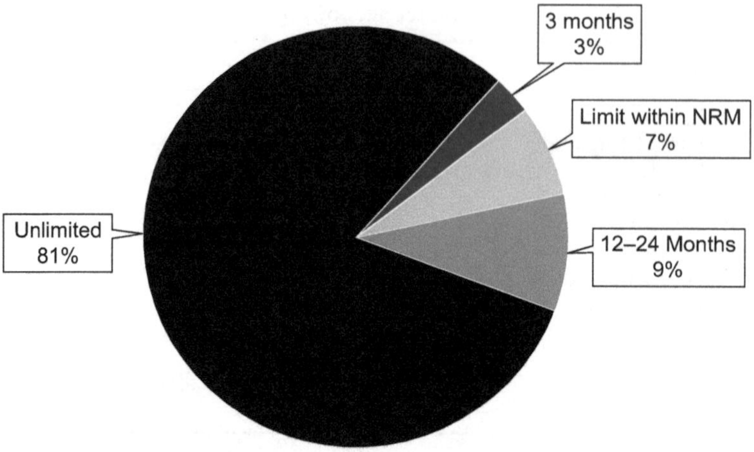


*Figure 3.6* Timeframe of support offered

> whoever is investigating has got to travel hundreds of miles in order to see that victim again or you're asking an agency or a police force that's in that area to take up that investigation. Already it becomes fragmented.[63]

This paucity of service availability in some areas also largely matches the findings of a Rights Lab study that identified the prevalence of anti-slavery networks and partnerships across the UK.[64] Norfolk and Cumbria were shown to have no partnerships in place, leaving these areas ill equipped to support survivors who have been identified locally (see Chapter 4 for further discussion).

In terms of time limits on support, an overwhelming majority of services were available on an unlimited or indefinite basis to survivors. This included everything from drop-in centres and dance classes to legal advocacy and emotional support.

Time-limited support was more likely to be offered by an organisation that provided a service to NRM service users only or to survivors who had completed the NRM process. Some time limits related to the set length of a service; for example, Northern College in Barnsley offers a ten-week educational programme that has been designed specifically for modern slavery survivors (see Section 8.2.2). Notably, every time-limited service identified is also an accommodation provider; this amounts to half of all the accommodation available to survivors $(n = 14)$, and for those in the NRM, that amounts to only ninety days of guaranteed housing. For services operating under government

63 Diana, Bristol, UK, 22 February 2019.

64 Office of the Independent Anti-Slavery Commissioner and University of Nottingham's Rights Lab, *Collaborating for Freedom: Anti-slavery Partnerships in the UK* (University of Nottingham and the Independent Anti-Slavery Commissioner 2017).

contracts (either directly or indirectly), this creates pressure to find suitable accommodation at the end of the NRM when many survivors are still processing trauma and in the midst of legal processes regarding their immigration status or criminal justice case. Once again, this creates problems for both the survivor and those working to secure a prosecution.

Finally, this discussion merits consideration of the prevalence of faith-based organisations (FBOs) in this sector. The Charity Commission considers an organisation faith based if one of its core aims is 'the advancement of religion for the public benefit.' This can include charities that operate under the ethos of their faith but do not facilitate overtly religious activities.[65] Overall, 18% of registered UK charities are faith based;[66] however, in the anti-modern slavery sector, the proportion is 27%, the majority of which are Christian.[67] Filtering the results to frontline, single-issue charities only raises the figure to 33%, meaning that FBOs play a substantial role in the delivery of support. This point is even more significant in respect of the government's choice of primary support provider, the Salvation Army. Further, to concerns from some quarters upon the awarding of the contract, the Home Affairs Committee hearing on Human Trafficking included the following exchange with Ann-Marie Douglas, the then-project director of the Salvation Army:

*Chair:* Could I start with the question of whether the Salvation Army is the best organisation to deal with these issues? Clearly, you have won the contract from the Ministry of Justice. You are now conducting this work, but there has been criticism of the fact that you are a religious organisation. I think very recently on your website you were quoted as saying that you believed, in terms of unwanted pregnancies, that it is best for the foetus to be carried to term-not you, personally. On your website, you also made reference to sexuality, saying, 'homosexual conduct is controllable and may be morally evaluated . . . society should be ordered on the basis of heterosexual unions'. You will understand why people were concerned about the Salvation Army perhaps having these contracts, bearing in mind those comments.

*Ann-Marie Douglas:* I can fully appreciate why there would be concern among certain sections of society about statements such

65 Sofia Yasmin and others, 'Communicated Accountability by Faith-Based Charity Organisations' (2013) 122 *Journal of Business Ethics* 103, 104.

66 ibid 103.

67 Hannah Lewis and others, *Faith Responses to Modern Slavery* (Economic and Social Research Council 2020).

> as that. However, the Salvation Army is a church as well as a charity, and the Salvation Army has particular religious views that it is not ashamed to declare and is not afraid to articulate. However, in terms of the delivery of this contract, we are bound by the terms of the contract, and within that contract there are very specific and very explicit requirements around equality and diversity to which we adhere. These are also extended to our sub-contractors, and it is a requirement that we provide a service that is equal to all victims of trafficking, irrespective of their religious beliefs.[68]

However, following the initiation of the Big Society, religious leaders expressed their enthusiasm for the 'leading part' faith was to play in plans for the scheme, with then–Archbishop of Canterbury Rowan Williams stating that 'the plans represented "an extraordinary opportunity" for the Church of England to advance a distinct Christian political and moral agenda,'[69] while the Evangelical Alliance saw it as an opportunity to promote 'a vision where biblical values . . . become, once again, part of the fabric of society.'[70] In the modern slavery sector, Lewis et al.'s research has found that proselytism is 'something that [FBO] staff had heard about happening at other organisations,'[71] but there was no hard evidence of this, as all charities in this sector were keen not to be 'tarnished' by this implication.[72] That said, Unseen's 2018 Helpline Assessment report found an emerging trend that churches or places of worship were often used as recruitment locations for potential trafficking victims. Faith was also utilised as a coercion technique, 'with the mention of cults and religious beliefs as a way of increasing the psychological controls over potential victims.'[73] It would be unfair to say that FBOs are an unhelpful influence in this sector – without their financial might and commitment, there would be far less support available for vulnerable people – but it is crucial that survivor needs take priority over religious agendas.

## 3.5 Conclusion

This chapter aimed first to examine the successes and limitations of the UK's legislation and policies, as well as exploring the support systems that are

68 Home Affairs Committee, *Human Trafficking* (HC 2013–14 72-i).

69 Steven Kettell, 'Let's Call the Whole Thing Off' (*Public Spirit*, 19 June 2013) <https://web.archive.org/web/20140814232737/www.publicspirit.org.uk/lets-call-the-whole-thing-off/> accessed 24 June 2020.

70 ibid.

71 Hannah Lewis and others (n 67) 13.

72 ibid.

73 Unseen, *Modern Slavery Helpline Annual Assessment* (Unseen 2018) 76.

currently in place to fulfil these policies in practice. The overall landscape of the UK's voluntary sector has undergone significant changes over the past decade. Many charities now operate along similar lines to business, with larger, well-established organisations benefitting from an advantageous starting point. Specialist and grassroots charities are therefore compelled to seek more creative and competitive ways to continue their work, with some small organisations finding that they are unable to survive in a saturated market. These changes have been the result of several factors, such as austerity and an increasing reliance from government on the voluntary sector. As with many customers, however, those responsible for the distribution of government funding are looking for a bargain. Unfortunately, this perception of 'value for money' does not take into account the specialist and complex needs of modern slavery survivors and opts instead for the lowest bidder, whether or not they offer the best service. There is also evidence that the current system has created something of a divide between *government-funded* and *independent* organisations, with the latter claiming that their operational freedoms outweigh any financial restrictions they face. Even more viscerally, the analysis of the differences between regional support provisions demonstrates that survivors encounter a 'postcode lottery' following intervention, where those picked up in urban regions with strong networks are far more likely to have their support needs met. Nonetheless, even these survivors will be moved to another area at least once during recovery due to the lack of relevant, specialist support in their current location.

Finally, while the charity sector has undoubtedly become more accountable and transparent over time, there are still question marks over the operational strategy of some organisations. Some organisations have benefitted from the skills and knowledge of individuals who have many years' experience and who can help to build robust, survivor-centred services that understand the nature of the support required. Others unwittingly replicate existing services and create unnecessary competition; worse still, without statutory regulations on best practice, some providers run the risk of causing additional harm through 'saviour complex' cultures or, with well-meaning intentions, doing what they think is best, regardless of survivors' own wishes. Goodwill alone is not enough to support the full range of complex needs that can be presented by traumatised and vulnerable individuals. The following chapter therefore explores the short-term care provisions that are available for modern slavery survivors, highlighting areas of good practice and identifying areas for possible development.

# 4 Short-term support

## 4.1 Introduction

Intervention from authorities is a crucial first step in the victim's ability to leave slavery and begin the process of recovery. While it seems, *prima facie*, that removal to a place of safety would be a welcome move, the reality for survivors is frequently far more complicated. Chapter 7, for example, discusses wariness of law enforcement officers and genuine fears of repercussions for both the victim and their families. For others, cultural norms and societal influences may result in survivors not associating their experiences with criminal or human rights abuses.[1] On a more fundamental level, economic security is a core concern, and many victims place alternative employment opportunities and accommodation above the prospect of simply ending their current exploitative situation without a safety net.[2] Combined with these survivor-based concerns, the previous chapter demonstrated the problems faced by the voluntary sector in achieving sustainable resources that can ensure the level of support required by survivors of modern slavery. Following intervention, survivors are generally referred to an independent charitable organisation, which is then tasked with providing housing, care and support.

This chapter focuses on the immediate and short-term support of modern slavery survivors by discussing their commonly identified core needs. By building on findings from the previous two chapters, it evaluates how government guidelines and policies work in practice across the UK's service delivery systems. It provides a deeper examination as to the effectiveness of these policies, particularly in relation to the National Referral Mechanism, which is the key statutory mechanism for identifying survivors in the UK. It also begins to explore areas of good practice and barriers to success in frontline support services, alongside consistencies and disparities in service delivery and potential improvements or alternative systems that would benefit the UK's

1 Jordan J Steiner and others, 'Providing Services to Trafficking Survivors: Understanding Practices across the Globe' (2018) 15(2) *Journal of Evidence-Informed Social Work* 151.

2 Alexandra C Duncan and Dana DeHart, 'Provider Perspectives on Sex Trafficking: Victim Pathways, Service Needs, & Blurred Boundaries' (2019) 14(4) *Victims & Offenders* 510.

DOI: 10.4324/9781032639895-4

survivor support pathways. It considers examples of good practice, linking to findings from other relevant sectors and asking how this information can benefit the wider modern slavery support system. It then moves on to addressing areas of limitation, picking up themes from the qualitative study and evaluating statutory aims and objectives in line with actual practice. The theme of multi-agency partnerships straddles both of these discussions, and there is a final, separate section dedicated to this topic.

## 4.2 Moving towards models of best practice

Over a decade ago, US-based scholars Macy and Johns designed a framework for a continuum of aftercare services,[3] and their work continues to be drawn from by academics interested in this area of research. While the Macy and Johns framework was focused on victims of sex trafficking, the study itself was based on international support mechanisms and thus provides some universality. The researchers divided survivor support needs into three phases: *immediate*, *ongoing* and *long-term*, and identified seven 'core' requirements in assisting recovery:

- Basic sustenance (food and water);
- Secure and safe accommodation;
- Physical healthcare;
- Mental healthcare and wellbeing;
- Legal assistance and immigration advocacy;
- Substance abuse support;
- Education and employment.[4]

Some of these (accommodation, healthcare and legal assistance) have been incorporated into the Government's Recovery Needs Assessment,[5] which provides the guidelines for assessing individual support requirements under the Victim Care Contract. The first two core needs – basic sustenance and shelter – also reiterate the foundation of Maslow's hierarchy of needs,[6] which establishes the elements required for an individual to attain full psychological wellbeing (see Figure 6.1 in Chapter 6). In terms of immediate care, both provisions are essential and form the basis of any fundamental support package. Accommodation, however, is one of the costliest aspects of any frontline support framework and as such, is often rigidly time limited. Typically, this accommodation is part of a wider charitable service that either specialises

3 Rebecca J Macy and Natalie Johns, 'Aftercare Services for International Sex Trafficking Survivors: Informing US Service and Program Development in an Emerging Practice Area' (2011) 12(2) *Trauma, Violence & Abuse* 87.

4 ibid.

5 Home Office, *Recovery Needs Assessment (RNA) v2.0* (Home Office 2020).

6 Abraham H Maslow, 'A Theory of Human Motivation' (1943) 50(4) *Psychological Review* 370.

in supporting modern slavery survivors – for example, Unseen – or provides a more overarching housing service for vulnerable people, such as Hestia. A 2017 policing inspection report, carried out by Her Majesty's Inspectorate of Constabulary, Fire and Rescue Services (HMICFRS), also found that in constabulary areas where links to voluntary support services were poor, forces were accommodating victims in hotels. The cost of this, which includes food and hygiene essentials, not only places pressure on already limited budgets, but 'carries the risk of the police being seen to be offering inducements to victims in supporting prosecutions.'[7] In any event, support provider capacity is already at a premium – Ayesha stated that her organisation is 'really small so we work with up to eight women, up to five men, and three children.'[8] Only 40% $(n = 28)$ of all anti-slavery frontline services are able to offer housing, and half of those $(n = 14)$ provide accommodation under the National Referral Mechanism, meaning that safehouse places are only currently guaranteed to an individual for ninety days (see Section 3.4). Although this is double the previous 'reflection and recovery' period, participants unanimously stated that it was 'still not long enough'[9] given the complex and ongoing needs of this population. Furthermore, in terms of psychological security, this provision is not enough to move survivors forward in the hierarchy of needs, and, at worst, survivors can become homeless 'so therefore they become perfect victims because they are very vulnerable, only to be re-trafficked again.'[10] The suggestions from practitioners regarding how to address this issue were varied:

> The accommodation issue doesn't have to be forever, it only has to be for a very short period of time, and once they've earned money they can find their own accommodation. It is only a small stopgap. It is something I've personally thought that the churches could climb on board with, is about this protecting vulnerable people, actually providing accommodation and actually doing something that could really make a difference within this arena.[11]

> Statutory housing, so the recent vote in Parliament about discretionary leave for survivors . . . cos obviously that entitles benefits, therefore they're given a proper twelve-month reflection period, not 90 days. But if there is a statutory requirement for housing then survivors would be

7 Her Majesty's Inspectorate of Constabulary, Fire and Rescue Services (HMICFRS), *Stolen Freedom: The Policing Response to Modern Slavery and Human Trafficking* (HMICFRS 2017) 72.

8 Ayesha, Portsmouth, UK, 30 October 2018.

9 Diana, Bristol, UK, 22 February 2019.

10 ibid.

11 ibid.

> much better off because they're . . . it's the basic roof over your head isn't it?[12]

> There's some brilliant charities and they will try wherever possible to try and help with work and help with their accommodation issues so if business can link up with those charities with that ongoing, that ability to be able to feed in the accommodation and support, you'll be quite a long way there.[13]

This suggests that, while longer-term statutory housing would certainly afford more security for survivors, the call for businesses, churches and other organisations to contribute is in keeping with the value that is placed on multi-agency partnerships. Given the prevalence of Christian-based organisations in this sector (see Chapter 3), there is certainly potential for the church to focus more of its energies towards supported accommodation for survivors.

In terms of access to healthcare, government guidelines stipulate that:

> All confirmed and suspected victims of modern slavery will have access to free emergency medical treatment regardless of their immigration status. The NHS Charging Regulations exempts victims and suspected victims of modern slavery from charges for specified NHS hospital treatment.[14]

Despite this, evidence presented to the Home Affairs Committee enquiry on modern slavery[15] and identified in other research[16] would suggest that access to physical healthcare may be something of a lottery depending on the immigration status of the survivor; individuals are often required to produce documentation for GP registration, without which they are refused an appointment. Support workers frequently assist with this by negotiating with medical administration staff and obtaining ID; however, language barriers can also create difficulties once survivors are able to get their appointments.[17] This is even more problematic with access to mental healthcare, as discussed in Chapter 6. Many frontline support organisations thus offer informal and holistic healthcare in their support packages:

> We have things like a 'sleep session' in the evening. Lots of survivors struggle to sleep and it's optional, obviously all these things are optional,

12 Donna, Nottingham, UK, 10 May 2019.

13 Diana, Bristol, UK, 22 February 2019.

14 Home Office, *Recovery Needs Assessment (RNA) v2.0* (n 5) 22.

15 Witness C, *Oral Evidence, Modern Slavery*, HC 1460 (6 November 2018) Q97.

16 Joanne Westwood and others, 'Access to, and Experiences of, Healthcare Services by Trafficked People: Findings from a Mixed-methods Study in England' (2016) *British Journal of General Practice* 794.

17 ibid.

> but we have yoga, and relaxation sessions in the evening so if people are struggling to sleep they can come and work with somebody to relax and do some meditative practices before bed and try and get themselves ready for that.[18]

Even where survivors are British and do not face these hurdles, they can experience misunderstanding from care workers who are not educated in modern slavery issues.[19] Principally, human trafficking is still frequently perceived to be something that happens to other nationalities – the popular concept of trafficking across international borders, for example, reinforces this stereotype, while sociological theories on colonial discourse concerning 'otherness' offer further explanation regarding unconscious biases.[20] Thus, many patient-facing staff across health and social care simply cannot conceive that their British patients and service users could be victims of the crime. The lack of survivor awareness in this vital frontline demographic has been identified as a significant gap in the system, but moves are underway to improve education and training in this area (see Section 2.3).

The remaining aspects of Macy and Johns' 'core' recovery requirements – legal assistance and immigration advocacy, and education and employment – are discussed in more detail across the immigration chapter and long-term care chapter, respectively, while substance misuse support is addressed in the following.

Another criticism of current support systems is that survivors of sex trafficking are often placed in provisions that have been specifically created for survivors of other gender-based crimes like domestic abuse or sexual violence.[21] Although there are multiple similarities between the groups (psychological abuse, violence, power imbalance),[22] sex trafficking survivors experience the additional, unique abuses of 'financial exploitation, participation in a particular subculture, specific societal stigma, exposure to victimizers outside of the primary relationship, and sexual activity outside of the primary relationship.'[23] Furthermore, services for domestic and sexual abuse survivors have been able to develop their support provisions through constant evaluation over many years, whereas stakeholder feedback for modern slavery support is still in its nascent stages.[24] What this means for current survivors, unfortunately, is that many support provisions

18 Ayesha, Portsmouth, UK, 30 October 2018.
19 *Oral Evidence, Modern Slavery*, HC 1460 (6 November 2018) Q100–103.
20 Homi K Bhabha, 'The Other Question: The Stereotype and Colonial Discourse' in KM Newton (ed), *Twentieth-Century Literary Theory* (Palgrave 1997).
21 Duncan and DeHart (n 2) 510.
22 Kathleen E Krieger and others, 'Evaluating Human Trafficking Service Programs: What Can Be Learned from Domestic Violence Service Program Evaluations' (2020) 8(2) *Journal of Human Trafficking* 157–183 <https://doi.org/10.1080/23322705.2020.1784686>.
23 Duncan and DeHart (n 2) 510, 513.
24 Krieger (n 22).

are a work in progress. This does not mean that models of support in domestic or sexual abuse services cannot be drawn on as frameworks for modern slavery support provisions.[25] Given the current understanding of other types of exploitative relationships, as outlined in Chapter 6, and the available evidence on best practice for assisting these survivor groups,[26] there is an argument for using existing knowledge as a foundation from which to build and develop tailored support. Some US-based research has begun to identify current models that can inform and develop human trafficking services.[27] These include the understanding that recovery is a 'staged' process, based on the Macy and Johns' continuum, while encouraging survivor empowerment throughout. It is also recognised that survivors can move back and forth in this process, for example, where events trigger re-trauma or vulnerability. One model was designed from mapping existing evidence-based practice onto an academic theory of survivor recovery,[28] complementing both practitioner and researcher expertise. The concept of knowledge exchange has also been adopted by the Modern Slavery and Human Rights Policy and Evidence Centre, a UK enterprise that 'aims to bring together academics, policymakers, businesses, civil society, survivors and the public on a scale not seen before in the UK.'[29]

Taking the experience of more established support provisions into consideration, an overarching aspect of any survivor support is that services should be ***trauma informed***.[30] This means that the organisation as a whole, and its individual practitioners, must have knowledge and understanding of the nature of trauma and how it manifests in survivors. This is woven into the support pathway from initial assessment to ending contact to facilitate the most appropriate intervention for the individual. Hopper, for instance, lists the elements of assessment with new referrals as:

> rapport-building and informed consent, safety assessment, needs assessment and goal-setting, history and vulnerability factors, trafficking narrative (including elements of force, fraud, and coercion) and trauma exposure, assessment of psychological symptoms, and strengths and coping.[31]

25 RL Curran and others, 'A Theory for Aftercare of Human Trafficking Survivors for Nursing Practice in Low Resource Settings' (2017) 35 *Applied Nursing Research* 82.

26 Krieger (n 22).

27 ibid.

28 ibid.

29 Modern Slavery and Human Rights Policy and Evidence Centre, 'Modern Slavery PEC' (*Modern Slavery PEC*) <www.modernslaverypec.org/> accessed 7 September 2020.

30 Sue Lockyer, 'Beyond Inclusion: Survivor-Leader Voice in Anti-Human Trafficking Organizations' (2020) 8(2) *Journal of Human Trafficking* 135–156 <https://doi.org/10.1080/23322705.2020.1756122>.

31 Elizabeth K Hopper, 'Trauma-Informed Psychological Assessment of Human Trafficking Survivors' (2017) 40(1–2) *Women & Therapy* 12, 15.

From these foundations, ongoing support should then seek to incorporate the following:

- applying principles of safety,
- encouraging the survivor to make his/her own choices,
- working in collaboration with the survivor,
- building a trusting relationship, and
- providing language access and cultural sensitivity.[32]

Through a trauma-informed model of support, practitioners can facilitate survivor empowerment and build towards the long-term goals of self-sufficiency and independent living. Government guidance states that anyone working with survivors must try to avoid retraumatising them[33] and links to the *Trauma-Informed Code of Conduct*[34] for trafficking survivors, which places emphasis on building trust and communicating in language that emphasises safety and security. In general, the concept of survivor empowerment is integral to frontline support services, based on a survivor-centred approach.[35] This means that the needs of the survivors are paramount to the service's mission statement, and care pathways are designed in collaboration with the survivor. Practitioners are therefore required to communicate honestly and effectively with survivors, even under negative circumstances:

> 'I don't want to sound as harsh as this but one of the outcomes from this time in the contract may be that you are only here for 45 days and this is an immediate crisis response for you and please use it as much as you can take everything you can from it but on day 45 we have to accept the reality that you may be able to reside, but you may be street homeless, you may have some supported accommodation, you may be able to seek asylum, or you may have to return home.' . . . None of those conversations are easy to have with someone that has just arrived with you, but are we doing that person a disservice because we are not in essence empowering them to have a choice because we are not giving them all the options and those options are horrific, but this is the situation we find ourselves in, but in my mind there is no point in protecting someone and saying it'll be ok then on day 43 saying 'by the way . . .'[36]

32 Steiner and others (n 1) 151, 153.

33 Home Office, *Modern Slavery Act 2015: Statutory Guidance for England and Wales* (Home Office 2020).

34 Rachel Witkin and Katy Robjant, *The Trauma-Informed Code of Conduct* (Helen Bamber Foundation 2018).

35 Steiner and others (n 1) 151.

36 Ayesha, Portsmouth, UK, 30 October 2018.

This feeds into the need for building trusting relationships with survivors:

> The initial needs and the importance of providing consistent advocacy for potential victims when they are first identified, so it was that initial contact on recovery and the time it takes to engage and gain trust.[37]

> And the one last year I remember when he was really traumatised, 'Do I trust you?' so I would say the trust relationship that they have with us, I would say that's probably the most important thing for them because they know that we won't let them down and obviously so many people have. I think that is what survivors would say is the most important thing that we've helped them with because once they trust us they then learn to trust themselves again, because it's their judgement that is the thing that is mostly impacted, in my view.[38]

As well as honesty, these quotes implicitly promote the idea of adult-to-adult conversations rather than viewing the survivor as someone to be protected from the realities of their situation. This type of relationship between practitioner and survivor also facilitates a more survivor-centred support pathway, as individuals feel they have agency in their own care plan. A level of consistent support, communication and trust-building is also logically best achieved by establishing one key practitioner with whom the survivor can address their recovery needs. The 'importance of the collaborative single point of contact model'[39] has already been demonstrated in areas such as social work, and this was likewise mentioned by several participants as a key factor in assisting the recovery of survivors. Frontline practitioners who work with service users from the time of referral until the end of their support journey are a first port of call for survivors, providing information and assistance on all aspects of their care pathway, additionally giving survivors access to a range of otherwise potentially unknown services:

> I think having an advocate who is well trained, knowledgeable about trafficking and about the rights of that individual is so important because the person you're supporting may not necessarily know those rights and facts, sadly usually doesn't, and then that person can adapt to the needs of the individual.[40]

37 Puja, Leeds, UK, 8 January 2019.
38 Donna, Nottingham, UK, 10 May 2019.
39 Steiner and others (n 1) 151, 154.
40 Caroline, Nottingham, UK, 22 November 2019.

> Obviously a survivor, once they're in their journey, the less people they're introduced to the better. So we're a constant in that part of the journey.[41]

> The most important aspects, which covers it all, I guess, is victim pathways. Knowing what provisions there are and ensuring that those provisions are in existence from the point of identification all the way through to recovery.[42]

Several non-statutory organisations have established advocacy roles as part of their frontline team, for example, Justice and Care have victim navigators who work within police forces across England,[43] while the Passage established a team of modern slavery navigators to complement the modern slavery arm of their overall homeless support services.[44] However, this is another area in which good practice frameworks can be built on from other recognised parallel fields:

> I don't think it's reinventing the wheel because we have ISVAs [Independent Sexual Violence Advisers] and IDVAs [Independent Domestic Violence Advisers] and so I don't necessarily think it's rocket science to say, 'Could we think about Independent Modern Slavery Advocates who have a similar type of role?'[45]

In 2010, the Stern Review noted the success of independent domestic violence advisors (IDVAs), demonstrating that it was 'therefore logical and to be greatly welcomed that the concept has now been extended to provide support to those who have suffered rape'[46] in the form of independent sexual violence advisers. The review noted that ISVAs provided a continuity of support that engendered trust and confidence in survivors, aiding their psychological recovery and significantly reducing withdrawal from the criminal justice system (see Section 7.5). Despite finding that ISVAs were 'cost-effective and affordable,'[47] the review made reference to unstable funding streams for the role: the Home Office was at the time providing conditional grants of up to £20,000, but for those charities that had to apply elsewhere for their ISVA funding, valuable

41 Donna, Nottingham, UK, 10 May 2019.
42 Caroline, Nottingham, UK, 22 November 2019.
43 Justice and Care, 'A Day in the Life of a Victim Navigator' (Justice and Care) <www.justiceandcare.org/a-day-in-the-life-of-a-victim-navigator/> accessed 9 September 2020.
44 Julia Tomas, 'The Passage Anti-Slavery Project 2018/2020: Findings and Recommendations from the First Two Years of the Passage Anti-Slavery Project' (The Passage, 2020).
45 Caroline, Nottingham, UK, 22 November 2019.
46 Baroness Vivien Stern, *The Stern Review: A Report by Baroness Vivien Stern CBE of an Independent Review into How Rape Complaints Are Handled by Public Authorities in England and Wales* (Government Equalities Office and Home Office 2010) 103.
47 ibid 105.

time was taken up with bidding contracts rather than carrying out the support work itself.[48] This echoes the status of the charity sector as a whole and how the increasingly competitive market is diluting some service quality in lieu of tackling the challenge to stay financially afloat. The victim navigator and modern slavery navigator roles mentioned previously are funded by two separate donors, and although the respective overall charity aims are diverse, there is a case to be made for uniformity of support.

> There needs to be better management of whoever is in charge of victims so it's uniform. Wherever anyone goes, the same forms are filled in, the same support is given, the same exit interview is given. And if they're going to leave, where are they going to go?[49]

In 2014, the Human Trafficking Foundation (HTF) addressed this issue by publishing a set of Survivor Care Standards (updated in 2015 and again in 2018).[50] Noting that there were 'no publicly available standards of care for victims of trafficking found in the UK,'[51] a range of experts from anti-slavery organisations and academia contributed to the ninety-three-page document, which aims to produce a consistent approach across all survivor care pathways. The standards draw on international legal mechanisms and human rights, promoting multi-agency working and trauma-informed, victim-centred approaches. Additionally, in response to reports from the Committee of Public Accounts[52] and National Audit Office,[53] which identified an 'absence of clear care standards and an inspection regime,'[54] the government announced that it was working with key stakeholders to develop a set of care standards which would then be incorporated into the Victim Care Contract. The HTF standards have now been written into government guidance for those working with survivors in the NRM, and the general move towards a minimum standard was described as a 'really positive step forward.'[55] Nonetheless, the government continues to outsource responsibility for safeguarding checks to the Salvation Army, although it stated that it was 'also consulting with experienced care sector inspectorates and colleagues in UK Visas and Immigration to design an inspection regime for modern slavery victim care.'[56] The concern with the

48 ibid.
49 Diana, Bristol, UK, 22 February 2019.
50 Kate Roberts (ed), *The Slavery and Trafficking Survivor Care Standards 2018* (Human Trafficking Foundation 2018).
51 ibid 10.
52 Committee of Public Accounts, *Reducing Modern Slavery* (HC 2017–19 886).
53 National Audit Office, *Home Office: Reducing Modern Slavery* (HC 2017–19 630).
54 HM Treasury, *Treasury Minutes: Government Response to the Committee of Public Accounts on the Thirty First to the Thirty Seventh Reports from Session 2017–19* (Cm 9643, 2018) 26.
55 Puja, Leeds, UK, 8 January 2019.
56 HM Treasury (n 54).

latter move, of course, is that the government is once again attaching survivor support to immigration, which has been shown to be counter-productive (see Chapters 2 and 5). Again, drawing on good practice from other similar service providers can be of use in this field. Research on service user experiences of domestic violence shelters found that survivors appreciated the concept of shared values, norms and practices within the organisation.[57] What this means is that 'from executive director to board of directors to "people who clean the floors",'[58] everyone involved understood and demonstrated a clear set of survivor-centred, trauma-informed philosophies. Examples included 'safety, relationship, emotional intelligence, awareness, intentionality, and belief in resilience, growth, and change'[59] and were designed to create a consistent, safe environment. Organisational values can be developed and enhanced through survivor input, as well as being used to empower those who use the service. This ethos can be maintained throughout a survivor's time within an organisation, established through more informal means:

> We try and encourage people to come together for a house meeting, as a touch point every morning just to make sure everyone's ok and then we get survivors to come together for a house meeting on a Friday to take control and say 'this is our space, this is our community and this is what we want to see.'[60]

Uniformity does not, however, mean that stakeholder organisations should adopt a 'one size fits all' mentality. Survivors come from a diverse range of backgrounds and support providers are encouraged to individualise care plans that take into account survivors' personal experiences and individual needs.[61]

> What that looks like when that is delivered on the front line needs to be kept quite flexible in terms of how each area needs to respond appropriately to . . . the response that they need to provide to victims in their area.[62]

For instance, one charity that helps survivors to find employment stated that they would never place someone in the same industry that they had previously

57 Shanti Joy Kulkarni and others, 'Successful Rules Reduction Implementation Process in Domestic Violence Shelters: From Vision to Practice' (2019) 64(2) *Social Work* 147.
58 ibid 147, 148.
59 ibid 148.
60 Ayesha, Portsmouth, UK, 30 October 2018.
61 Steiner and others (n 1) 151.
62 Puja, Leeds, UK, 8 January 2019.

been trafficked into.[63] Another government-funded organisation has amended their time-limited service delivery:

> We said let's cap it at hours because you might have someone who moves out of a safehouse into asylum and they might not know the area they're in and they might need loads of support so the hours they need might be really high in the beginning and then tapers off. You might have someone who moves from a safehouse into local authority supported accommodation, they might have a key worker who might not know much about trafficking but they know housing, benefits and all the other elements so they might not need as much support then but when they come to independent living they might need more, so now we say each survivor can get 200 hours as and when they need it, so they can dip in and out.[64]

Tailored support may also include something as simple as providing service users with a means of keeping in touch with their support workers, a practice that at least one charity has adopted as part of their support plan.[65] A study on trafficking victims' access to technology[66] identified that many victims were either prevented from using mobile phones during their captivity or that traffickers used the technology to maintain coercion and control. Therefore, offering newly referred survivors a secure mobile phone could give them an additional level of support that they otherwise would not have access to. From a practical point of view, this also ensures that communication flows both ways between practitioners and survivors, especially if the survivor leaves the geographical area.

Research also emphasises the 'importance of providing culturally appropriate services, suggesting that providers discuss with survivors their preferences regarding food, clothing, and basic needs in a culturally sensitive manner.'[67] However, organisations need to be alert to the level of interaction that individual survivors are comfortable with:

> It's not a natural group of people, you've got some that struggle with trusting people, they might know a couple from the particular business they're working in, but they won't all know each other, some are happy to converse or find it quite easy to converse in English, there will be others that really struggle, we've got some who are happy talking to people

63 Rachel, London, UK, 11 May 2019.
64 Ayesha, Portsmouth, UK, 30 October 2018.
65 Donna, Nottingham, UK, 10 May 2019.
66 Jessica Elliott and Kieran McCartan, 'The Reality of Trafficked People's Access to Technology' (2013) 77(3) *Journal of Criminology Law* 255.
67 Steiner and others (n 1) 151, 155.

> who share the same nationality, but we've also got those who are very fearful of those that have the same nationality.[68]

The latter point alludes to the fact that some survivors will fear encountering people who were involved in their trafficking, although there are equally those who feel more safe dealing with practitioners and communities with whom they have more in common.[69]

For survivors, a consistent and secure support pathway, paired with a collaborative practitioner approach that affords them autonomy, has been demonstrated to enhance recovery. This in turn benefits the overall aims of the government's criminal justice strategy:

> We've found that wherever they get accommodation, they can go on and live quite successful lives, and they give evidence and we get successful prosecution at court.[70]

> Supporting victims of modern slavery is extremely complex and the delivery of consistent advocacy on the frontline to make sure that victims are engaged with services so they don't drop off that cliff edge of support that's so often spoken about or falling through the gaps or disengaging or going missing, disengaging with not just services but police investigations, managing victim support when their witnesses and victims in a prosecution case.[71]

## 4.3 Barriers to service delivery

One of the central aims of this research was to examine how legislation and policy actually works in practice. In an ideal world, frontline organisations and practitioners would be able to fulfil policy requirements to the most beneficial outcomes; however, there are strong indications that regional differences, funding variations, time limitations and individual agendas can lead to an 'implementation gap' on the ground.[72] The NRM, as the statutory mechanism for identifying survivors in the UK, is the fundamental means through which most survivors will access early post-intervention support so an exploration of

68 Rachel, London, UK, 11 May 2019.
69 Steiner and others (n 1) 151, 155.
70 Diana, Bristol, UK, 22 February 2019.
71 Puja, Leeds, UK, 8 January 2019.
72 Alison Gardner, 'An Idea Whose Time Has Come? Modern Slavery, Multiple Streams Approach and Multilayer Policy Implementation' (2018) 10 *Journal of Human Rights Practice* 461.

its 'on the ground' effectiveness is pertinent here. The Home Office describes the NRM as:

> the UK's system for identifying and providing access to support for potential victims of modern slavery. The aim of the NRM is to lift victims out of a situation of exploitation, provide them with a period of intensive support to assist with their recovery, and get them to a position where they can begin to re-build their life. If required, the NRM can provide for adult victims (through the Victim Care Contract (VCC) in England and Wales): safe and secure accommodation, financial support and an allocated support worker who advocates for the victim as necessary.[73]

The Victim Care Contract, therefore, has been designed as a 'bridge' between intervention and ongoing care and, as such, is not intended to provide support beyond a survivor's immediate needs.[74] However, recognising that the majority of individuals will not recover within the reflection period, government guidance states that no one should leave the VCC without alternative means of support *if* they have ongoing recovery needs.[75] Key support workers are then tasked with undertaking the assessment by completing a form, which is forwarded to the prime contractor[76] of the VCC for 'quality assurance.' Provided the prime contractor is satisfied with the details outlined on the form, it is then passed to the single competent authority, who 'determine[s] whether or not the support worker's recommendations for any continuation of VCC support are appropriate and reasonable, based upon all the available evidence . . . and should be implemented.'[77] This is the same SCA that determines whether a person is considered to have been a victim of trafficking (see Chapter 2). One section of the form, however, requests information:

> which may impact on their access to alternative services and the level of support that they may require. This includes questions about immigration status, recourse to public funds, asylum claims, voluntary returns to country of origin, pregnancy and/or dependents and ongoing criminal proceedings.[78]

While this appears to simply establish vulnerability factors, this information can be used further along in the process to obstruct access to support or even detain survivors under immigration regulations (see Chapter 5). In other

73 Home Office, *Recovery Needs Assessment (RNA) v2.0* (n 5) 7.
74 Home Office, *Modern Slavery Act 2015* (n 33).
75 ibid.
76 At the time of writing, this would be the Salvation Army.
77 Home Office, *Recovery Needs Assessment (RNA) v2.0* (n 5) 13.
78 ibid 14.

words, the nature of this 'fact finding' would appear to have ulterior motives, a theme that emerges with alarming frequency in the NRM process.

Despite these rather implicit concerns that individuals may attempt to take advantage of state-funded support, one of the messages that has filtered through from survivors is that most of them, especially men, just want to work. It is frequently the reason they first responded to the offer of employment that led to their enslavement, and, where survivors have travelled from another country, they may have dependents back at home that rely on the funds they send.

> Specifically the men that I've met in factories and on car wash forecourts, if I was able to say 'I have got a job for you tomorrow that pays the minimum wage and we can get you accommodation and you would be safe and free to do what you want to do', I think they'd jump at that opportunity.[79]

The NRM does not recognise this need, however, preventing survivors from working while they are awaiting a decision and leaving many survivors at risk of destitution in the event that they do not receive a positive Conclusive Grounds decision. This was reported to the Home Affairs Committee during the modern slavery enquiry:

> If I can only have the support coming from the Hestia award of £35 a week, that's only £5 a day. How can I budget with £5 a day – for my transport, for my food, thinking of my [number] children back home and the [***] with £35 a week? If I gave you £5 and told you, 'Budget it for yourself,' can you budget it for yourself?[80]

Meanwhile, access to legal aid and assistance runs into difficulties under the NRM:

> They need a solicitor and it takes time to have a solicitor. Also, because there are those who have the right to work and they are earning some money and they need to declare that, they need to make sure they don't really have money for legal aid. That's the fact. Of course, their salary is for their family, so they couldn't really afford to pay a solicitor.[81]

Following a positive Conclusive Grounds decision, survivors are entitled to a further forty-five days of 'move on' support, while those who receive a negative CG decision are offered nine working days of transitional support. While

79 Ayesha, Portsmouth, UK, 30 October 2018.
80 Witness B, *Oral Evidence, Modern Slavery*, HC 1460 (6 November 2018) Q84.
81 ibid Q91.

'[t]he expectation is that the CG decision will be made as soon as possible after the 45 calendar days Recovery period,'[82] the reality for survivors is that they are waiting for months and sometimes years for their decision (see Chapters 2 and 8). Nonetheless, the government is quite effusive in its commitment to move survivors on quickly, stating that survivors 'should exit VCC support as soon as other sufficient services are in place.'[83] Although it goes on to say that there should be no gap between exiting the VCC and accessing alternative support, in reality, this is not always possible. One of the key messages from frontline practitioners is the importance of a clear and consistent survivor pathway. While the introduction of advocates for survivors would go some way to ensure this, other aspects of survivor journeys could counter-balance or even negate this role. The analysis of individual survivor support provisions in Chapter 3 showed that services are heavily weighted in London and Yorkshire and the Humber, while the North East and East of England are under-represented. This can sometimes occur as an indirect result of other policy or economic factors: Sheffield, for example, has cheaper statutory accommodation for asylum seekers, so a large majority of survivors get sent to the area upon applying for asylum.[84] Variations in funding, policy limitations (for example, NRM-only services) and lack of other local support networks can thus result in unpredictable outcomes:

> We get phone calls from other parts of the country where they're saying 'we've got a difficulty with this client or with this particular person and we don't know where they can get help from' or people literally ringing up saying 'I am supporting somebody and this is their story or situation, what do I do?', so that happens relatively regularly as well.[85]

> And it depends on which part of the country as to whether you can get the advocacy support because the trouble is with the NRM providers and a lot of the other people who work in this field, they're not there for the long haul, they've then got six months funding, they've only got . . . you know they're restricted to what services they can provide.[86]

This is partially because modern slavery challenges were initially addressed almost exclusively through a national lens, using overall UK data rather than seeking to understand local patterns.[87] A participant from law enforcement recalled how some police forces continued to state that 'it doesn't happen

82 Home Office, *Recovery Needs Assessment (RNA) v2.0* (n 5) 8.
83 ibid 16.
84 Frontline practitioner, in conversation.
85 Caroline, Nottingham, UK, 22 November 2019.
86 Donna, Nottingham, UK, 10 May 2019.
87 Gardner (n 72) 461.

here' even two years after the Modern Slavery Act was enacted.[88] Ultimately, these regional differences and inconsistencies lead to a significant number of survivors moving from place to place in order to access the support they need:

> As part of our NRM contract we will receive people from all over the UK and then usually they will reside here if they are resettling so they would move from a safehouse into the community but that doesn't mean they were found or recovered here.[89]

Thus, should a survivor be assigned an advocate in Leeds, they will be unable to fully access this support if they are moved to London three months later. The implementation of these transfers, particularly the way they are communicated to survivors, can also be reminiscent of their previous trafficking experiences and consequently very damaging:

> We did ask people about safehouse experiences and there's way too much travel and movement of people without any sufficient support . . . not telling where they're getting moved to until the day of, not telling them who's gonna pick them up, I mean things that when survivors will say they feel like they're being re-trafficked are no small statement. Some random person showing up saying 'I'm gonna move you somewhere and you don't know where.'[90]

In December 2017 the Home Office and the Department for Communities and Local Government announced a funding bid for local authorities to participate in twelve-month pilot programmes to test 'transition pathways' for survivors leaving the NRM.[91] Six authorities were granted this funding, including Leeds, Birmingham and Croydon, but participants did not find the pilots to be particularly edifying:

> I admire the fact that it's been a year-long pilot and I admire the fact that somebody's recognised it but why did you need a pilot? To prove there was a need, we all know there was a need! Did nobody count the homeless people that all turned up in night shelters that had got a conclusive grounds decision? That information is already out there. And actually why did it need a Home Office pilot, I don't get it, I don't understand why it needed a twelve month pilot. Maybe it needed to prove what statutory services need to provide, that's fine as long as it changes in July,

88 Puja, Leeds, UK, 8 January 2019.
89 Ayesha, Portsmouth, UK, 30 October 2018.
90 Jenni, Manchester, UK, 13 August 2019.
91 British Red Cross, *After the National Referral Mechanism – What Next for Survivors of Trafficking? Initial Findings from the STEP Project* (British Red Cross 2018).

> because if that's the case, then it will change in July, if it's not, then the pilot will end, they'll take three years producing a report about it and in the meantime, all of those other victims will then be re-traumatised by our statutory services.[92]

> The pilot work they're doing at the moment is very restricted to only supporting those after the NRM who have got a positive decision CG and have recourse to public funds immediately and that's very, very limited, that's a very small amount of people and they're actually, usually, the simpler cases, that's the ones who have the least difficulties.[93]

In fact, the latter quote flags an issue that has been raised in other research – as well as service gaps for pre- and post-NRM support – for 'those individuals who did not wish to enter the NRM,'[94] the available support is even more restricted. The government guidance, for example, provides that individuals who do not consent to the NRM may still be able to access statutory housing support but *only where they have recourse to public funds.*[95] This automatically excludes a vast number of foreign nationals, and, given that other avenues of support such as a key worker may not be present, survivors are unlikely to be aware of these rights, rendering them at further risk:

> So the gaps that I still see are people who are offered the NRM and don't want to go in but are survivors of trafficking, it might be that they're still working with the police but they've chosen not to go into the NRM, there are no routes of support for those people. This means the police are acting as social workers or those people are just disappearing and going back into either exploitation or becoming homeless or other chaotic circumstances, so I don't think we're doing any kind of justice to those people and that's simply because they don't want to go into the NRM and that doesn't seem particularly fair.[96]

The nascency of modern slavery legislation and policy in the UK also means that many organisations are still developing best practice through trial and error. Statutory agencies and government-funded charities will sometimes find that their guidance fluctuates after Cabinet re-shuffles and the subsequent change in ministerial agenda. Part of the difficulty in creating robust and workable policies that can be translated coherently into practice is that the UK

92 Donna, Nottingham, UK, 10 May 2019.
93 Caroline, Nottingham, UK, 22 November 2019.
94 Office of the Independent Anti-Slavery Commissioner and University of Nottingham's Rights Lab, *Collaborating for Freedom: Anti-slavery Partnerships in the UK* (University of Nottingham and the Independent Anti-Slavery Commissioner 2017) 24.
95 Home Office, *Modern Slavery Act 2015* (n 33) 45.
96 Caroline, Nottingham, UK, 22 November 2019.

government is still ascertaining which anti-modern slavery model it wants to adopt. Fundamentally, the UK operates under a criminal approach, but increasing attention to post-intervention support and domestic structural and societal factors is changing the modern slavery landscape, 'albeit in a piecemeal way.'[97] Even when funding was first distributed after the enactment of the Modern Slavery Act, survivor support was prioritised as highly as law enforcement,[98] although the National Audit Office recorded that the full extent of spending was not known.[99] While any progress must be welcomed, it is crucial that changes are made from the perspective of the survivors themselves:

> I spend a lot of time speaking with Parliamentarians, speaking with Home Office civil servants, thinking especially at the moment about the new Adult Care Contract and all the silos of money they want to put into it and how that looks and talking with our staff teams about 'if we did this what would the impact be?' and trying to work out the changes and trying to view that survivor journey from start to finish and encourage the Home Office to do the same because at the moment we try and look at this little bit and that little bit and try and mash it together and it doesn't really work.[100]

In addition, modern slavery survivors will very often present with additional issues such as alcohol and/or substance addiction or other mental health problems.[101] This raises immediate difficulties from a referral perspective:

> So, there's a conversation to be had around if someone presents as a victim of trafficking, what's the greater need? Is sorting out the addiction a bigger need than the trafficking and is that an appropriate crossover of services?[102]

Furthermore, survivors themselves will not necessarily view a referral into the NRM as beneficial if they are experiencing personal difficulties. If those needs cannot be met by specific post-slavery support providers, individuals are unlikely to engage:

> She was referred into the NRM, but she was extremely chaotic in her behaviour, very traumatised, she exhibited mental health issues, alcohol dependency and she was in and out of the NRM . . . she disengaged and

97 Gardner (n 72) 461, 464.
98 ibid 461.
99 National Audit Office, *Home Office: Reducing Modern Slavery* (HC 2017–19 630).
100 Ayesha, Portsmouth, UK, 30 October 2018.
101 Duncan and DeHart (n 2) 510.
102 Ayesha, Portsmouth, UK, 30 October 2018.

> engaged inconsistently really with services, for quite a long period of time.[103]

Rachel explained that this sometimes means having to decline referrals if the organisation believes that they are not the most appropriate service for a survivor.

> Someone who's got an alcohol dependency that they're not willing to address, then actually [this service] isn't a realistic option, it's not a priority for them so I think there are other services that better suit those individuals and actually it's about us using our funding wisely to make the maximum impact.[104]

Echoing the aforementioned problems in healthcare, she went on to describe the difficulties survivors face when language barriers come into play:

> And I think the other thing would be interpretation, so where there are services in the city, for example alcohol addiction, those services are there but can be hard to access if you haven't got the language ability and there are times when interpretation is funded so often we have to advocate on their behalf to get an interpreter, but as a vulnerable adult they should be entitled to that. But often it takes quite a lot of advocacy to get that interpreter for them and that's something they may not be able to do on their own. There's things like that which are holes in services, or struggles where we find that the services might be there but helping someone access them is difficult.[105]

Furthermore, where an individual has been coerced into slavery or made to commit crime in the course of their enslavement, the perception of oneself as a 'victim' is not always straightforward. Women and girls who have been pressured into sexual exploitation by 'Romeo pimps'[106] (traffickers who initially seduce their victim by playing the role of boyfriend) may feel loyalty towards their trafficker or believe that they themselves are responsible for their situation and therefore undeserving of assistance[107] (see also Chapter 7). Part of the role of service providers is thus enabling survivors to understand and appreciate what has happened to them. At the same time, support that also aims to

103 Puja, Leeds, UK, 8 January 2019.
104 Rachel, London, UK, 11 May 2019.
105 Rachel, London, UK, 11 May 2019.
106 Duncan and DeHart (n 2) 510.
107 ibid.

empower its recipients has to be designed in a way that respects the autonomy and agency of survivors:

> It's also interesting if someone doesn't see themselves as a victim, which again you get quite a lot. I think survivors are incredibly pragmatic and then the hardest discussion to ever have is 'well it's better than I had at home'. I can't argue with that because I can't change the situation in Albania or Romania or Vietnam.[108]

> Now, it's victim-centric, the NRM is victim-centric, they can turn around and say 'Thank you very much but do you know what? I know I'm in a bit of bother, but this is a lot better than I'm getting at home and I don't want to go anywhere.'[109]

Striking the balance between creating a unified care pathway and allowing survivors to ultimately become self-sufficient is thus a double-edged sword. The problem for any agency that supports individuals with complex needs is how to prioritise those needs and whether they are the best organisation to do so. Support providers are, by their nature, in the business of assisting people and when this becomes untenable, it must be hard to turn them away. Nonetheless, where strong multi-agency partnerships have been established, the ability to provide individualised, specialist support packages across several organisations can go some way to mitigate this problem.

## 4.4 Multi-agency partnerships

Multi-agency partnerships (MAPs) have always been considered a vital part of the anti-modern slavery sector;[110] all participants discussed joint initiatives with other organisations and pointed to the benefits of sharing responsibility and expertise:

> Well, the Salvation Army have the main contract for the National Referral Mechanism, so clearly we have to work closely with them around the decisions and the referrals into that process, but sitting below that, there's a whole host of groups that have got engaged through our West Yorkshire network.[111]

> As part of an investigating, wider investigation, we may need work as in partnership with other agencies. Once the victim has been identified,

108 Ayesha, Portsmouth, UK, 30 October 2018.
109 Diana, Bristol, UK, 22 February 2019.
110 Steiner and others (n 1) 151.
111 David, Birmingham, UK, 20 October 2018.

> our number one priority, as with our strapline is the protection of that vulnerable person, so it's about safeguarding.[112]

Although this attitude has been endorsed by the government,[113] there is limited guidance as to how it is best achieved.[114] A 2017 mapping study, under the purview of Kevin Hyland, the then-IASC, found that MAPs existed in most areas of the UK although there were significant variations 'in terms of structure, leadership, membership, activities, funding and the degree of formality in partnership arrangements.'[115] Most of the partnerships were chaired and co-ordinated by the police, reflecting the role of law enforcement in this field,[116] and the wider criminal model as adopted by the UK in its anti-slavery approach. Consequently, this placed the strongest emphasis on intelligence sharing within the key activities. Wales and Northumberland were found to have at least five active partnerships in place, where other regions (including Norfolk, Surrey and Cumbria) had not established any multi-agency networks at that point. Even where partnerships existed, the researchers found that the range of models and working patterns had resulted in a 'limited consistency'[117] which translated into varying and inconsistent practices of survivor support. Donna, who works across two different cities, had identified a clear regional difference:

> So, in Birmingham there's a lot of multi-agency working, they've got a very good West Midlands Anti-Slavery Partnership that's been operating for many years. Whereas, that's not the case in Derby, it's very siloed, it's like 'This is mine, I'm going to deal with this', that's how it feels. It's not about partnership working, it doesn't work like that.[118]

Interestingly, Derbyshire was shown by the mapping study to have two multi-agency networks in place: Derby and Derbyshire Modern Slavery Partnership and East Midlands Anti-Human Trafficking Partnership. The former of these reported the following activities in its partnership operations:

- Community awareness-raising
- Frontline staff training
- Intelligence sharing

112 Diana, Bristol, UK, 22 February 2019.
113 Home Office, *Modern Slavery Act 2015* (n 33).
114 Office of the Independent Anti-Slavery Commissioner and University of Nottingham's Rights Lab (n 94).
115 ibid 9.
116 ibid.
117 Office of the Independent Anti-Slavery Commissioner and University of Nottingham's Rights Lab (n 94) 12.
118 Donna, Nottingham, UK, 10 May 2019.

- Planning for joint enforcement
- Joint commissioning of services
- Co-ordinating referrals
- Survivor support
- Monitoring and analysis of progress[119]

Although the Derby and Derbyshire Modern Slavery Partnership was established in 2014,[120] it is possible that a partnership is only as effective as the people in charge. The Rt Revd Dr Alastair Redfern, Bishop of Derby, formed the initial partnership group and later created the Clewer Initiative, a 'project to encourage other dioceses to replicate the modern slavery work of Derby and Derbyshire Modern Slavery Partners'[121] across the rest of the UK. Donna spoke positively of the bishop's work at that time, describing how he got everyone together and was 'the driving force.' However, in August 2018 Dr Redfern retired, and 'it stopped.'[122] Although the partnership includes representations from organisations such as the British Red Cross, the Gangmasters' and Labour Abuse Authority (GLAA) and the YMCA,[123] without an enthusiastic and focused leadership, networks can rapidly disintegrate. As Diana observed: 'this framework will only be as good as either the people running it or the people in it or the numbers of people that can provide that support.'[124] The IASC mapping exercise also made reference to 'reticence on the part of other partners to take leadership roles.'[125] It did not elaborate on this point but stated that access to support from the voluntary and community sectors was inconsistent across partnerships. Where a partnership was demonstrated to be working well, the researchers found that there was a 'natural' lead, regardless of sector (law enforcement, voluntary, local government etc.), around which the work could be co-ordinated. This somewhat reiterates the point that networks are only as strong as the people involved.

Ayesha, who represents a government-funded charity, said how difficult it had been to engage some local partners 'just because it's not their usual

119 Independent Anti-Slavery Commissioner, 'Multi-agency Anti-slavery Partnerships: Mapping Locations and Activities for Anti-slavery Partnerships across the UK' (*IASC*) <https://iasc-map.nottingham.ac.uk/index.html> accessed 7 May 2020.

120 Clewer Initiative, 'The Derby Story' (*The Clewer Initiative*) <www.theclewerinitiative.org/derby> accessed 7 May 2020.

121 Rt. Rev Dr Alastair Redfern, *Derby and Derbyshire Modern Slavery Partnership Newsletter* (2nd edn, Derby and Derbyshire Modern Slavery Partnership 2018) <https://static1.squarespace.com/static/58f723af1b631bc0c1e17415/t/5bb1fa570d929713f2ace98e/1538390625703/BoD+Modern+Slavery+Newsletter+05 + 18+%28004%29.pdf> accessed 7 May 2020.

122 Donna, Nottingham, UK, 10 May 2019.

123 Independent Anti-Slavery Commissioner (n 119).

124 Diana, Bristol, UK, 22 February 2019.

125 Office of the Independent Anti-Slavery Commissioner and University of Nottingham's Rights Lab (n 94) 8.

population that they'd work with,'[126] although she stated that through perseverance, the organisation now had collaborative partnerships with policing, health and local authorities and safeguarding teams 'to make sure that when we don't have the answers, we have a wealth of other people around to do multi-agency work.'[127] This accumulation of knowledge, skills and expertise across various services also highlights the fact that individual budgets simply do not stretch far enough to provide an all-encompassing service:

> We need to constantly keep reviewing that because I do worry around the squeeze on funding generally, not only in local authorities but across different organisations, so that integrated approach is more important than ever because of the reduction in funding, and it does get more complicated and more complex added to the funding issues as well.[128]

Gaps in funding and resources were acknowledged by all participants, and although, for some, this did not detract from 'a real desire to work together to be collaborative,'[129] some sectors received criticism for their lack of involvement:

> There's a real lack of appropriate health or social care, those that aren't, their lives aren't in immediate danger but actually they can't cope on their own living independently, they need some support and there's just nothing available.[130]

> I think at least the heart is there to be caring for these victims. Local authority, it's less. I dunno! It's just less, that we see happening, but I think that's just the state of social care.[131]

> Generally, at a time of austerity, local authorities are struggling across the board which means that we are, under the Care Act, adding another population that they are responsible for looking after at certain points, they haven't had any extra funding to do that.[132]

This does, in some respects, reflect the impact of cuts on public services and the consequent stretch on resources,[133] as outlined in Chapter 3. However, where a statutory organisation is ordinarily responsible for the social care of

126 Ayesha, Portsmouth, UK, 30 October 2018.
127 ibid.
128 David, Birmingham, UK, 20 October 2018.
129 Donna, Nottingham, UK, 10 May 2019.
130 Rachel, London, UK, 11 May 2019.
131 ibid.
132 Ayesha, Portsmouth, UK, 30 October 2018.
133 See also discussion on NHS waiting times for mental health appointments in Trauma chapter.

vulnerable people, particularly with regard to basic needs like accommodation, it creates a chasm in the overall system if the responsibilities cannot be met. If the government wishes to fulfil its commitment to eradicating modern slavery, it must therefore consider investing appropriately in all aspects of survivor support.

Communication is an especially significant issue, with practitioners from all sectors emphasising the importance of establishing strong dialogue between one another. The government acknowledges that Domestic Homicide Reviews, Adult Death Reviews and Serious Case Reviews persistently expose a lack of clear communication and information sharing amongst relevant agencies and states that '[o]rganisations involved in identifying and supporting victims need to understand how and when they can share information in support of victims.'[134] Despite this, however, the evidence suggests that some agencies are not always able or willing to maintain those links:

> At the moment you've got individuals that are making decisions without referring to anyone else because the trouble with this arena is there is a lot of people doing a lot of stuff in silos, nobody's actually talking to each other.[135]

> If you improve that expertise, if you improve communication between agencies so that you're not retraumatising your victim with every different person they deal with. So I will make a referral, an informed referral to an agency, to a solicitor, then when they come in all they do is ask clarity questions, it's not 'Tell me all about yourself'. Re-trauma – 'tell me how you got to the UK, tell me who sold you'. None of that goes on, it's very much focused questions based on what information they need, so it's much better for the survivors.[136]

> I think we've had a couple of referrals in the past where perhaps we weren't given all the information we would have liked, or made aware of certain issues. Because someone's keen to get someone moved on and it's good progression, but I think by having relationships with those referral partners, that's improved because obviously if we get bad referrals or inaccurate referrals, it affects our willingness to work with somebody later on.[137]

134 Home Office, *Modern Slavery Act 2015* (n 33) 38.
135 Diana, Bristol, UK, 22 February 2019.
136 Donna, Nottingham, UK, 10 May 2019.
137 Rachel, London, UK, 11 May 2019.

These comments point out that reliable communication is not only valuable to the respective organisations but to the welfare and well-being of the survivors themselves. Participants also indicated that some agencies were struggling to strike an appropriate balance between confidentiality and information sharing. Given the sensitive nature of the information and the vulnerability of survivors, it is reasonable that some organisations will be reluctant to discuss details on request, but collaborative relationships should instil a mutual trust and understanding that benefits the individuals they aim to support.

> What we've found is, charities and NGOs that have been working in this arena, whilst they will spend their energy, quite rightly, safeguarding and looking after that victim, those very simple and basic questions get missed, or even if they're asked, they're never recorded, or they're never passed on anywhere. And without intelligence you won't be able to fight this problem.[138]

> A lack of communication between support providers and [my organisation] is one issue. And I understand disclosure and confidentiality, but . . . *every time* . . . so I've got three new clients, they've signed our forms of authority with informed consent and I'm still not getting co-operation from the support providers so I'm then having to go back to the victim and ask them. Well, that's retraumatising the victim and I'm not willing to do that.[139]

Note that these quotes, although they fundamentally raise the same problem, are from two very different frontline perspectives and demonstrate how withholding disclosure specifically impacts the respective work of each agency and, consequently, the survivor. In fact, one of the ways to improve communication between organisations could be for them to have a greater understanding of each others' remits:

> I would again come back to the multi-agency approach, understanding each agency's roles and responsibilities and the limitations of those and make sure you are working with agencies who have something to bring to the table, who offer specialist support services, who are going to be able to provide the right kind of victim care and services and agencies that understand their role within that.[140]

138 Diana, Bristol, UK, 22 February 2019.
139 Donna, Nottingham, UK, 10 May 2019.
140 Puja, Leeds, UK, 8 January 2019.

Law enforcement participants, for example, wanted charities and non-profit organisations to understand the role of policing and the challenges of investigating modern slavery crime. They talked about the *complex, labour-intensive, resource-intensive* nature of investigations and how it can take years to achieve successful prosecutions. Diana described a case where one NGO worker had booked tickets for a group of survivors to fly to a third country; he had not informed any other services of his decision, and it was only by a chance telephone call that Diana's agency was able to swiftly intervene:

> That decision-making process was made by that individual, on behalf of that charity, with no redress or information given to the wider investigating police force, or us, or anyone else. Now, all that money, all that organisation, all the operational work and the ongoing case, court case, *would have been destroyed overnight*[141].

Likewise, charity representatives expressed the need for statutory agencies to appreciate the more nuanced challenges that survivors face:

> I think it's really important to understand where NGOs and charities are coming from in terms of how they see the importance and stability to provide consistent victim care in those in the frontline perspective.[142]

> We've had survivors talk to police and they are keen to get their story across and keen to help justice and then the police will say there's not enough evidence, there's no further action and no one's thought to explain that might be an outcome to the survivor in the first place, so it's setting those expectations.[143]

Other respondents made observations on the experienced reality of finding oneself in the middle of a system that makes regular demands from a multitude of avenues:

> We expect a traumatised individual, whatever that level of trauma, we expect them to be able to understand the difference between their caseworker, key worker and their Police officer, and their lawyer, and their GP, and often these job roles and the segregation of them from the culture they come from are not understood, so it's really hard to understand what info they are giving to which person. They often say I've told you this already, and it's like no you've told the police officer that, and

141 Diana, Bristol, UK, 22 February 2019.
142 Puja, Leeds, UK, 8 January 2019.
143 Ayesha, Portsmouth, UK, 30 October 2018.

> that's your criminal case and again it's helping people understand the parameters.[144]
>
> I think there is an awful lot of sitting around waiting with nothing happening for them but then, when things do happen, it's like you need to be . . . G4S are coming tomorrow, or this solicitor, we've had a letter from the Home Office and we need to see you right now so you need to come for an appointment tomorrow.[145]

The final quote flags another difficulty, again related to communication between agencies. Governmental organisations have been found lacking in this area, as articulated by the CEO of the Medaille Trust at the Home Affairs Committee enquiry on modern slavery:

> To give some examples: we have two of our safe houses in Manchester, one in Merseyside, and clients are given appointments to report at Lunar House in Croydon at 9.15 am, which means that they have to be up at 4.00 am; they have to get an expensive train ticket, which is reimbursed through the Government, but at great expense, and they have to report, perhaps, with a support worker. An expensive return from Manchester to London at peak hours is about £390, I think, on the train for a victim and a support worker. It does not make sense to us. If they have medical or mobility issues they can report to Liverpool and it is £12 return, but other clients are just told, 'No, it is 9.15 am. It is Croydon. Get on with it.'[146]

While different partner agencies have distinct agendas by design, it is clear that a greater understanding of each other's roles and responsibilities, alongside the limitations of those remits, will forge stronger lines of communication. City Hearts, for example, operates in the north of England and acts as a 'gateway' agency to integrating survivors in communities. The organisation works with survivors to prepare them for employment, at which point they connect with the Co-op's 'Bright Futures' programme (see Section 8.2.3) to identify work opportunities for the survivor. Equality of involvement also seems to strengthen these partnerships, as 'this clearly raises the interest of everyone concerned, it fosters better working relationships and generates enthusiasm within the subject area.'[147] West Yorkshire's Anti-Slavery Network is an excellent example of collaborative, engaged partners headed by a driven lead.

144 ibid.
145 Becky, Sheffield, UK, 19 December 2018.
146 Garry Smith, *Oral Evidence, Modern Slavery*, HC 1460 (6 November 2018) Q115.
147 Office of the Independent Anti-Slavery Commissioner and University of Nottingham's Rights Lab (n 94) 32.

Following his election as police and crime commissioner (PCC) for West Yorkshire, Mark Burns-Williamson established the network, as 'it was a fact that modern slavery and trafficking was happening in West Yorkshire and it was clearly a real threat, not only to individual victims but wider communities.'[148] He also identified the importance of working with NGOs and other local agencies to jointly tackle the problem, and later forged a nationwide PCC Anti-Slavery Network. His proactive approach has facilitated strong multi-agency relationships across West Yorkshire, which were evidenced in this work and have been acknowledged in other pieces of research.[149] Participants that were involved with other successful multi-agency partnerships were also very positive about the experience:

> We've got a joint project with the police, where that intelligence is passed on directly to the police and then rescues, you know raids, and such like occur and [my organisation] are usually one of the parties that help.[150]

> We work really closely with the local housing association, who offer supported accommodation so that's a really good partnership and yeah, it's really about people's needs, so we work with [area] Women's Aid, we work with the local provider in [city] so they offer the NRM support and a lot of the women from there are asylum seekers, so we will have referrals from them quite often for a volunteer placement. It's about that meaningful activity and that is very much tailor-made around the individual.[151]

Although successful partnerships highlight how well a system can work with the right people on board, this does appear to let the government off the hook in terms of its own responsibilities. Not only has the outsourcing of social welfare to voluntary organisations led to regional inconsistencies (see Section 3.4), the government can now look to networks and agencies that are working well and simply ask other organisations to replicate those models rather than undertake any strategic development work. Thus far, the reforms to the NRM could be seen as little more than tinkering, and do not appear to have taken structural challenges into account. The following quote from

148 David, Birmingham, UK, 20 October 2018.
149 Gardner (n 72) 461; Office of the Independent Anti-Slavery Commissioner and University of Nottingham's Rights Lab (n 94).
150 Donna, Nottingham, UK, 10 May 2019.
151 Rachel, London, UK, 11 May 2019.

Caroline, for example, illustrates the ongoing difficulties with communication, which have not been resolved by the digitalisation of the NRM:

> There should be the ability, if you're a First Responder you should have your own log in and password, so that you can log in to the system and you should have your own identifiable ID as a First Responder, you go in and you're the one who has to fill that in and you sign that off with your own ID to say I've opened up the system and I've completed this form. Again, I just think, if we're going to do that, you put people who you want to be First Responders on a training course and at the end of that they get their own unique log in code and password which ensures that we've got some quite of quality assurance of the people who are the First Responders and who are doing that but as far as I'm aware, that's not what we're deciding to do – it's just going to be electronic and anyone can fill it in, rather than a paper form.[152]

Ultimately, clear and fluid communication channels between agencies who all have the same fundamental aims is to the benefit of the survivors each organisation is motivated to support.

## 4.5 Conclusion

For vulnerable and traumatised individuals, who are often fresh from exiting captivity, it is imperative that their initial interactions with support providers provide foundations of trust and respect. From there, survivor pathways should be consistent while allowing for individual agency and flexibility. Security of accommodation is by far the most crucial aspect of this pathway; however, it is the biggest obstacle for support organisations to overcome. Cost, space limitations and statutory time restrictions mean that no survivor can be guaranteed the same housing from intervention to independence, and this highlights both the disparities and barriers to success in consistently supporting survivors throughout the pathway. There are conversations to be had regarding who could realistically step up and improve this issue, but, as with any matter concerning large financial output, a strong incentive would likely have to be presented. In terms of the government's own policies, the current NRM system also gives survivors a stark choice: exiting slavery in exchange for support while being prevented from engaging in paid employment; or surviving alone in a precarious situation where at least the 'freedom to work' exists. This creates a dilemma for some survivors whose *raison d'être* is providing for themselves and their families, and, for those who choose not to enter the NRM, their support options become severely limited. There is a growing awareness of this demographic among frontline organisations, and many

152 Caroline, Nottingham, UK, 22 November 2019.

do offer services even for non-NRM survivors, as indicated in the previous chapter.

Further potential improvements identified in the data regard greater consistency and trust-building. There is also a sound call for advocacy and the establishment of a designated key support worker to assist individual survivors through to recovery and independence; however, until more regions are able to cater for a significant majority of ongoing needs, the single advocate would only be valuable for as long as the survivor remains in that particular geographical area. One of the most positive findings from my research, however, was the existence of active, well-run multi-agency partnerships across several regions of the UK. Practitioners within these networks view them as a positive addition to the modern slavery support sector, and, for regions that have yet to develop MAPs to their fullest capacity, they have the benefit of some good working models from which to build their own networks. The evidence suggests that it is not necessary to limit MAP leadership candidacy to one particular professional background; the most important qualities are enthusiasm, drive and the ability to bring everyone together for agreed aims and objectives. Where all representatives in a MAP respect and understand each other's roles and responsibilities, the potential for valuable information sharing and clear communication is increased, leading to more consistent support pathways and benefitting survivors overall. It is odd that the health and social care sector is largely absent from this landscape, particularly with regard to the NRM. While it could be argued that they are already stretched to capacity under austerity, the same can be said for the voluntary sector, which is absorbing a lot of the responsibility for managing complex and serious support needs. This responsibility is not supported by statutory uniform standards, meaning that some organisations are reliant on the integrity and expertise of their workers to design appropriate services.

While many of these areas can be improved through communication and relationship-building, the survivor pathway faces a far bigger challenge from government policy. This is because, despite the issue of modern slavery being the subject of high-profile campaigns, Select Committee enquiries and ultimately its own piece of legislation, a more controversial policy area can render all support null and void. The next chapter thus explores the alternative pathways for those survivors who are also subject to the UK's immigration regulations.

# 5 Immigration

## 5.1 Introduction

Chapters 2 and 4 highlighted how successive UK governments have made a point of pledging their commitment to tackling modern slavery and the stated policy aims of supporting survivors have been announced with some fanfare. Based on the government's own figures,[1] a significant number of trafficking and slavery referrals into the National Referral Mechanism are for non-British nationals, and this has remained consistent every year. Moreover, eight of the top ten most represented nationalities amongst referred adults are from outside the EU. These statistics, however, provide only a tiny insight into the overall picture – as official figures, they show only those individuals who have been formally identified as potential victims *and* who have given their consent to be referred into the NRM. A deeper examination of these figures further reveals emerging patterns that seem to favour UK nationals and EU nationals in the Conclusive Grounds decision-making process, while broader research raises discrepancies and questions as to how foreign national survivors are treated within the UK's modern slavery support systems. This contributes to the book's overarching examination of consistencies and disparities in the support available to survivors, as well as further identifying the successes and limitations of the UK's legislation, policies and practices.

The topic of immigration is now part and parcel of any discussion on human trafficking and modern slavery, and it would be remiss to ignore the fact that so many survivors in the UK have arrived here from other countries. It would thus be disingenuous to discuss the issue without examination of the UK's immigration regulations and their relationship with modern slavery policy and legislation. Through analysis of statistical data and independent reports, this chapter aims to understand the avenues a survivor pathway can take when their immigration status is uncertain. This includes commentary on the Rwanda policy and the UK government's feverish endeavours to stop

1 Home Office, *National Referral Mechanism Statistics – End of Year Summary 2023* (Home Office 2024).

DOI: 10.4324/9781032639895-5

small, refugee-carrying boats from landing on British shores, initiatives which have been met with condemnation by campaigners in the anti-slavery field.

## 5.2 A tale of two policies

Hodkinson and others, taking an historical perspective on the UK's conflation of immigration and modern slavery, observe that the 'hostile environment' has been shaped and developed through successive legislation since the 1905 Aliens Act.[2] Over a century later, the distinct preference for white migrants is evident. When the EU granted membership to ten new states in 2004,[3] the expansion opened up employment opportunities for 75 million citizens,[4] but the then-Labour government chose not to put transition measures in place, which would have regulated immigration from the new member states. This decision, combined with a gross underestimate of the number of anticipated arrivals, led to increasingly vocal media concerns about the strain on public resources.[5] The government did, however, curtail the arrival of low-skilled migrants from third countries with the introduction of a points-based system.[6] The Borders, Citizenship and Immigration Act[7] additionally ensured that non-EU nationals were prevented from claiming benefits until they attained British citizenship or permanent residence. When, in 2006, it was found that the Home Office was neglecting to deport non-nationals convicted of serious crimes, the voices of dissent grew louder and the government reflexively toughened its stance on deportation and immigration in general.[8] The emerging viewpoint saw 'immigrant' – or more specifically, 'illegal immigrant' – as synonymous with 'criminal,'[9] an attitude that has pervaded mainstream discourse ever since.

The moves dovetail with deep-rooted efforts to immobilise and criminalise society's poor.[10] Where Victorian poor laws and vagrancy laws once demonised

2 Stuart N Hodkinson and others, 'Fighting or Fuelling Forced Labour? The Modern Slavery Act 2015, Irregular Migrants and the Vulnerabilising Role of the UK's Hostile Environment' (2020) 00(0) *Critical Social Policy* 1.

3 Bridget Anderson, 'Where's the Harm in That? Immigration Enforcement, Trafficking, and the Protection of Migrants' Rights' (2012) 56(9) *American Behavioural Scientist* 1241.

4 Jean-Claude Trichet, President of the European Central Bank, 'EU Enlargement: Challenges and Opportunities' (Speech at 'Europe's Frontiers: EU Enlargement – Its Implications and Consequences' Conference, Lisbon, 27 October 2004) <www.ecb.europa.eu/press/key/date/2004/html/sp041027.en.html> accessed 2 November 2020.

5 Anderson (n 3) 1241.

6 Hodkinson and others (n 2) 1.

7 Borders, Citizenship and Immigration Act 2009.

8 Anderson (n 3) 1241.

9 Ieke de Vries and others, 'Anti-immigration Sentiment and Public Opinion on Human Trafficking' (2019) 72 *Crime, Law and Social Change* 125.

10 Julia O'Connell Davidson, 'New Slavery, Old Binaries: Human Trafficking and the Borders of "Freedom"' (2010) 10(2) *Global Networks* 244.

'those who managed to move from their birthplace in an attempt to eke out a living on the margins of the legally regulated economy,'[11] UK policies have shifted their attentions to restricting migrant movement and rights.[12] These structural changes have laid the foundations for a system that not only plays into the hands of potential traffickers but also seriously diminishes the security that survivors of modern slavery are afforded. Successive Conservative home secretaries have thus maintained an even harsher low-tolerance position, from Theresa May's controversial 'Go home or face arrest' campaign[13] to Priti Patel triumphantly announcing that she intended to end freedom of movement 'once and for all.'[14] Under the Conservative's hostile environment policies, the 2018 'Windrush scandal' targeted members and descendants of the post-war Caribbean migration wave 'with the result that some lost their homes and jobs, were refused healthcare, pensions and access to social security, held in immigration detention centres and even refused re-entry to or deported from the UK.'[15] The fact that citizens who had lived, worked, paid taxes and created families in the UK for decades were at risk of sudden deportation highlights the vulnerability of more recent arrivals with no support networks and limited English who are under the control of traffickers and slaveholders.

Significantly, the state has placed an increasing amount of emphasis on the public's role in flagging immigration concerns; those employed in the state sector even have a duty to identify and report breaches of immigration control,[16] effectively meaning that 'public bodies have been turned into a border force.'[17] The right-wing media continued to reinforce their anti-immigration message with growing intensity, to the extent that the Daily Mail and the Sun have been accused by the European Commission against Racism and Intolerance of fuelling hate crime and xenophobia.[18] While these policies may play to the crowd, the reality of deportation or detention is rarely examined in public discourse. It also ignores the cognitive dissonance of simultaneously raising

11 ibid 244, 253.

12 Cliodhna Murphy, 'Enforcing Employment Standards for Undocumented Domestic Workers in the UK and Ireland: Rethinking Illegality in Zones of Invisibility' (2015) 29(4) *Immigration, Asylum and Nationality Law* 349.

13 Patrick Wintour, '"Go Home" Billboard Vans Not a Success, Says Theresa May' *The Guardian* (London, 22 October 2013) <www.theguardian.com/politics/2013/oct/22/go-home-billboards-pulled> accessed 5 August 2020.

14 Richard Ballout, 'Priti Patel Firmly Intends to End Free Movement of People' (*Immigration News*, 3 October 2019) <https://immigrationnews.co.uk/priti-patel-end-of-free-movement/> accessed 27 October 2020.

15 Hodkinson and others (n 2) 1, 3.

16 Anderson (n 3) 1241.

17 Ahmed Aydeed, *Oral Evidence, Modern Slavery*, HC 1460 (2 July 2019) Q246.

18 Lizzie Dearden, 'The Sun and Daily Mail Accused of "Fuelling Prejudice" in Report on Rising Racist Violence and Hate Speech in UK' (*The Independent*, London, 8 October 2016) <www.independent.co.uk/news/media/press/sun-and-daily-mail-fuelling-prejudice-racist-violence-hate-crime-speech-uk-ecri-report-a7351856.html> accessed 8 November 2020.

awareness and sympathy for victims of modern slavery and human trafficking. Compare the moves for engagement on immigration issues to calls for the public to be vigilant about signs of modern slavery: campaigns highlight the indicators to be aware of, and people are encouraged to call helplines even if their concerns seem trivial – 'it is better to be safe than sorry.'[19] The Sun, meanwhile, declared its support for Lord McColl's Modern Slavery (Victim Support) Bill[20] and launched its own 'Stamp out Slavery' campaign.[21] None of these initiatives dare to mention the obvious contradiction, as identified by Ayesha:

> I think we have to start tapping at the elephant in the room that links immigration with trafficking and slavery. We have to accept the elephant is there and then is there a way around the elephant or is it remaining, and if so, what does that mean? I don't think government are quite ready to engage in that conversation yet and we all know it's there but we're just kind of hoping it's going to stay quiet and be pushed over there.[22]

Theresa May, who introduced the Modern Slavery Act and has continued to publicly declare her support for the cause, has repeatedly associated trafficking with illegal immigration;[23] however this entrenches the polarised images of 'bad' immigrants (traffickers and people smugglers) with 'good' immigrants (unwitting victims and those who want to work). As well as muddying the policy waters, the conflation of policy issues thus creates a feedback loop of attitudes around 'ideal victims,' which is unhelpful to both survivors and their wider support systems (see Sections 5.5 and 7.4).

It should also be noted that anti-modern slavery campaigns are not born of a drive to improve general employment conditions for all. This can be evidenced by the fact that resources for immigration enforcement are far greater than the funding afforded to the protection of employment rights.[24] Concurrent to this policy trend, aggressive moves by large multi-national corporations to reduce wages, employment rights and workplace regulations have helped to facilitate the rise of recruitment agencies, zero-hour contracts and the gig economy.[25] This type of temporary casual employment differs to the seasonal work traditionally pursued by foreign students and younger people wishing to earn

19 Anderson (n 3) 1241, 1254.

20 Modern Slavery (Victim Support) HL Bill (2019–21).

21 The Sun, 'Stamp Out Slavery' (*The Sun*) <www.thesun.co.uk/topic/stamp-out-slavery/> accessed 8 November 2020.

22 Ayesha, Portsmouth, UK, 30 October 2018.

23 Caroline Robinson, 'Claiming Space for Labour Rights within the United Kingdom Modern Slavery Crusade' (2015) 5 *Anti-Trafficking Review* 129.

24 Anderson (n 3) 1241.

25 Steve French, 'Between Globalisation and Brexit: Migration, Pay and the Road to Modern Slavery in the UK Hospitality Industry' (2018) 8(1) *Research in Hospitality Management* 23.

money as they travel; it is increasingly becoming a more permanent means of livelihood for other demographics.[26] The Anti-Trafficking Monitoring Group (ATMG) has warned that risks of exploitation 'are exacerbated when coupled with a labour market that favours deregulation and flexibility.'[27] Specifically, migrant workers are 'disproportionately concentrated in lower-end, insecure or precarious jobs,'[28] mainly within the hospitality, construction and agricultural sectors.[29] A 2017 report outlined how this increases their vulnerability to exploitation:

> Lack of knowledge about employment rights, limited language skills and little or no access to training and support networks can place migrant workers at particular risk of abuse. Debt bondage arising from excessive recruitment fees, debt servicing and wage deductions can entrap migrant workers within circles of abuse. These factors mean that migrants, along with other vulnerable workers, frequently lack the leverage or knowledge that would allow them to assert their basic rights.[30]

One of the key means of exploitation is through undercutting pay, as illustrated by the discovery of Leicester-based textile sweatshops.' Migrant workers there were earning an average of £4.25 an hour,[31] additionally demonstrating the grey area between legitimate employment and modern slavery as defined by UK law, which is explored in Chapter 2. Commentators have also noted an increasing policy stance that favours central and eastern European migrant workers in lower-skilled employment, while squeezing non-EU nationals out of this end of the labour market.[32] This is a worrying trend that poses serious risks given the changes to EU worker rights in a post-Brexit UK. Traditionally, non-EU nationals were acknowledged to have had a greater vulnerability to exploitation as their immigration status was often linked to employer sponsorship.[33] However, post-Brexit, EU migrant workers based in the aforemen-

26 ibid.

27 Anti-Trafficking Monitoring Group, *Brexit & the UK's Fight against Modern Slavery* (ATMG July 2017) 2.

28 Hannah Lewis and Louise Waite, 'Migrant Illegality, Slavery and Exploitative Work' in G Craig and others (eds), *The Modern Slavery Agenda: Policy, Politics and Practice in the UK* (Policy Press 2019) 220.

29 French (n 25) 23.

30 CORE Coalition, *Risk Averse? Company Reporting on Raw Material and Sector-specific Risks under the Transparency in Supply Chains Clause in the UK Modern Slavery Act 2015*' (CORE 2017) 51.

31 Sarah O'Connor, 'Dark Factories: Labour Exploitation in Britain's Garment Industry' *Financial Times* (London, 17 May 2018) <www.ft.com/content/e427327e-5892-11e8-b8b2-d6ceb45fa9d0> accessed 1 July 2020.

32 Alex Balch and Andrew Geddes, 'Opportunity from Crisis? Organisational Responses to Human Trafficking in the UK' (2011) 13 *BJPIR* 26.

33 French (n 25) 23.

tioned insecure and precarious jobs will also face the uncertainty of whether their immigration status is actually legal (see also Chapter 2). Immigration charities further warned that the government's proposed bans on low-skilled EU workers could 'lead to a boom in a black market for low-paid workers that will be exploited by criminals and lead to coercion and abuse.'[34] The social care sector then suffered the compounded impacts of Brexit *and* COVID, leading the Home Office to relax immigration rules in 2021 in order to recruit desperately needed care workers.[35] In December 2023, James Bullion, the chief inspector of adult social care and integrated care, indicated to the Health and Social Care Committee that the previous fears had been borne out, stating that 'exploitation and modern slavery were becoming a more common feature of alerts to us.'[36]

The dichotomy is compounded by legislation that also appears to run counterintuitively to anti-modern slavery efforts. The Immigration Act 2016,[37] for example, included provisions that criminalised undocumented migrant workers themselves, in direct conflict with concerns around labour abuse. Anyone who is subject to immigration control thus commits an offence if they know or have reasonable cause to believe that they are not entitled to work because of their immigration status.[38] The weaker efforts to protect labour rights are also apparent as the definition of 'work' includes activity that is not covered by employment protection legislation.[39] This is not an oversight: the government 'intended the definition to be broad enough to include informal arrangements without a contract.'[40] Given the casual, insecure and illegitimate nature of exploitative labour, this is exactly the type of 'illegal work' that corresponds to offences listed in the Immigration Act. Common law principles such as the 'doctrine of illegality' exacerbate this issue by rendering victims of modern slavery – who are not employed under legal contracts – ineligible to claim through employment tribunals. This issue was epitomised in *Hounga v Allen*,[41] a case that is examined in Chapter 7.

34 Lisa O'Carroll, 'Immigration Rules Post-Brexit Could Fuel Modern Slavery, Say Charities' *The Guardian* (London, 21 February 2020) <www.theguardian.com/uk-news/2020/feb/21/immigration-rules-post-brexit-could-fuel-modern-slavery-say-charities> accessed 29 October 2020.

35 Department of Health and Social Care/Home Office, 'Biggest Visa Boost for Social Care as Health and Care Visa Scheme Expanded' (*Gov.uk*, 24 December 2021) www.gov.uk/government/news/biggest-visa-boost-for-social-care-as-health-and-care-visa-scheme-expanded accessed 5 April 2024.

36 James Bullion, *Oral Evidence, Social Care: Changes to Legal Migration Measures*, HC 411 (19 December 2023) Q16.

37 Immigration Act 2016.

38 s34 Immigration Act 2016.

39 ibid.

40 Judy Fudge, 'Why Labour Lawyers Should Care About the Modern Slavery Act 2015' (2018) 29(3) *King's Law Journal* 377, 397.

41 [2014] UKSC 47.

2023's Illegal Migration Act then increased restrictions on the level of support and protection available to modern slavery survivors, swiftly following the Nationality and Borders Act 2022, which also reduced the extent of temporary leave to stay in the UK for positive CG victims. Suella Braverman, the home secretary responsible for both these statutes, claimed that 'modern slavery laws are being abused by people gaming the system.'[42] The Office for Statistics Regulation and the Home Affairs Select Committee both requested specific evidence of these abuses, but say that none was provided, and even the Home Office's own referral data contradicts the idea, given the proportion of positive conclusive grounds decisions (see Chapter 2). The Joint Committee on Human Rights report was not sparing in its criticism at the Bill stage, citing its departure from many of the UK's commitments to international law;[43] the home secretary was unmoved. It is the Rwanda policy, however, that has received the most vocal condemnation from across a range of actors and organisations. The policy, a response to the numbers of refugees arriving to the UK via small boats across the English Channel, aims to redirect the refugees to Rwanda as a 'third party' processing centre. As well as once again breaching international legal standards,[44] the scheme is undiscerning and risks removing victims of modern slavery to a country whose human rights record is notoriously poor. The government line appears to be that the choice of passage to the UK negates any access people may have to support and protection as victims of trafficking. Given that 80% of NRM referrals from small boat arrivals have received positive Conclusive Grounds decisions since 2018,[45] it is evident that immigration enforcement is the greater priority. A cynical interpretation may even suggest that this is an expedient method of NRM referral reduction.

The Home Office has also designated UK Border Force (UKBF) Officers as 'first responders' (see Section 2.3) on the basis that they are situated in a strong position to identify potential victims of trafficking.[46] The logic to this is sound enough, but commentators have noted that 'neither their professional culture as a law enforcement agency nor their prior training or experience has

42 Emily Dugan, 'Watchdog Disputes Braverman's Claim Modern Slavery Laws Being "Gamed"' *The Guardian* (London, 9 October 2022) <www.theguardian.com/uk-news/2022/oct/09/watchdog-disputes-bravermans-claim-migrants-gaming-slavery-laws> accessed 26 March 2024.

43 Joint Committee on Human Rights, *Legislative Scrutiny: Illegal Migration Bill* (HC 2022–23 1241).

44 [2023] UKSC 42.

45 Home Office, 'Official Statistics: Irregular Migration to the UK, Year Ending March 2023' (*Home Office*, 25 May 2023) <www.gov.uk/government/statistics/irregular-migration-to-the-uk-year-ending-march-2023/irregular-migration-to-the-uk-year-ending-march-2023#data-tables> accessed 5 April 2024.

46 Independent Chief Inspector of Borders and Immigration, *An Inspection of Border Force's Identification and Treatment of Potential Victims of Modern Slavery: July to October 2016* (Williams Lea Group on behalf of the Controller of Her Majesty's Stationery Office 2017).

*Table 5.1* Annual referral figures for UKBF and UKVI

| | *2016* | *2017* | *2018* | *2019* | *2020* | *2021* | *2022* | *2023* |
|---|---|---|---|---|---|---|---|---|
| UKBF | 3% | 2.7% | 2% | 2.4% | 1.3% | 1.4% | 1.3% | 1.4% |
| UKVI | 38% | 38.3% | 30% | 23.5% | 16.4% | 21.6% | 30% | 30.1% |

involved significant focus on the protection of vulnerable adults.'[47] It consequently appears to create a conflict of interest. The primary function of the UKBF is to 'sort' people according to their immigration status, maintaining an alert for those who would pose a threat to border integrity. Sorting people by vulnerability – that is to say, recognising the signs of vulnerability – is essentially not compatible with the UKBF's *raison d'être*. The new focus on human rights has been seen as an imposition by some border officers, with a number of them actively resisting their change in role;[48] former survivor support organisation Eaves secured seventeen successful appeals against UKBF during its first two years as a first responder, as well as forcing 'countless reassessments.'[49] Referral rates over the past four years would suggest that, despite the UKBF's unique opportunities to identify potential victims, their actual contribution to the National Referral Mechanism process is persistently negligible. Taking data from the NRM annual statistics,[50] Table 5.1 shows the percentage of overall referrals to the NRM from the UKBF, with the same from UK Visa and Immigration shown for comparison.

A more sympathetic reading of these percentages is the fact that many people, at the point of crossing the border, have not yet been exploited.[51] Moreover, given that individuals are required to give their consent to enter the NRM by signing a form that identifies them as a victim of crime (as well

47 Katerina Hadjimatheou and Jennifer Lynch, 'UK Anti-slavery Policy at the Border: Humanitarian Opportunism and the Challenge of Victim Consent to Assistance' (2018) 00(0) *European Journal of Criminology* 1, 5.

48 ibid 1.

49 Mark Townsend, 'Sex-trafficked Women's Charity Poppy Project in Danger as Funding Withdrawn' *The Guardian* (London, 17 April 2011) <www.theguardian.com/society/2011/apr/17/prostitution-human-trafficking> accessed 18 May 2020.

50 Data taken from: National Crime Agency, *National Referral Mechanism Statistics – End of Year Summary 2016* (National Crime Agency 2016); National Crime Agency, *National Referral Mechanism Statistics – End of Year Summary 2017* (National Crime Agency 2017); National Crime Agency, *National Referral Mechanism Statistics – End of Year Summary 2018* (National Crime Agency 2018); Home Office, *National Referral Mechanism Statistics – End of Year Summary 2019* (Home Office 2019); Home Office, *National Referral Mechanism Statistics – End of Year Summary 2020* (Home Office 2021); Home Office, *National Referral Mechanism Statistics – End of Year Summary 2021* (Home Office 2022); Home Office, *National Referral Mechanism Statistics – End of Year Summary 2022* (Home Office 2023); Home Office, *National Referral Mechanism Statistics – End of Year Summary 2023* (Home Office 2024).

51 Hadjimatheou and Lynch (n 47) 1.

as consenting to their details being shared with other state authorities), there is an understandable reluctance for them to do so. Additional barriers to consent will also come into play, such as emotional ties to their traffickers, fear of repercussions and the overriding need or desire to earn money. A 2018 study also found that UKBF officers generally waved EU nationals through immigration sorting because they were deemed to be legal migrants travelling under freedom of movement rights.[52] This may previously have resulted in many potential trafficking victims falling under the radar of the authorities at several junctions, meaning that the changing immigration status of EU nationals could actually help to identify victims sooner – although this too has yet to bear out in official NRM statistics. In any event, the view that UKBF is able and willing to assist with anti-slavery measures may need revising.

Meanwhile, a positive Conclusive Grounds decision does not afford survivors any legal immigration status (see Chapters 2 and 8). In the years 2014–16, only 384 out of 2563 individuals with positive CG decisions were granted discretionary leave to remain in the UK[53] – 15% of all confirmed victims. Not all survivors wish to stay in the UK, while others will opt to apply for asylum instead (UKVI are responsible for a large proportion of NRM referrals, 'predominantly made as part of an asylum claim').[54] Nevertheless, the Home Office will automatically consider discretionary leave for confirmed survivors of modern slavery 'if they are not granted asylum or humanitarian protection or leave on the basis of their family or private life.'[55] Bearing in mind that this only relates to *positive* CG decisions, this suggests that far higher numbers are left without a legal immigration status and no statutory means of support. There is no way of knowing what happens to these survivors as there is no official outcome monitoring or statistical analysis available.[56] Even support providers who work long-term with survivors are unable to shed much light on this issue:

> I mean someone who is a UK citizen who just climbs the NRM, they have citizenship so they have access to some other things, or they agree to go back to family or they really don't have . . . maybe they return or

52 ibid.

53 Patrick Burland, 'Smoke but No Fire: How Not to Read UK Government Trafficking Statistics' (*Open Democracy*, 28 April 2017) <www.opendemocracy.net/en/beyond-trafficking-and-slavery/smoke-but-no-fire-how-not-to-read-uk-government-trafficking-statistics/> accessed 28 October 2020.

54 Department of Justice, The Scottish Government and The Welsh Government, *2018 UK Annual Report on Modern Slavery* (HM Government 2018) 12.

55 Home Office, *Discretionary Leave for Victims of Modern Slavery v3.0* (Home Office 2020) 9.

56 Any available statistics on discretionary leave to remain in the UK do not specify figures for potential or identified victims of trafficking and slavery.

> they go underground, or they marry someone and become a UK citizen. All kinds of things.[57]

The government, in the meantime, have consistently ignored calls to automatically grant the automatic right to remain for survivors who receive a positive CG decision. Submitting evidence as part of the Work and Pensions Committee's inquiry, 'Victims of Modern Slavery,'[58] Sarah Newton MP warned against introducing a blanket policy that could encourage false trafficking claims:

> If all victims of modern slavery were granted automatic [Discretionary Leave], we expect that abuse of the NRM would increase by people seeking access to benefits to circumvent recent restrictions (EEA nationals), and by those who have exhausted other options to remain in the UK (failed asylum seekers).[59]

There is a rather unfortunate inference to be drawn from this, and from Suella Braverman's belief that the NRM is being 'gamed,' which cast aspersions on the government's ability to effectively process NRM referrals and therefore eliminate fraudulent or false claims. Ms Newton's concerns also failed to acknowledge that victims who have been trafficked from another country will have been told, in most cases, that their 'employer' will arrange all the necessary visas and documentation.[60] Kevin Hyland, in his capacity as IASC, also provided evidence to the Work and Pensions Committee Victims of Modern Slavery inquiry, highlighting the clear problem with the current system:

> If you have been locked up in a farm, or locked up in premises being forced into labour or being sexually exploited, you are not going to be able to produce pay slips, or a P45, or whatever. That is the basics of where we are getting this wrong, even to that level.[61]

More recently, the Independent Chief Inspector of Borders and Immigration report stated that while the Home Office had 'taken steps to tackle the exploitation of migrant workers and abuse of the visa route by unscrupulous

57 Jenni, Manchester, UK, 13 August 2019.

58 Work and Pensions Committee, *Victims of Modern Slavery: Twelfth Report of Session 2016–17*, HC 803 (30 April 2017).

59 Letter from Sarah Newton MP to Chair of Work and Pensions Committee (17 February 2017) <https://old.parliament.uk/documents/commons-committees/work-and-pensions/Letter-from-Sarah-Newton-MP-to-Chair-re-modern-slavery-session-17-2-2017.pdf> accessed 27 October 2020.

60 David M Doyle and others, '"I Felt Like She Owns Me": Exploitation and Uncertainty in the Lives of Labour Trafficking Victims in Ireland' (2019) 59 *British Journal of Criminology* 231.

61 Kevin Hyland, *Oral Evidence, Victims of Modern Slavery*, HC 803 (11 January 2017) Q130.

employers,'[62] the efforts had resulted in visa caseworkers identifying cases of modern slavery on a daily basis. Furthermore, the implication that undocumented migrants who are aware of their illegal immigration status would present themselves to the authorities is somewhat unrealistic. Anti-immigration attitudes permeate victims' own fears while in confinement,[63] a factor that traffickers themselves are keenly aware of. Threat of deportation is one of the most commonly utilised means of coercion by slaveholders to their victims.[64] Reflecting Biderman's theory of coercion, as outlined in Table 6.1 (Section 6.3), this invokes a known fear within the victim and can be repeatedly used with very little effort required on the part of the abuser. The deployment of this threat serves multiple purposes: alongside psychological intimidation and reinforcement of the power imbalance, regular reminders of the victim's precarious immigration status will instil a fear of state authority. Should a law enforcement officer arrive to investigate the site, victims will be too scared to speak up and risk drawing attention to themselves.[65] Consequently, this fear will be at the forefront of victims' minds even when the authorities arrest their captors and remove them from the site, and, instead of revealing details of the slavery and abuse, their focus will be centred on their immigration status.[66] Kevin Hyland's evidence at the Victims of Modern Slavery inquiry further emphasised this:

> A victim of modern slavery comes forward, they are presented with a number of forms that they have to sign, then their immigration status is looked at, and then there is a process to decide whether they are a victim or not. If we did the same for a victim of domestic abuse or a victim of rape I am sure people, parliamentarians and others, would be standing there in shock and horror.[67]

However, it is the government's decision to transfer responsibility for identifying victims of modern slavery to the Home Office that has attracted the strongest criticisms. Initially, this responsibility was given to the National Crime Agency's Modern Slavery and Human Trafficking Unit and UK Borders Agency[68] – later to UKVI – as Competent Authorities to process NRM

62 David Neal, *An Inspection of the Immigration System as It Relates to the Social Care Sector: August 2023-November 2023* (Independent Chief Inspector of Borders and Immigration 26 March 2024) 52.
63 de Vries and others (n 9) 125.
64 Doyle and others (n 60) 231.
65 Observational data from interactions with survivors and law enforcement officers in the field.
66 de Vries and others (n 9) 125.
67 Kevin Hyland, *Oral Evidence, Victims of Modern Slavery,* HC 803 (11 January 2017).
68 Jessica Elliott, 'The National Referral Mechanism: Querying the Response of "First Responders" and the Competence of "Competent Authorities"' (2016) 30(1) *Journal of Immigration, Asylum and Nationality Law* 9.

claims and determine whether an individual could be confirmed as a victim of trafficking or slavery. Following several administrative changes, this decision-making procedure is now the domain of caseworkers under a Single Competent Authority and Immigration Enforcement Competent Authority, which sit within the Home Office (see Chapter 2). The SCA is also tasked with deciding whether to issue Discretionary Leave to Remain to a survivor following a positive CG decision.[69] In other words, the immigration status of confirmed victims is in the hands of a governmental department whose principal responsibility is the control and criminalisation of immigration. The Home Affairs Committee inquiry on modern slavery revealed the extent of frustration regarding the decision:

> The lack of independence in terms of first responders but also the competent authority we think is a major issue and major conflict of interest, with both those parties being normally the Home Office.[70]

> It is not always even communicated within the Home Office. We had somebody who was given a positive reasonable grounds decision but then it did not appear in his monthly report from the Home Office, and it was still enacting processes to deport him so he had the interview around travel papers all within the same time period. They do not communicate it within the Home Office. In theory, having one body, which is the same body, at least one of the benefits, you would imagine the Home Office might argue, is making it efficient. That is not even the case because they do not communicate even within the same organisation.[71]

Sarah Teather went on to express concerns that the information gathered by the SCA was at risk of being used for immigration enforcement rather than to implement the anti-modern slavery measures. This concern is not new: a 2013 review by the Anti-Trafficking Monitoring Group found evidence that the then-CAs were conflating victims' trafficked status with their immigration status, citing that this 'inappropriately influences NRM decisions and that hence the decision making is unfair and discriminatory.'[72] The 2017 National Audit Office (NAO) report on modern slavery additionally claimed that 'potential victims from the UK are the most likely to receive a positive conclusive grounds decision (88 per cent of the cases that have received a

69 Home Office, *Modern Slavery Act 2015: Statutory Guidance for England and Wales* (Home Office 2020).

70 James Wilson, *Oral Evidence, Modern Slavery*, HC 1460 (2 July 2019) Q208.

71 Sarah Teather, *Oral Evidence, Modern Slavery*, HC 1460 (2 July 2019) Q243.

72 The Anti-Trafficking Monitoring Group, 'Hidden in Plain Sight – Three Years on: Updated Analysis of UK Measures to Protect Trafficked Persons' (Executive Summary) (ATMG 2013) 8.

Conclusive Grounds decision),'[73] whereas the National Crime Agency's 2015 data showed that only 30% of Albanian cases resulted in a positive CG decision.[74] The same data reported positive CG decisions for 50% of Vietnamese cases and 37% of Nigerian cases, while referrals from the UK received positive decisions in 90% of cases. Referrals for Polish, Romanian and Slovakian nationals were positive in 90.5%, 85% and 78% of cases, respectively. This is despite evidence that a majority of source states for human trafficking are situated outside the EU.[75] However, these decisions were made under the former system, where CA responsibilities were split between the MSHTU, who processed claims where immigration was not a concern, and the UKVI, who were tasked with determining cases for EEA and non-EEA nationals. To put this data into clearer context, the past six years of available data[76] are presented in the following table, which provides an overview of the top five most referred nationalities.

Note that Albanians, consistently one of the most commonly represented nationalities amongst NRM referrals, only had a one in three chance of receiving a positive CG decision in 2015. Unfortunately, the NCA statistics that provide a breakdown of CG decisions by nationality are no longer available,[77] and from 2017 the annual summaries only provided information on decisions for UK nationals, EU nationals, 'Other' and 'Not known.' This tendency by the government not to publish disaggregated data reflects other grey areas of official statistical recording (see Sections 2.3 and 8.3), and it has not gone unnoticed by agencies and commentators.[78] Even more frustratingly, the published NRM data no longer even includes this level of information breakdown, so it is difficult to establish a comparison for more recent years.

However, in the data that was available for the years 2017–2019, UK and EU nationals were more likely to be confirmed as victims than those in the

73 National Audit Office, *Home Office: Reducing Modern Slavery* (HC 2017–19 630) 30.

74 Fudge (n 40) 377.

75 United States Department of State, *Trafficking in Persons Report 2019* (Publication Office of the Under Secretary for Civilian Security, Democracy and Human Rights 2019).

76 Data taken from: National Crime Agency, *National Referral Mechanism Statistics – End of Year Summary 2017* (n 50); National Crime Agency, *National Referral Mechanism Statistics – End of Year Summary 2018* (n 50); Home Office, *National Referral Mechanism Statistics – End of Year Summary 2019* (n 50); Home Office, *National Referral Mechanism Statistics – End of Year Summary 2020* (n 50); Home Office, *National Referral Mechanism Statistics – End of Year Summary 2021* (n 50); Home Office, *National Referral Mechanism Statistics – End of Year Summary 2022* (n 50); Home Office, *National Referral Mechanism Statistics – End of Year Summary 2023* (n 50).

77 The National Crime Agency is exempt from Freedom of Information requests, which further closes off this avenue of investigation.

78 After Exploitation, 'Analysis: Trafficking Decisions on Non-EU Nationals "Nearly Five Times More Likely" to Be Rejected Than British Claims' (After Exploitation 2020) <https://after-exploitation.files.wordpress.com/2020/04/after-exploitation-analysis-nrm-statistics-2020.pdf> accessed 29 October 2020; Burland (n 54).

*Table 5.2* Top five most-referred nationalities 2018–2023

| *2018* | | | *2019* | | | *2020* | | |
|---|---|---|---|---|---|---|---|---|
| *Nationality* | *Referrals* | *% of total* | *Nationality* | *Referrals* | *% of total* | *Nationality* | *Referrals* | *% of total* |
| British | 1625 | 23 | British | 2836 | 27 | UK | 3560 | 34 |
| Albanian | 946 | 14 | Albanian | 1705 | 16 | Albanian | 1638 | 15 |
| Vietnamese | 697 | 10 | Vietnamese | 887 | 8 | Vietnamese | 653 | 6 |
| Chinese | 451 | 6 | Chinese | 798 | 8 | Sudanese | 460 | 4 |
| Romanian | 427 | 6 | Indian | 467 | 4 | Romanian | 368 | 3 |

| *2021* | | | *2022* | | | *2023* | | |
|---|---|---|---|---|---|---|---|---|
| *Nationality* | *Referrals* | *% of total* | *Nationality* | *Referrals* | *% of total* | *Nationality* | *Referrals* | *% of total* |
| UK | 3952 | 32 | Albanian | 4613 | 27 | UK | 4289 | 25 |
| Albanian | 2511 | 20 | UK | 4185 | 25 | Albanian | 4051 | 24 |
| Vietnamese | 991 | 8 | Eritrean | 1171 | 7 | Vietnamese | 991 | 6 |
| Eritrean | 712 | 6 | Sudanese | 851 | 5 | Sudanese | 922 | 5 |
| Sudanese | 505 | 4 | Vietnamese | 768 | 5 | Eritrean | 890 | 5 |

'Other' group. 2019's data, which also provided a differentiation between negative Reasonable Grounds decisions and other outcomes, shows the starkest contrast between UK and 'Other' nationals: in line with the NAO's earlier findings, British nationals were almost five times more likely to receive positive CG decisions than non-EU citizens. Further unpacking of this data additionally reveals consistent trends that favour UK and EU nationals over non-EU nationals. In 2017, 'Other' accounted for 71% of all referrals into the NRM but received only 18% of all positive CG decisions, while the UK and EU groups combined made up 28% of cases but received 82% of positive decisions. In 2018, the disparity reduced slightly, with 'Other' making up 64% of cases and receiving 25% of all positive decisions, and UK/EU nationals receiving 75% of positive decisions from an overall referral proportion of 36% ; 2019's figures show an almost identical 65 / 35 split between each group, although the amount of 'Other' receiving positive decisions rose to 30% alongside the UK/EU's 69%.

Charities in this field have pointed out these discrepancies for many years,[79] and the combined challenges of language barriers, trauma and lack of paper trails will obviously complicate an already difficult investigation. Nevertheless, the starkly contrasting figures suggest that where survivors would require a visa to remain in the UK, they are far less likely to be confirmed as a victim of trafficking or slavery. One inference to be drawn from this is that the 'Home Office's overall goal of reducing net immigration into the UK may be influencing how it determines victim status.'[80] A 2014 UK review, conducted largely by personnel from the Home Office, refuted this, claiming that the proportion of individuals from the top ten countries of origin who received a positive decision were 'fairly similar and do not suggest a nationality bias.'[81] Information on 'top' source countries is, however, drawn from NRM referral data and the nationalities of those who do not consent to the NRM – and those who are not identified as potential victims at all – are unpublished.[82] Yet again, the failure of the government to provide a full picture is skewing figures.

## 5.3 Detention and deportation

The government's efforts to develop and reform the NRM system since its inception in 2013 would imply that it has identified flaws and taken steps to eradicate them. Given the proportion of foreign nationals that are referred into the NRM each year, these efforts should include a substantial focus on identifying and protecting migrants who are potential victims of modern

79 After Exploitation (n 78).
80 Fudge (n 40) 377, 384.
81 Home Office, *Review of the National Referral Mechanism for Victims of Human Trafficking* (Home Office 2014) 23.
82 After Exploitation (n 78).

slavery. Nevertheless, independent research and the Home Office's own data shows that many survivors from outside the UK are getting caught up in immigration control instead. For instance, a 2019 report by charity Women for Refugee Women (WRW) identified fourteen cases of women who had been trafficked prior to their detention in Yarl's Wood immigration centre.[83] All fourteen women were originally from China and had been held at the centre 'for months on end.'[84] The report reiterated the Home Office's Adults at Risk policy, which aims to safeguard and protect vulnerable people including, *inter alia:*

- Survivors of torture
- Survivors of sexual or other gender-based violence, e.g. female genital mutilation
- Survivors of human trafficking or modern slavery
- Individuals experiencing post-traumatic stress disorder (PTSD)[85]

The policy itself states that any person identified as being at risk within these parameters 'should not be detained.'[86] Nonetheless, the WRW report stated that previous research had found survivors of rape, domestic abuse, forced marriage, sexual exploitation and female genital mutilation in immigration detention and alleged that the Home Office was not only failing in its promise to protect vulnerable people but 'deliberately refusing to protect them, and is knowingly inflicting further harm and trauma on them.'[87] The report also pointed to the Home Office's guidance for assessing trafficking claims, which outlines the effects of trauma. Despite acknowledging that potential victims of modern slavery may not disclose immediately and will often appear to have inconsistencies in their narrative, WRW found specific incidents where the Home Office 'said they didn't believe the women's accounts on the basis of "internal inconsistencies", and/or because of late disclosure.'[88] In the same year, After Exploitation produced an independent mapping report which found that 507 potential victims of trafficking had been detained under immigration powers in 2018.[89] The report raised concerns that even where potential victims had already been identified as such, they were 'knowingly held in

83 Gemma Lousley and others, *"From One Hell to Another" The Detention of Chinese Women Who Have Been Trafficked to the UK* (Women for Refugee Women 2019).

84 ibid 2.

85 Home Office, *Immigration Act 2016: Guidance on Adults at Risk in Immigration Detention* (APS Group on behalf of the Controller of Her Majesty's Stationery Office 2018).

86 ibid 9.

87 Lousley and others (n 83) 2.

88 ibid 8.

89 Maya Esslemont, *Supported or Deported? Understanding the Deportation and Detention Data Held on Human Trafficking and Slavery'* (After Exploitation 2019).

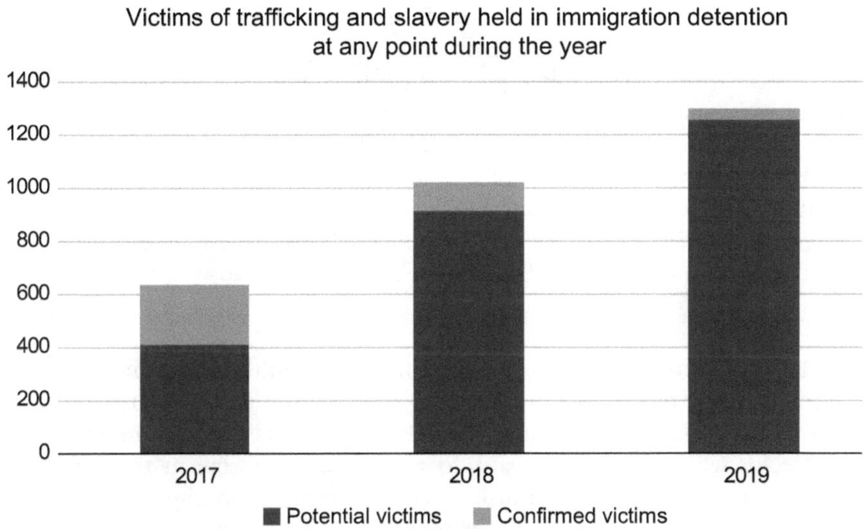


*Figure 5.1* Victims of trafficking and slavery held in immigration and detention

immigration detention for any length of time.'[90] This is hardly conducive to a 'recovery and reflection' period, not least because the very nature of being in detention 'reminds them of their experience of being held in captivity.'[91] At a Parliamentary debate on detaining trafficking and slavery victims under immigration law, then-Immigration Minister Caroline Nokes denied this evidence, stating that the figure of 507 was 'for people who had a positive decision on reasonable grounds to remain when entering detention, or while in detention.'[92] This distinction between *potential* and *confirmed* victims does nothing to detract from the detail that vulnerable individuals are nonetheless at risk of being placed in detention. It also exposes the fact that government authorities are not carrying out the appropriate checks prior to detention, and – as the report's author has suggested – implies that immigration targets are the highest priority.[93] Since the presentation of both sets of findings to the UK government, there appear to have been no moves to improve the situation, and After Exploitation's continued monitoring revealed a worrying trend towards exponentially increasing numbers of victims in immigration detention (see Figure 5.1).[94] The organisation also noted that in 2018, eight individuals

90 ibid 3.

91 Sarah Teather, *Oral Evidence, Modern Slavery*, HC 1460 (2 July 2019) Q208.

92 HC Deb 9 July 2019, vol 663, col 85.

93 Maya Esslemont, 'The Detention Of Trafficking Victims Is Soaring – We Need Transparency' (*Each Other*, 17 February 2020) <https://eachother.org.uk/trafficking-victims-detained-we-need-transparency/> accessed 16 March 2020.

94 ibid.

were forcibly removed from the UK during their NRM-mandated 'recovery and reflection' period.[95] There is no further information on the reasons for these deportations; the government has yet to implement a system of recording and publishing data on trafficked individuals in immigration detention, despite numerous Parliamentary questions. Responding to a written question from Frank Field MP, Caroline Nokes stated that 'NRM referrals, Reasonable Grounds and Conclusive Grounds decisions are considered separately from immigration enforcement action,'[96] while the most recent question on this matter, from Lord McColl of Dulwich, received this answer from Baroness Williams of Trafford:

> [NRM] information does not distinguish between those detained under immigration powers and those living in the community. The reason for this is two-fold, firstly because the NRM referral is not an immigration route by which individuals should regularise their stay in the United Kingdom and secondly, because a person's status in immigration detention is not permanent and can change.[97]

Both responses imply that there is no intention to consider linking this data in the near future. In her final Prime Minister's Questions in July 2019, Theresa May was asked by Vernon Coaker MP about the detention of potential modern slavery victims as immigration offenders, reiterating the previous concerns.[98] Unfortunately, rather than addressing the question, Mrs May referred to a general independent review of the MSA[99] and assured the House that government would be taking 'most' of the recommendations on board. In January 2020, however, the newly elected Conservative government abandoned the previous Parliament's commitment to reunite child refugees with their families under the Withdrawal Agreement Bill.[100] Vulnerable children are at particular risk from trafficking and exploitation, and this move would only worsen the danger.[101]

The previous chart represents the number of potential and confirmed victims who were held in immigration detention at any point during the year over a three-year period, according to the Home Office's own statistics

95 Esslemont (n 89).

96 HC Deb, 24 June 2019, col 266715W.

97 HL Deb, 11 March 2020, col 1944WA.

98 Oral answers to questions 24 July 2019, vol 663, col 1301.

99 This is most likely to refer to the *Independent Review of the Modern Slavery Act: Final Report*, presented to Parliament in May 2019.

100 Amelia Gentleman and others, 'MPs Vote to Drop Child Refugee Protections from Brexit Bill' *The Guardian* (London, 8 January 2020) <www.theguardian.com/world/2020/jan/08/mps-vote-to-drop-child-refugee-protections-from-brexit-bill> accessed 10 January 2020.

101 Helen Connelly, *Without My Family: The Impact of Family Separation on Child Refugees In the UK* (Refugee Council, Save the Children and Amnesty International UK 2019).

(obtained via a Freedom of Information request from After Exploitation).[102] In 2017, the number of potential victims was 410 , with 225 confirmed victims; the ratio of potential victims to confirmed victims was higher in 2018, at 914 and 106 , respectively, and higher again for the first three quarters of 2019, with 1256 potential victims to 42 confirmed victims. As discussed, the identification of victims can take months, which may account for the higher proportion of confirmed victims in the 2017 statistics (simply put, the authorities have just had more time to process referrals from that year than more recently identified potential victims), but the overall figures demonstrate that the amount of victims in detention – potential or confirmed – doubled in less than 36 months. Taking into consideration 2019's positive RG figures ( $n = 8429$ ), this indicates that 15% of all potential victims were held in immigration detention that year. It is possible that high numbers of trafficking victims have always been subjected to detention and that identification figures are increasing due to better awareness of modern slavery. Nonetheless, this does not detract from the fact that identification does not occur *before* victims have been detained. Even in the event that a positive RG or CG decision is recognised by immigration centre staff, survivors are not necessarily given the support they need. WRW identified a victim who was detained for an additional fortnight due to lack of available space in a safehouse and another who was released back to the address where she had previously been sexually exploited.[103]

It is worth reiterating here that, upon receiving a positive CG decision, survivors are ***not automatically granted leave to remain***. In fact, some individuals who are confirmed as victims of trafficking 'simultaneously receive a letter informing them that this finding does not mean that they have a right to remain in the UK.'[104] Instead, they are required to submit a new immigration application in order to stay in the UK and prevent the risk of future detention.[105] Despite the efforts of organisations like WRW, however, the nature of detention means that it is difficult to access survivors in order to offer them support and assistance; this applies even to lawyers who could provide the necessary advice for immigration claims. Legal aid is also unavailable for unconfirmed victims who have not applied for asylum following the enactment of the Legal Aid, Sentencing and Punishment of Offenders Act[106] (LAPSO). Presently, this law has an even greater effect on EU nationals who

102 After Exploitation, 'After Exploitation Data Shows 1,256 Potential Trafficking Victims Detained Last Year' (*After Exploitation*, 14 February 2020) <https://afterexploitation.com/2020/02/14/1256-potential-trafficking-victims-detained-last-year/> accessed 2 November 2020.

103 Lousley and others (n 83).

104 Virginia Mantouvalou, 'The UK Modern Slavery Act 2015 Three Years on' (2018) 81(6) *Modern Law Review* 1017, 1027.

105 Esslemont (n 89).

106 Legal Aid, Sentencing and Punishment of Offenders Act 2012.

are less likely to apply for asylum.[107] Uncertainty over whether they will be paid then whittles down the pool of lawyers who would be willing to take on a survivor's case. A 2019 survey found that only 64% of respondents had access to a solicitor, while only 42% were taken on as clients following a free legal advice appointment in detention.[108] Even where legal representation has been secured, transfer to another detention centre will usually put an end to this, as experienced by 29% of respondents to the survey. This echoes the traumatic effects of 're-trafficking,' which denotes the experiences of survivors who are transferred from area to area over the course of their support pathway. Furthermore, survivors who are unfamiliar with their legal rights are thus less likely to pursue them:

> It is not really in the Home Office's interest, is it, in a way? It is difficult to tell whether or not that is genuinely affecting decisions, but if somebody [who has been detained] is found subsequently to be a victim of trafficking, there is a potential for quite a significant damages claim.[109]

Some lawyers have taken to advising their non-EU clients to file an asylum application as soon as possible in order to circumnavigate the LAPSO provisions.[110] However, pursuing this claim before entering the NRM can backfire by raising questions as to the credibility of the trafficking claim.[111] Inevitably, this exacerbates an already hard-line stance on immigration by the government.

The final destination for some survivors may ultimately be their native country, whether this occurs through repatriation or deportation. While this can be a positive as they are reunited with their family, it frequently means returning to the conditions that led to their trafficking in the first place, for example, a poor socio-economic climate[112] or even a family that was complicit in their original trafficking.[113] Furthermore, emotional and practical support for continuing recovery is not guaranteed. The cultural stigma attached to being a victim of slavery could result in social rejection by a survivor's home

107 Thanos Maroukis, 'Keeping Up Appearances: The British Public Policy Response to the Trafficking of Domestic Workers in a Changing Regime of Social Protection' (2017) 15(2) *Journal of Immigrant & Refugee Studies* 155.

108 Bail for Immigration Detainees, 'Legal Advice Survey – Spring 2019' (BID UK) <www.biduk.org/pages/106-bid-legal-advice-surveys> accessed 9 November 2020.

109 Sarah Teather, *Oral Evidence, Modern Slavery*, HC 1460 (2 July 2019) Q246.

110 Maroukis (n 107) 155.

111 ibid.

112 Mantouvalou (n 104) 1017.

113 David Gadd and Rose Broad, 'Troubling Recognitions in British Responses to Modern Slavery' (2018) 58 *British Journal of Criminology* 1440.

community,[114] or, as Ayesha commented, the support structures simply don't exist:

> Just because the UK has decided you're a victim, that doesn't mean everyone else will accept you as a victim, so again there's this disconnect of victims being returned – the UK government deems you to be a victim but the Albanian government might say 'there's no evidence that you're a victim' so you don't get access to any of the services that a victim would get access to.[115]

For this reason, it is vital that the government and its statutory authorities have a plan for the safe repatriation of survivors, even where returning home is at the request of the survivor. At present, there is no monitoring mechanism to collate information on any individuals who have been returned to high-risk countries of origin, including survivors of trafficking.[116] This reiterates the need for both cross-border co-operation and multi-agency communication amongst UK partnerships (see Chapters 2 and 4).

## 5.4 Impact of current policies

Chapter 4 showed that a common theme that underpins post-intervention vulnerability for survivors is that of subsistence, especially for those who have entered the UK from non-EU countries. The fact that most survivors will have made their original journey in the hope of earning money will be a huge concern to those who do not wish to return home empty-handed. Consequently, some of those facing deportation will knowingly 'subject themselves to further exploitation in desperate bids to conceal the economic failure of their journeys.'[117] Others, who hope to stay in the UK and have applied for asylum, struggle to survive on the state-allocated £49.18 a week.[118] Prevented from legally working, many survivors will resort to taking on the type of casual, insecure labour described previously rather than fall into destitution. Somewhat inevitably, the precariousness and illegality of this employment is often a swift route back into labour exploitation. Furthermore, the knowledge that they are undertaking illegal work means they are no longer protected under modern slavery legislation. Home Office guidance specifies that for modern slavery to be present, there has to be a 'menace of penalty,' which includes 'threat or use of force, coercion, abduction, fraud, deception, abuse

114 Hadjimatheou and Lynch (n 47) 1.
115 Ayesha, Portsmouth, UK, 30 October 2018.
116 Esslemont (n 89).
117 Gadd and Broad (n 113) 1440, 1451.
118 UK Government, 'Asylum Support' (*UK Government*) <www.gov.uk/asylum-support/what-youll-get> accessed 14 March 2024.

of power or vulnerability.'[119] Although the guidance recognises that individuals may consent to a situation where there is no other viable option, this only acknowledges alternatives such as harm to the victim or their families; in other words, it 'expressly excludes from consideration forms of involuntariness and menace from economic compulsion or coercion.'[120] It is unclear whether this is simply an oversight by the Home Office, but alongside the criminalisation of undocumented migrant workers, there is a consistent message that foreign nationals' economic difficulties are not the concern of the UK government. This could raise questions of legality under the European Convention of Human Rights, under which a 2006 case[121] found that leaving asylum seekers without social support while their asylum application is pending violated the right to freedom from inhuman or degrading treatment.[122] The government would of course argue that they do provide financial assistance, but the severely limited means afforded to survivors – combined with the prohibition on paid employment – render them dangerously close to actual destitution. Once again, policies that keep traumatised individuals in a position of uncertainty and economic difficulty are at odds with the notion of 'reflection and recovery,' as confirmed by Jenni:

> Since Brexit happened, EU citizens, they reach out to us, they're between a rock and hard place. So we get the folks interested in us because they don't have the right to stay or they don't have the right to work. And as a survivor of slavery and trafficking, it is really important for folks that they have stability, that there is opportunity to build a new life, and so this idea of being sent back to a home country or that one can just sit and reflect and not be busy or if people came potentially for a job and they want, after they leave a forced labour situation, an actual job, so being stripped of the capacity to work is counter to everything that they were seeking.[123]

Caroline also described how frightening the system can be for those who do not fully understand what is happening to them:

> A lady who we took on at a point where she was a negative CG decision and she was dispersed under the asylum system from [city], she came to us through a friend that she was living with, she was very distressed, she

119 Home Office, *Victims of Modern Slavery: Frontline Staff Guidance v3.0* (Home Office 2016) 34.
120 Hodkinson and others (n 2) 1, 16.
121 Limbuela, Tesema and Adam [2006] 1 AC 396.
122 Art 3, Council of Europe Convention for the Protection of Human Rights and Fundamental Freedoms (European Convention on Human Rights, as amended) (adopted 4 November 1950, entered into force 3 September 1953) ETS 5 (ECHR).
123 Jenni, Manchester, UK, 13 August 2019.

> didn't read or write English, or speak it, and she had loads of letters that she didn't understand, she had no idea what was going on.[124]

Moreover, one frequently overlooked group experiences even more stringent controls under the current system. The Immigration Rules, updated in 2012, state that Overseas Domestic Workers are only eligible to stay in the UK under a sponsored visa that prohibits them from changing employer[125] (see Section 2.2). Although this restriction is not unique to domestic workers, the nature of their employment in private households exposes them to higher risk of abuse and exploitation with fewer opportunities to report to authorities.[126] While there is very little information on the nationality of the domestic workers, Home Office figures indicate that the overwhelming majority of employers are from the Middle East,[127] who bring domestic workers with them under the Tier 5 visa. Therefore, should those ODWs choose to leave a household where they are being abused or exploited, they automatically become undocumented, putting them at risk of deportation or detention. Virginia Mantouvalou's extensive research in this area indicates that, once in the UK, 'these workers are trapped in ongoing cycles of exploitation by subsequent employers who know about their status as undocumented migrants.'[128] Even where they have been legally identified as a victim of trafficking or slavery, leave to remain will only be granted under these conditions:

(i) no recourse to public funds; and
(ii) no employment except:
  (a) as a domestic worker in a private household;
  (b) as a private servant in a diplomatic household working only in the household of the employer recorded by the Certificate of Sponsorship Checking Service in the Tier 5.[129]

The Immigration Rules consequently place ODWs who have been confirmed as victims of trafficking or slavery between destitution or returning to an abusive employer if they are unable to find domestic work elsewhere. Mantouvalou goes as far as suggesting that the UK's restrictive treatment of ODWs may be

124 Caroline, Nottingham, UK, 22 November 2019.
125 Home Office, 'Immigration Rules Part 5: #orking in the UK' (*UK Government*, updated 5 October 2020) <www.gov.uk/guidance/immigration-rules/immigration-rules-part-5-working-in-the-uk> accessed 4 November 2020.
126 Amy Weatherburn, 'The Impact of the 2012 Domestic Workers in a Private Household visa on Human Trafficking for Domestic Servitude' (2016) 30(3) *Journal of Immigration Asylum and Nationality Law* 204.
127 Virginia Mantouvalou, '"Am I Free Now?" Overseas Domestic Workers in Slavery' (2015) 42(3) *Journal of Law and Society* 329.
128 ibid 329, 331.
129 Home Office (n 125) para 159J.

in violation of article 4 of the ECHR by creating a 'visa of enslavement.'[130] By allowing foreign employers to retain their own poor labour and human rights standards during their stay in the UK, and by tying ODWs to these employers, the government has effectively imported the slavery and abuse of domestic migrant workers. In the meantime, more nuanced legal issues continue to leave victims of domestic servitude without remedy. In *Nambalat v Taher*,[131] the UK Court of Appeal, following the National Minimum Wage Regulations, applied the test of whether a worker is 'integrated into the family.'[132] The Court was satisfied that the employer met the basic requirements to provide the worker with food and accommodation but did not question the quality of meals and living conditions.[133] As a result, abusive households are sanctioned to provide the bare minimum subsistence to domestic workers in order to qualify as reasonable employers. This type of legal reasoning places ODWs in a similar position to that of the Leicester textile workers (Section 2.4): the audit trail appears to demonstrate legitimacy while providing a smokescreen for the reality.

It is undeniable that the impacts of detention, however, are likely the most devastating and far-reaching for survivors of trafficking and slavery. People are often detained without warning, following what may have been a forcible arrest in which they were placed in handcuffs.[134] Even prior to entering the detention centre, individuals have reported being left – in a cell or a vehicle – for an entire day without food or water.[135] They are rarely given information as to what will happen next and, as the UK is the only country in Europe not to legislate time limits on immigration detention,[136] detainees face daily uncertainty in the shadow of indefinite incarceration. As well as reliving the conditions of imprisonment that they experienced during their illegal confinement, violence towards immigration detainees is common, and access to medical healthcare is poor.[137] Immigration detainees are often employed to undertake cooking and cleaning tasks to assist the running of the centre, however, they are statutorily disqualified from receiving the minimum wage[138] and

130 Mantouvalou (n 127) 329.
131 (2012) EWCA Civ 1249.
132 Cliodhna Murphy, 'Enforcing Employment Standards for Undocumented Domestic Workers in the UK and Ireland: Rethinking Illegality in Zones of Invisibility' (2015) 29(4) *Immigration, Asylum and Nationality Law* 349, 357.
133 Ismail Idowu Salih, 'Viewing Domestic Workers Problems through a Human Rights Lens' (2015) 34(7) *Equality, Diversity and Inclusion: An International Journal* 622.
134 Jesuit Refugee Service, *Detained and Dehumanised: The Impact of Immigration Detention* (JRS UK 2020).
135 ibid.
136 Bail for Immigration Detainees, *"Nothing Good Comes from Detention": Voices from Detention* (BID 2019).
137 ibid.
138 Immigration, Asylum, and Nationality Act 2006, s59.

usually earn an average of £1 an hour.[139] For detainees who are also survivors of modern slavery, this will feel remarkably similar to the exploitation they had previously endured. Moreover, the conditions of detention include confinement to particular areas for long periods of time and a restrictive regime that allows very little time for relaxation or activity, all of which exacerbate existing trauma symptoms – many detainees self-harm and experience suicidal feelings.[140] Combined with the realisation that they can be deported without notice at any point, most detainees spend their days in constant fear. Survivors in immigration detention also have far less access to support systems and wait considerably longer for assistance than those who are not detained.[141] If support becomes available, it is not only logistically difficult, but frontline practitioners have reported that repeated hostile encounters with authority figures and institutions make survivors extremely wary of engaging with those who offer genuine support.[142] From a criminal justice perspective, survivors who are eventually released as confirmed trafficking victims are therefore unlikely to provide a statement:

> [W]hat victims are told by their traffickers and by their enslavers is that, 'If you escape the Home Secretary will detain you'. If you are then found in a detention centre, what has happened to you is exactly what the trafficker has told you. How is that going to be conducive to you to disclose information that might be helpful to the Secretary of State in terms of making a decision on your claim and, also, informing the police for that to be investigated?[143]

Even where individuals present a willingness to give evidence, the potential to gather sufficient information for prosecution is severely diminished by the effects of compounded post-traumatic syndrome; this is discussed in more detail in Chapters 6 and 7.

Finally, it should be noted that the government's tendency to withhold data (or at best, publish limited statistics) is a growing concern both amongst independent organisations and within Parliament. Since the enactment of the Modern Slavery Act, MPs and Peers have been refused data on modern slavery survivors in immigration detention on nine separate occasions.[144] The government has often held back this information on the basis that it is not held centrally, wilfully ignoring the fact that there is evidently a need for this data.

139 Jesuit Refugee Service (n 134).
140 Bail for Immigration Detainees (n 136).
141 Home Affairs Committee, *Modern Slavery* (HC 2017–19 1460).
142 Sarah Teather, *Oral Evidence, Modern Slavery*, HC 1460 (2 July 2019) Q220–1.
143 Ahmed Aydeed, *Oral Evidence, Modern Slavery*, HC 1460 (2 July 2019) Q214.
144 After Exploitation, 'Immigration Detention' (*After Exploitation*) <https://afterexploitation.com/detention-2/> accessed 9 November 2020.

## 5.5 From victim to offender (part I)

The crime of breaching immigration law appears to take priority over any other crime that may be reported to the authorities. This has led to authorities often dealing with potential trafficking victims from a position of suspicion as to their motives for reporting exploitation. Take, for example, ODWs. Many of these workers were already subject to abuse by their employer before they came to the UK but felt unable to escape while in the Middle East due to the lack of human rights provisions there.[145] Criminal justice professionals, either during the investigation stage or on behalf of a defendant in court, will ask questions that seek to challenge the claimant's credibility: 'Why did you choose not to escape? Why didn't you report this in the country that you were before? And why did you agree to join them here knowing what they are?'[146] It is not just domestic workers, however: evidence provided to the Home Affairs Committee hearing on modern slavery found that the police were often referring potential victims on to the Home Office following self-reports of trafficking and slavery.[147] Instead of referring individuals into the NRM, the Home Office detained them. Were it not for the fact that charitable organisations like WRW routinely check immigration detention centres to offer assistance, cases like this would not be picked up at all.

The suspicion with which potential victims are viewed also means that, rather than being interviewed as a witness, they often find themselves the subject of criminal investigations. Furthermore, anyone who has been found guilty of criminal offences will not be granted discretionary leave 'because it is a Home Office priority to remove them from the UK.'[148] Although the Modern Slavery Act offers a statutory defence for confirmed victims who commit crimes under duress whilst in captivity,[149] this does not translate to automatic immunity from punishment or deportation. A 2017 policing inspection report, carried out by Her Majesty's Inspectorate of Constabulary, Fire and Rescue Services, found that many police officers were not even aware of the defence and therefore do not investigate crime scenes for evidence that will help to determine whether trafficking or slavery has taken place.[150] Where officers were aware of it, they were cynical as to its merits, stating that workers in cannabis factories had been trained to rely on the defence in the event of police intervention.[151] In fact, many reports suggest that offences committed

145 Mantouvalou (n 127) 329.
146 Maroukis (n 107) 155, 162.
147 Ahmed Aydeed, *Oral Evidence, Modern Slavery*, HC 1460 (2 July 2019) Q246.
148 Home Office, *Discretionary Leave for Victims of Modern Slavery v3.0* (n 55) 12.
149 Modern Slavery Act 2015 s45.
150 Her Majesty's Inspectorate of Constabulary, Fire and Rescue Services (HMICFRS), *Stolen Freedom: The Policing Response to Modern Slavery and Human Trafficking* (HMICFRS 2017).
151 ibid.

by victims of trafficking and slavery are deliberately being used as justification for removing them from the UK.[152] Primarily, though, the most common criminal offences relate to immigration. The HMICFRS report stated that it was 'seriously concerned' that

> potential victims of modern slavery and human trafficking were identified and treated from the outset primarily as immigration offenders. This focus on immigration status means that many victims are not being informed of the support to which they may be entitled during the 45 days' reflection and recovery period (if they receive a positive reasonable grounds decision through referral to the NRM). It also means that opportunities for gathering intelligence and developing investigations and prosecutions are being lost.[153]

In fact, one of the reasons the SCA may offer discretionary leave to a confirmed victim is for the purpose of providing evidence in a criminal prosecution;[154] this is not dissimilar to the USA's T visa, which allows survivors the right to remain in return for compliance with criminal justice procedures.[155] However, as discussed, in the event that survivors are removed from detention and given the opportunity to provide evidence, they may ultimately decline. This reluctance to co-operate with the authorities, along with the emphasis on survivors' crimes rather than those of their captors, means there are fewer prosecutions taking place that require witnesses to be granted such leave. A cynical reading of this would infer that once again, the priority is immigration control rather than eradicating the 'great human rights issue of our time.'[156] Furthermore, the SCA is also mandated to grant discretionary leave for survivors when 'it is necessary to pursue compensation.'[157] Compensation can be ordered through the Courts as part of a criminal case, as outlined in Chapter 7, or – even if there is no prosecution – it can be awarded through the government's own Criminal Injuries Compensation Authority (CICA) (see Chapter 8). However, both routes take a considerable amount of time and, with minimal legal assistance, most survivors are unlikely to be aware of or have the capacity to pursue this avenue. Yet again, it is unclear whether this is simply an unintended omission by the Home Office.

152 Home Affairs Committee, *Modern Slavery* (HC 2017–19 1460).

153 Her Majesty's Inspectorate of Constabulary, Fire and Rescue Services (HMICFRS) (n 150) 45.

154 Home Office, *Discretionary Leave for Victims of Modern Slavery v3.0* (n 55).

155 Stephanie Hepburn and Rita J Simon, 'Hidden in Plain Sight: Human Trafficking in the United States' (2010) 27(1) *Gender Issues* 26.

156 Theresa May, 'Defeating Modern Slavery' (*Home Office/Prime Minister's Office*, 31 July 2016) <www.gov.uk/government/speeches/defeating-modern-slavery-theresa-may-article> accessed 7 November 2020.

157 Home Office, *Discretionary Leave for Victims of Modern Slavery v3.0*' (n 55) 7.

In any event, the persistent focus on immigration above all other presenting factors does appear to belie the underlying aims of the UK's modern slavery legislation, leading to a stark realisation: 'It comes down to, if you don't have status in the UK, what's the point? You're prolonging the inevitable. If our approach is removal, why are we bothering?'[158] Moreover, the cognitive dissonance created by competing policies and practices sends mixed messages to those on the frontline. Individual stakeholders within multi-agency partnerships may interpret their roles in a way that counteracts the efforts of partner organisations, undoing months of effort and trust-building.[159] Ayesha demonstrated that even within the same organisation, there is some confusion as to what they are required to do:

> It doesn't make it any easier for staff members who are in essence in a holding pattern until someone is removed but it would make it easier in terms of we actually know what the approach is and at the moment we have asylum claims that are in for year upon year and living in a safehouse for a long time is not ideal but you've got nowhere else to go, so some of the systemic issues make the issues on the frontline even harder.[160]

Fundamentally, a realistic and honest approach from government would at least offer some clarity, even if it is not the desired strategy of support providers.

## 5.6 Conclusion

While the general theme of immigration did not emerge as heavily in my research interviews as it does in academic literature, I feel that its inclusion in this book is justified. A critical exploration of the UK's modern slavery survivor pathways should investigate those journeys that diverge from the support route and fall steadily into another altogether different area of policy. This not only casts light on the limitations of the UK's legislation and policies but flags major discrepancies and barriers to success in survivor support pathways. The additional question is, then: which of these approaches is the government favouring when it comes to foreign modern slavery survivors? Through enacting two conflicting pieces of legislation, the state has left authorities with a crude binary choice between enforcing immigration and supporting a victim of horrific crime. Unfortunately, the competing responsibilities are heavily weighted by available resources and overarching policies and targets that err strongly towards the first option. The aims of each Act have also 'blurred the

158 Ayesha, Portsmouth, UK, 30 October 2018.

159 Alison Gardner, 'An Idea Whose Time Has Come? Modern Slavery, Multiple Streams Approach and Multilayer Policy Implementation' (2018) 10 *Journal of Human Rights Practice* 461.

160 Ayesha, Portsmouth, UK, 30 October 2018.

lines between criminal, immigration and labour law,'[161] leaving survivors themselves to navigate through the no man's land between victim and offender. Meanwhile, the government has repeatedly delivered a message to the public that condemns traffickers who coerce and imprison vulnerable migrants while simultaneously fuelling anti-immigration sentiments and placing increasingly restrictive rights on the same group. Prohibiting paid employment for survivors ultimately (re)creates exactly the type of conditions that lead to risk of slavery in the first place. Furthermore, the refusal to automatically grant discretionary leave to remain to confirmed trafficking victims from overseas increases their likelihood of facing deportation. These policies, and the subsequent experiences of life in immigration detention centres, potentially breach at least two fundamental human rights while doing very little to support individuals who have already suffered the worst human rights abuses.

The issue of poor government monitoring is also documented throughout this book, but the problem appears to be more serious in this policy area than anything else under discussion here. Incompetent monitoring leads to inaccurate recording of statistics, and the government's explanations for total lack of publication in some cases belie the repeated Parliamentary and independent calls for data evidence. Moreover, the justifications for refusing discretionary leave to remain appear to be based on fears that the NRM system will be abused, yet the indications suggest it is the government themselves who are abusing the mechanism for the purposes of immigration enforcement. One of the most concerning outcomes of these findings is how detrimental this is to survivor justice. The Modern Slavery Act was created to strengthen punitive measures against perpetrators of trafficking offences, demonstrating the UK's commitment to tackling the crime as well as providing support for its victims. Yet when those victims are effectively removed from the criminal justice process, or even placed into the 'offender' sphere of the system, that commitment begins to look weak. Overall, there is very little consideration for the reality of survivor's lives; what they have already been through and how their experiences of the NRM and beyond may continue to feed into their trauma. The following chapter therefore addresses this extremely pertinent aspect of survivor support and asks what is currently being done to manage it.

161 Fudge (n 40) 377, 378; the overall issue of survivors and labour law in the UK additionally holds the potential for future research.

# 6 Trauma and therapeutic intervention

## 6.1 Introduction

The need for services to be trauma informed has already been discussed in this book, while the previous chapter demonstrates how the impacts of poor monitoring and conflicting policies can re-traumatise survivors, negating any positive support experiences they previously had. The issue of trauma and therapeutic intervention is a major facet in survivors' lives, and the need to address mental and emotional health needs is a core part of survivor support. In psychological terms, trauma is defined by the Diagnostic and Statistical Manual of Mental Disorders (DSM-IV) as where an individual has 'experienced, witnessed, or was confronted with an event or events that involved actual or threatened death or serious injury, or a threat to the physical integrity of self or others';[1] this includes repeated exposure to such events. The diagnostic term post-traumatic syndrome disorder (PTSD) therefore refers to people exhibiting symptoms directly related to those traumas, such as sleeplessness, flashbacks, avoidance of certain stimuli and anxiety[2]. Survivors within the NRM are statutorily entitled to counselling as part of their support package, so the research questions addressed in this chapter are concerned with good practice models and barriers to success and the potential for improvements or alternative systems that would benefit survivors.

This chapter identifies the current legislative and policy guidelines concerning how trauma should be addressed in victims of modern slavery and examines how this works in practice in the UK. There is a discussion on trauma in survivors and how the manifestation of post-trauma symptoms can affect short- and long-term recovery, followed by an exploration of the therapeutic intervention that survivors are currently entitled to and able to access. This part of the book aims to show how the psychological effects of trafficking and

1 American Psychiatric Association, *Diagnostic and Statistical Manual of Mental Disorders (DSM-IV)* (4th edn, American Psychiatric Association 1994) 463.
2 ibid.

DOI: 10.4324/9781032639895-6

slavery impact survivor recovery if they are not addressed appropriately and examines whether current policy approaches in this area are fit for purpose.

## 6.2 International and domestic legislation and policy on trauma in victims

The Council of Europe (CoE) Convention on Action against Trafficking in Human Beings[3] provides that '[e]ach Party shall adopt such legislative or other measures as may be necessary to assist victims in their physical, psychological and social recovery'[4] to include, at the least, 'counselling and information . . . in a language that they can understand.'[5] Additionally, EU Directive 2011/36/EU[6] calls on member states to ensure that survivors are given assistance and support measures, including 'psychological assistance, counselling and information'[7] before, during and for 'an appropriate period of time after the conclusion of criminal proceedings.'[8] The length of this timeframe would appear to be at the discretion of the relevant member state and can, therefore, be taken to mean that those survivors who are not engaged in the criminal justice system will not be eligible for statutory psychological assistance. The Directive also specifies that this assistance should be offered 'as soon as the competent authorities have a reasonable-grounds indication for believing that the person might have been subjected to [trafficking, slavery, servitude or labour exploitation].'[9] Again, this potentially excludes those survivors who are not deemed, by law or policy, to be victims. Meanwhile the UK, notwithstanding its ratification of the CoE Convention – significantly three years after it opened for signature[10] – has been slow to develop a comprehensive support system for trafficking and slavery survivors. The 2015 Modern Slavery Bill incorporated the core provisions of the Directive but was pushed through Parliament hastily during an election year, with requests from the government that proposed amendments be kept to a minimum. While this is not unusual for anti-trafficking legislation, it often results in flawed statutes with

3 Council of Europe Council of Europe Convention on Action Against Trafficking in Human Beings (adopted 16 May 2005, entered into force 1 February 2008) CETS 197.

4 ibid art 12(1).

5 ibid art 12(1)(d).

6 Directive 2011/36/EU of the European Parliament and of the Council of Europe on preventing and combating trafficking in human beings and protecting its victims (replacing Council Framework Decision 2002/629/JHA) (5 April 2011).

7 ibid art 11(5).

8 ibid art 11(1).

9 ibid art 11(2).

10 Council of Europe, 'Chart of Signatures and Ratifications of Treaty 197: Council of Europe Convention on Action against Trafficking in Human Beings' (*Council of Europe*) <www.coe.int/en/web/conventions/full-list/-/conventions/treaty/197/signatures?p_auth=baA8DUjQ> accessed 15 October 2017.

glaring omissions. In the case of the Modern Slavery Act,[11] the lack of support provisions for survivors is striking.[12] Any references to support are vague and uninstructive, merely assigning the guidance and regulation of assistance to the Secretary of State:

> (1) The Secretary of State must issue guidance to such public authorities and other persons as the secretary of state considers appropriate about –
>
> (a) the sorts of things which indicate that a person may be a victim of slavery or human trafficking;
> (b) arrangements for providing assistance and support to persons who there are reasonable grounds to believe may be victims of slavery or human trafficking;
> (c) arrangements for determining whether there are reasonable grounds to believe that a person may be a victim of slavery or human trafficking.[13]

At any given time, there is no guarantee that the responsible minister has a reasonable level of expertise on mental health welfare and psychological intervention – in fact, ministerial positions are frequently given to MPs who have no prior experience or knowledge of their departmental area. Since the Modern Slavery Act was enacted in 2015, the role of Secretary of State for the Home Department has been held by many different MPs.[14] Although Theresa May can take credit as the minister who introduced the Modern Slavery Bill, and for continuing to press for action on defeating slavery even after leaving the Home Office to become prime minister,[15] her résumé gives no indication that she has directly worked in this field – or even a related industry – for any discernible period of time.[16] Her successors, meanwhile, primarily have backgrounds in business and finance,[17] although Suella Braverman famously

11 Modern Slavery Act 2015.

12 Caroline Robinson, 'Claiming Space for Labour Rights within the United Kingdom Modern Slavery Crusade' (2015) 5 *Anti-Trafficking Review* 129.

13 Modern Slavery Act 2015 s49.

14 Home Office, 'Secretary of State for the Home Department' (*UK Government*) <www.gov.uk/government/ministers/secretary-of-state-for-the-home-department#past-role-holders> accessed 9 August 2020.

15 BBC News, 'Theresa May: Leaders Have 'a Moral Duty' to Act on Slavery' *BBC News* (11 June 2019) <www.bbc.co.uk/news/uk-politics-48589411> accessed 9 August 2020.

16 UK Government, 'The Rt Hon Theresa May MP' (*UK Government*) <www.gov.uk/government/people/theresa-may> accessed 9 August 2020.

17 UK Government, 'The Rt Hon Amber Rudd' (*UK Government*) <www.gov.uk/government/people/amber-rudd> accessed 9 August 2020; UK Government, 'The Rt Hon Sajid Javid MP' (*UK Government*) <www.gov.uk/government/people/sajid-javid> accessed 9 August 2020; UK Government, 'The Rt Hon Priti Patel MP' (*UK Government*) <www.gov.uk/government/people/priti-patel> accessed 9 August 2020.

qualified as a lawyer before going into politics.[18] It is unsurprising, therefore, that the majority of frontline support workers do not look directly to domestic legislation for guidance on providing this type of support for survivors. Only two interviewees referred to the legal requirements concerning psychological support; both mentioned the Council of Europe Convention,[19] citing it as a source of rights for survivors to access counselling. Nevertheless, even this provision was not deemed ideal, for example:

> The whole notion of person-centred and person-informed therapy would be that that individual decides when it's right for them to enter therapy, and yet our interpretation of [the CoE Convention] is 'every victim must have' and that's a really interesting concept but if they don't want it, are you then enforcing something that should be therapeutic on someone who doesn't want to have it?[20]

> The entitlements as presented in the European Convention are slightly woolly, so the interpretation of them because we haven't put the NRM onto statute yet, we haven't actually got a list of 'this is what you must do' so we've got best practice guidelines and under the [Adult Care Contract] those are expanded.[21]

Furthermore, the UK's National Referral Mechanism has been criticised for its rigidity and for failing to take into account the reality of victims' lives (see Chapter 2). Additionally, there are those survivors who simply do not wish to be referred into the NRM (see Chapters 4 and 8), which means that support is effectively offered on a conditional basis. Even where NRM-mandated support is available to survivors, once the brief 'reflection and recovery' period has ended, there is no formal guidance for survivor support.

> But [organisation] only looks after them until they've got conclusive grounds and then . . . I mean there's one survivor I'm still working with who was rescued in 2013 and we're now in 2019.[22]

> Someone in the system might decide that that individual isn't a victim of trafficking but that isn't saying they're not somewhere on the exploitative spectrum and then what do we do with that individual? So, you might

18 UK Government, 'The Rt Hon Suella Braverman KC MP' (*UK Government*) www.gov.uk/government/people/braverman accessed 15 March 2024.

19 Council of Europe Convention on Action Against Trafficking in Human Beings (adopted 16 May 2005, entered into force 1 February 2008) CETS 197.

20 Ayesha, Portsmouth, UK, 30 October 2018.

21 ibid.

22 Donna, Nottingham, UK, 10 May 2019.

> not have a label of trafficking that gives you access to all those bits and bobs.[23]

These issues were further raised by two participants in terms of their respective organisation's support provisions. Ayesha was based in a government-funded, first responder agency, and Caroline was from an independent organisation that relied on charitable funding only. The significance of these differences lies in their respective capacity for taking on new referrals. NRM organisations, even while they sit within the voluntary sector, are working under government contracts, which therefore place restrictions on the type of clients they can provide support to. Specifically, the clients will be those who have received a positive Reasonable Grounds decision and are now eligible to receive all available statutory assistance. Ayesha talked in terms of an 'exploitative spectrum' in which people may not have been formally identified as a potential victim of trafficking but have very likely experienced some levels of abuse and exploitation. She identified this as a serious gap in services that left many vulnerable people with nowhere to go: 'because you don't meet the threshold for one label that we have assigned or one piece of law . . . so where does the responsibility lie for people who get a negative decision, who still will have needs?'[24] Some of this responsibility is presently taken on by independently funded services such as the one Caroline represents, where approximately 25% of accepted referrals have previously received negative decisions. As a self-sufficient organisation, however, limited capacity and resources dictate the overall number of service users they can accommodate, which means they will only take on a negative decision referral if they believe 'there is legal weight to challenge the negative decision.'[25]

Nonetheless, one practitioner suggested that where a survivor accesses psychological intervention prior to a decision being made, it can result in a positive Conclusive Grounds decision:

> We've seen recently decisions on NRM status being made on not have or having had it so there's a disconnect between what we're trying to provide and the decisions that are coming out of government because you potentially are pushed down a route of therapy because it will help your claim which is interesting politically, I think.[26]

Although this quote is anecdotal, the implication is that there are now extra hidden conditions placed on the decision-making process. If this is the case in reality, it not only potentially impacts a survivor's progression through the

23 Ayesha, Portsmouth, UK, 30 October 2018.
24 ibid.
25 Caroline, Nottingham, UK, 22 November 2019.
26 Ayesha, Portsmouth, UK, 30 October 2018.

NRM but can result in unsuitable therapeutic support for people at a point when they are particularly vulnerable.

## 6.3 Symptoms of trauma in modern slavery survivors

Researchers unanimously conclude that the psychological effects of labour exploitation are devastating,[27] which raises the issue of post-trauma and how best to support survivors. In particular, strong links have been identified between the nature of abusive and coercive relationships, and the power imbalances that exist in labour exploitation.[28] The relationship between a trafficker and their victim bears many striking comparisons to other types of coercive relationship, for example, those where child sexual exploitation or domestic abuse occurs. In such relationships, the victim is subjected to fluctuating behaviours from their abuser: harsh physical or emotional abuse can give way to tenderness and acts of compassion or a system of punishment and reward. The confusion this creates in the victim frequently leads to 'traumatic bonding,' which manifests itself by significantly reducing their ability to psychologically detach themselves from their abusers.[29] Women and girls are said to be at higher risk from traumatic bonding, as female survival instincts include establishing a personal connection in order to protect themselves from danger.[30] Thus, when support is offered from outside agencies, even after the victim has physically broken free from the situation, it is not uncommon for them to return to their abuser. This is not only frustrating for support services but serves as a huge barrier to achieving justice against traffickers and slave-holders.[31] The primary challenge for anti-slavery policy makers is developing trust with survivors and creating a safe and secure environment to facilitate recovery. A 2009 report outlined some key principles for those responsible for supporting trafficked individuals through trauma recovery:

> Supporting psychological recovery often includes three stages, although there is no clear timeline for these stages in the recovery of trafficked persons and an individual may move between them multiple times. In the first stage, it is essential to restore an individual's sense of safety and

27 E.g. Coral J Dando and others, 'Perceptions of Psychological Coercion and Human Trafficking in the West Midlands of England: Beginning to Know the Unknown' (2016) 11(5) *PLoS ONE* e0153263; Paola Michelle Contreras and others, 'Psychotherapy in the Aftermath of Human Trafficking: Working through the Consequences of PsychologicalcCoercion' (2017) 40(1–2) *Women and Therapy* 31; Andrea Nicholson, and others, 'A Full Freedom: Contemporary Survivors' Definitions of Slavery' (2018) 18(4) *Human Rights Law Review* 689.

28 Susan SM Edwards, 'Coercion and Compulsion – Re-Imagining Crimes and Defences' (2016) *Criminal Law Review* 876.

29 ibid.

30 ibid.

31 ibid.

*Table 6.1* Biderman's theory of coercion

| *Method of coercion* | *Purpose of tactic* |
|---|---|
| **Isolation** | Deprives victim of all social support.<br>Victim develops an intense concern with self.<br>Victim becomes dependent on trafficker/abusive boss. |
| **Monopolisation of perception** | Fixes victim's attention on immediate predicament.<br>Eliminates stimuli competing with those controlled by trafficker.<br>Frustrates action not consistent with compliance. |
| **Induced debility and exhaustion** | Weakens mental and physical ability to resist. |
| **Threats** | Cultivates anxiety and despair. |
| **Occasional indulgences** | Provides positive motivation for compliance.<br>Hinders adjustment to deprivation. |
| **Demonstrating omnipotence** | Suggests futility of resistance. |
| **Degradation** | Makes cost of resistance more damaging to self-esteem than capitulation.<br>Reduces victim to 'animal level' concerns. |
| **Enforcing trivial demands** | Develops habits of compliance. |

> personal control over decision and events. At some point, those able to enter the second stage begin to address their traumatic experience and its impact on their mental health. The last stage includes receiving support reintegrating into their original or adopted community. However, mental health status may fluctuate during reintegration, e.g., if the trafficked person takes part in prosecution proceedings or has a difficult encounter with a family member. Severe mental distress may appear or reappear years later.[32]

Alongside the parallels with intimate abusive relationships, several studies have utilised Biderman's theory of coercion[33] – which was initially designed in relation to prisoners of war – to identify methods used by traffickers to enforce compliance in their victims. Table 6.1 presents those methods and their categorisations.

To test this theory, Baldwin et al. carried out semi-structured interviews with a small sample of trafficking survivors and analysed the responses against

32 Cathy Zimmerman and Rosilyne Borland, *Caring for Trafficked Persons: Guidance for Health Providers* (International Organization for Migration 2009) 138.

33 Albert D Biderman, 'Communist Attempts to Elicit False Confessions from Air Force Prisoners of War' (1957) 33(9) *Bulletin of the New York Academy of Medicine* 616.

Biderman's framework.[34] They found that each of his eight identified methods of coercion were present within the accounts of those trafficker-victim relationships. As cited in Table 6.1, each tactic serves its own purpose in creating compliance and breaking down resilience within the victim. Ultimately, victims can be threatened with death and, for those who have been trafficked from countries where disappearances and murder are commonplace, the threat is extremely real.[35] Unfortunately, the effects of a sustained campaign of abuse and coercion will remain with the victim long after they have been released from slavery, as Becky noted:

> I've had other people who've said that for ten years they've been enslaved to someone who's not allowed them to have any friends because that might allow them to escape and any sign of friendship has been the time that they've been moved on, so this is the first time that they might have made friends. It's quite strange because some of the people on the first week who might come across as being shy, it's actually the social skills and not knowing how to speak to somebody.[36]

Dando et al. reiterate Biderman's theory, stating that psychological coercion is 'known to be a dominant feature of human trafficking,'[37] and describing threats of violence, poor living and working conditions, and deprivation of basic needs such as food, water and sleep.[38] The 2017 high-profile English case against the Rooney family displayed every one of these hallmarks to an almost textbook degree, holding their victims in squalid caravans, providing them with only a bare subsistence of food and routinely beating them as both a punishment and deterrent.[39] Furthermore, the case highlighted the fact that the Rooneys' victims were deliberately targeted; most of their victims had come from the homeless population and in addition had drug and alcohol dependencies or learning disabilities.[40]

The awareness of underlying vulnerability in their victims also demonstrates a common feature in survivor profiles. Often, facets of this vulnerability can

34 Susie B Baldwin and others, 'Psychological Coercion in Human Trafficking: An Application of Biderman's Framework' (2015) 25(9) *Qualitative Health Research* 1171.

35 David M Doyle and others, '"I Felt Like She Owns Me": Exploitation and Uncertainty in the Lives of Labour Trafficking Victims in Ireland' (2019) 59 *British Journal of Criminology* 231.

36 Becky, Sheffield, UK, 19 December 2018.

37 Dando and others (n 27) 3.

38 ibid.

39 Janice Sutherland, 'The Modern British Slave Trade' [Television Broadcast] (Documentary, Channel, 4 January 2017).

40 Jamie Grierson, 'UK Family Found Guilty of Enslaving Homeless and Disabled People' *The Guardian* (London, 11 August 2017) <www.theguardian.com/uk-news/2017/aug/11/uk-family-found-guilty-of-enslaving-homeless-and-disabled-people> accessed 14 October 2017.

include dependencies on drink or drugs, frequently as a pre-existing issue which traffickers then exploit as a means to procure their victim:

> Anecdotally, we've got people turning up at homeless shelters, recruiting workers to either work block paving or roofing or any of those. Often they've got drink or drug, alcohol problems, deliberately chosen because of that, not really paid wages but given booze or drugs to sweeten the deal and after six weeks, they'll be dropped off at another homeless shelter.[41]

Therefore, where survivors already have an underlying addiction, service providers need to make crucial decisions on the correct care pathway in order to reduce the likelihood of this leading to the risk of further abuse and/or re-trafficking (see Chapter 4). First, however, frontline practitioners need to identify the dependency, which is not always a straightforward process; for instance, Rachel also highlighted the fact that addiction, by its very nature, will often be concealed by survivors during initial assessments. Overall, she felt that there was 'a degree of vulnerability that survivors will hide quite well. So, particularly mental health and alcohol issues that are quite well covered up to start with.'[42] Even when these issues are identified and the survivor is ready to address them, most frontline voluntary sector services do not have the capacity or resources to provide direct support. Given the correlation between substance misuse and mental health difficulties, particularly amongst modern slavery survivors,[43] specialist services are usually required for such high-intensity intervention. Unfortunately, as discussed in the following, this means referrers are then confronted with the issue of access problems and lengthy waiting times.

Nicholson et al.'s research has also acknowledged the lack of survivor narrative in academic and policy debate in this area and, through a series of interviews, set about identifying how survivors define slavery and freedom.[44] The findings highlight the erosion of a person's entire identity during their enslavement. This frequently occurs through the psychological elements of the exploitative relationship; never being referred to by one's actual name, deprivation of agency and choice, and prevention of meaningful human interaction all lead to feelings of isolation and inferiority and a deteriorated sense of self. Participants of the study described feeling like they were a 'nothing' and a 'non-person,' reduced to silence and numbness on a daily basis. This minimalisation of one's own self can in part be attributed to the intended effects of

41 Diana, Bristol, UK, 22 February 2019.

42 Rachel, London, UK, 11 May 2019.

43 Neil Parkes, *A Few Doors Down: The Links Between Substance Misuse and Modern Slavery* (Black Country Women's Aid, Salvation Army and Bright Day Consulting 2018).

44 Nicholson and others (n 27) 689.

coercion, but as a participant of my own research observed, it can also be an internal survival tactic,

> particularly when I think about some of the women who have been through domestic servitude, that making yourself invisible in the corner is a safe thing to do so you don't even know who you are really.[45]

Again, the long-term difficulties this creates for survivors require an intense amount of specialist therapeutic intervention. Learning to rebuild your identity and personality when you are unable to remember who you once were is a painstaking process. Additionally, any opportunity to rebuild autonomy is frequently hampered by the legal ramifications of a survivor's immigration status. One survivor participant in the previously mentioned study expressed his frustration at having no identification documents; thus he was unable to apply for citizenship or a passport, which severely impacted his ability to fully integrate in society.[46] This 'acceptance as a "legitimate" person'[47] not only the reveals the personal desire of an erstwhile victim to feel humanised, it further demonstrates the intertwined nature of immigration and slavery in UK law and policy.

## 6.4 Post-trauma support and therapeutic intervention

Currently, there is a small but steadily increasing base of academic research on post-intervention service needs for survivors of trafficking and modern slavery. Multiple authors who have researched post-trauma symptoms in victims of exploitation 'specifically identify shame and mistrust as obstacles to engaging in various types of services (e.g., legal, case management, vocational rehabilitation).'[48] Contreras posits that enabling a survivor to build a trusting relationship with support services is therefore essential to recovery and, consequently, justice. Typically, where survivors have experienced an abusive background prior to being trafficked, their mistrust towards others is ingrained. Survivors fear that, having been rejected or humiliated by those closest to them, they have little chance of being believed or accepted by authority figures who do not know them at all.[49] Aid and support often comes from a range of providers, for example, housing, food, healthcare and financial assistance, and these providers can themselves represent authority figures who have a great amount of power over survivors. For instance, their decisions are generally based on set criteria, albeit with an element of subjectivity. Thus, even

45 Becky, Sheffield, UK, 19 December 2018.
46 Nicholson and others (n 27) 689.
47 ibid 689, 700.
48 Contreras and others (n 27) 31, 34.
49 ibid 31.

unconsciously, providers may make judgments on whether they are presented with a 'deserving' or 'undeserving' victim, which will impact the level of support individual survivors receive.[50]

In 2015, the Human Trafficking Foundation conducted its own research into the government's long-term support provision strategies. Based on qualitative interviews with ten female survivors, the findings showed that each interviewee was 'still clearly affected by the psychological impact of their trafficking experiences.'[51] Social isolation was cited as an exacerbating factor to symptoms of trauma, and the report expressed the importance of mental health support as part of a survivor's recovery. Appropriate psychological intervention provided at the right point in a care pathway will not only improve the individual's quality of life and wellbeing but will reduce the inevitable strain on services further down the line, particularly in circumstances where those mental health difficulties would have increased and become more complex. These recommendations were reflected by the majority ($n = 7$) of respondents, who discussed the need to acknowledge trauma in survivors and to provide suitable means of support. This level of support, according to one participant, 'is not necessarily therapeutic intervention or psychiatric help or even counselling';[52] lower-level assistance, such as facilitated self-help, coping skills and sleep hygiene, can be offered to help survivors manage their symptoms if they do not yet feel ready to deal with the more deep-rooted psychological issues. Nonetheless, the need to address these issues as part of a comprehensive recovery pathway was prioritised by half of all respondents, with one interviewee stating that it was the most important aspect of a survivor's recovery, as they believed that 'trauma is often at the base of a lot of problems.'[53] The reasons for this followed a similar theme:

> If they had traumatised younger years and then suddenly they're being expected to live independently in an adult capacity and they don't and they may still be facing police investigations and potentially immigration difficulties or public law or compensation and they don't have any support that is a massive issue for me.[54]

> To be able to provide [trauma therapy] to a survivor before they're then let loose in the world because the trouble is, all of these survivors have gone through the programme and they're out the other side and they're now in normal jobs. So this happens when you're now in a mainstream

50 ibid.

51 Human Trafficking Foundation, *Life Beyond the Safehouse for Survivors of Modern Slavery in London* (Human Trafficking Foundation 2015).

52 Ayesha, Portsmouth, UK, 30 October 2018.

53 Rachel, London, UK, 11 May 2019.

54 Caroline, Nottingham, UK, 22 November 2019.

> employer, how does a mainstream employer react to that? It's very different to how we react to that because we recognise it, so it just . . . if we could allow people to express that trauma and go to therapy before being in mainstream employment, then that would be a lot better for survivors.[55]

This suggests that the potential implications of placing a survivor into independent living without fully addressing their psychological needs can be problematic, if not dangerous. One participant actually identified real examples of how a survivor's progress can rapidly unravel:

> it only takes something to happen, we had someone who'd been through [our service], they progressed to mainstream employment, then they witnessed something, it was retraumatising, they lost their job, they were quickly unable to pay rent, they got into massive housing arrears, their mental health was all over the place and within a couple of months they'd gone from being an almost textbook case of progression to being really high needs, needing lots and lots of support and I think that if that help to address the trauma had been there earlier on, maybe they'd have had the tools to cope with the situation they experienced.[56]

The worst-case scenario, therefore, is for a traumatised survivor to return to a state of economic and emotional vulnerability which once again places them at risk of being trafficked.

One of the additional difficulties frontline services face in dealing with this issue is the speed with which survivors are currently pushed through the NRM. Some participants commented on the limitations of timeframes for therapeutic intervention and general support provisions. Those participants were unanimous in their belief that survivors are not legally entitled to enough time in which to benefit from the support on offer. Even where survivors have been able to access therapeutic services during their statutory period of support, the 'new life' they establish for themselves can rapidly disintegrate if they have not established a long-term care plan:

> So although she was independent and she could manage a schedule and she could clean the house, and she could cook food, she didn't have friends or community and so she then fell into this manipulative and quite abusive relationship and then she turned to alcohol which then triggered flashbacks and it was just a really quick spiral downwards.[57]

55 Donna, Nottingham, UK, 10 May 2019.
56 Rachel, London, UK, 11 May 2019.
57 Caroline, Nottingham, UK, 22 November 2019.

One of the possible options for longer-term therapeutic intervention could therefore include rolling programmes of support, as opposed to a structured, time-limited course of counselling. As with established standards in other similar areas of support, this intervention could be developed from existing models of good practice (see also Chapter 4). The Freedom Programme,[58] for example, offers free weekly support groups for survivors of domestic abuse. Designed as a series of twelve individual sessions to explore relationship and gender dynamics, the programme does not need to be attended in any particular order, and individuals can access as many or as few group sessions as they wish. The programme runs continually, so as soon as one series of twelve has ended, facilitators start all over again the following week. This not only enables survivors to join the programme at any point in the cycle – meaning there is no waiting time – it gives them the autonomy to choose the groups they wish to attend, and they can easily pick up a missed session at a later date. Facilitators are trained to deliver the programme, and, as a support group, survivors can share their stories with each other in confidence as well as developing their understanding of what has happened to them. Theoretically, there is potential for this type of rolling programme to be adopted for modern slavery survivors, although more research would need to be undertaken to establish how it could be written and delivered.

In June 2017, Lord McColl introduced the Modern Slavery (Victim Support) Bill in acknowledgement of the lack of support provisions currently written into the Modern Slavery Act (see Section 3.5). The Bill makes more specific instruction on the type of assistance survivors should be provided with, including – and most significantly, not restricted to: '(c) medical advice and treatment (including psychological assessment and treatment); (d) counselling; (e) a support worker.'[59] Crucially, it extends a survivor's right to remain in the UK to twelve months, thereby providing greater opportunities to access the necessary means of support. The Bill was described in generally positive terms by those participants who discussed it, with particular emphasis on the longer leave to remain:

> What it means is they would get 12 months discretionary leave but that would also come with 12 months of support that goes along with that because the stability that we see that both discretionary leave combined with the support brings, and somebody's ability to process what's

58 'What Is the Freedom Programme?' (*The Freedom Programme*) <www.freedomprogramme.co.uk/> accessed 13 October 2020.

59 Modern Slavery (Victim Support) HL Bill (2017–2019) 3 (bold added by author).

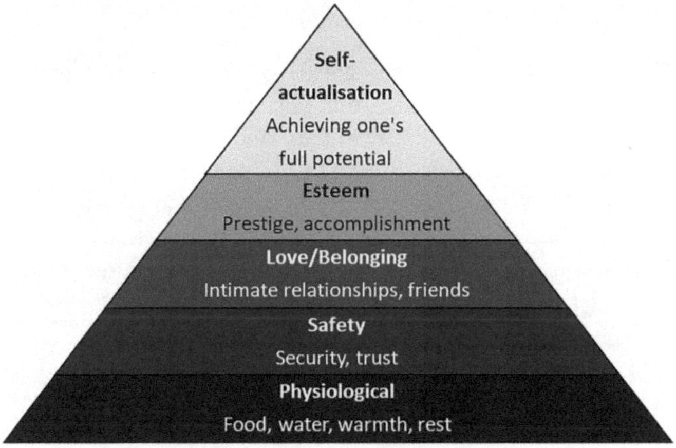


*Figure 6.1* Maslow's hierarchy of needs

> happened to them and start to recover and move forwards, is hugely different to a person who is still in a state of uncertainty and insecurity.[60]

> I think victims, if they've got enough time to – post-NRM – if they've got twelve months to really concentrate on recovery so they're not worrying about those immediate needs of housing and basic subsistence, but they can actually concentrate on getting the support that they need, whether that's medical or mental health, just to recover a little bit, then I think you've got a much higher chance of those support services that come in further down the line, of actually making a real long term difference.[61]

This also taps into Maslow's hierarchy of needs,[62] which establishes the foundations required for a person to attain full psychological wellbeing. Figure 6.1 shows a reproduction of the hierarchy pyramid model, taken from Maslow's original theory.

Starting with the basic human needs of sustenance, comfort and sleep, the means to reach an ideal state of being is realised through a succession of one's needs being achieved. Where a particular set of needs is not met, an individual is thus unable to reach the ultimate goal of self-actualisation. Lord McColl's

60 Caroline, Nottingham, UK, 22 November 2019.
61 Rachel, London, UK, 11 May 2019.
62 Abraham H Maslow, 'A Theory of Human Motivation' (1943) 50(4) *Psychological Review* 370.

Bill, in allowing for a longer secure period of recovery, would begin to fulfil the two foundation blocks identified by Maslow, as observed by Rachel:

> If their basic needs are met they can then begin to look at their other needs of recovery and trauma, but actually if employment could be offered later on and those basic needs had been met by government funding or statutory provision. . . . If they've got time to focus on those immediate needs, where those immediate needs are met, and they can concentrate on recovery, then all the other things that different charities and organisations can offer, I think will have a longer term impact if they're not part of that immediate crisis reaction point.[63]

In fact, one of the key support principles for practitioners and their respective organisations is that of survivor safety and, more crucially, the need for survivors to *feel safe*. As well as feeling secure and protected within their new environment – be that their safehouse, their support service building or their place of work or study – this means knowing that they have the liberty to leave that environment whenever they may wish to do so. For example, a US study focused on a New York-based legal aid agency that takes all new clients on a tour of their building as part of their initial assessment.[64] The tour includes an introduction to employees of the agency and ensures that survivors are shown the whereabouts of all available exits. The sole purpose of this tour is to make the client feel safe, 'because if they know who does what, they can better make requests for services themselves.'[65] One UK organisation employs a similar practice. As a residential service provider, its clients are given the opportunity to meet with representatives prior to moving in, and day visits are organised with survivors' key workers, who can also attend tours of the building:

> They get to feel the atmosphere of the place, they can see that the receptionists are friendly, they get to see the bedrooms, they can see how safe and secure the bedrooms are, so everything's there, it's all single occupancy. . . . I work with the accommodation manager to make sure that the [survivors] have always got en suite. There's actually three different locked doors before you can get to theirs. . . . So they feel really safe.[66]

This level of orientation is a simple practice that may often be overlooked by time-stretched services; however, it emphasises the importance of understanding and accommodating a survivor's needs right from the initial meeting. In

63 Rachel, London, UK, 11 May 2019.

64 Kristin Heffernan and Betty Blythe, 'Evidence-Based Practice: Developing a Trauma-Informed Lens to Case Management for Victims of Human Trafficking' (2014) *Global Social Welfare* 169.

65 ibid 169, 172.

66 Becky, Sheffield, UK, 19 December 2018.

the hierarchy of needs, 'safety' also includes feelings of security and trust. All but one of my study participants stressed the importance of building trust with survivors, acknowledging that recovery can only occur where survivors feel fully supported and have a sense of security from their key workers. Creating a partnership between practitioners and survivors that minimises any perceived power imbalances will help to build this trust; even offering food and drink and beginning each session with some small talk can establish a less authoritative and therefore more collaborative relationship with survivors.[67] This reflects the good practice examples discussed in Chapter 4 and reiterates the concept that an overall trauma-informed service is vital for survivor recovery. There is even some evidence to suggest that general health will improve in individuals who have a greater feeling of security.[68] This may be due to the psychosomatic nature of some physical ailments; however, the links between stress and poor physical health are also well documented.

The previously cited US study, focusing specifically on trauma-informed aftercare, also reiterated the universal prevalence of trauma symptoms in trafficked individuals. While this was true of all survivors, regardless of the nature of their enslavement, the researchers found that 'the emotions felt by each client, along with the client's cultural responses to her or his experiences, may be different for each victim or survivor of human trafficking.'[69] Therefore, while there is no doubt that survivors should be afforded therapy to help them address their trauma, any psychological interventions need to take account of the social and cultural backgrounds of individual clients. The implications of this mean that any therapeutic care plan must be carried out by a highly skilled specialist who understands the complex needs of modern slavery survivors. This would also, by necessity, include the ability to communicate with the survivor in an appropriate language, as one study participant observed: 'mental health is difficult to talk about; mental health with a telephone interpreter is really difficult.'[70] Donna, who had expressed the strongest desire for trauma therapy as a crucial aspect of survivor recovery, simply stated: 'Utopia would be language-specific group support and language-specific individual therapy.'[71] This level of 'cultural competency' would ensure a safe and collaborative space in which survivors could use their own narrative to work through their trauma and thus begin their recovery. A collaborative approach also places the client in control of their care pathway, providing them with the autonomy to make informed decisions and enable their empowerment;[72] this theme is explored further in Section 8.4.

67 Heffernan and Blythe (n 64) 169.
68 Cathy Zimmerman and others, 'The Health of Trafficked Women: A Survey of Women Entering Posttrafficking Services in Europe' (2008) 98(1) *American Journal of Public Health* 55.
69 Heffernan and Blythe (n 64) 169, 170.
70 Rachel, London, UK, 11 May 2019.
71 Donna, Nottingham, UK, 10 May 2019.
72 Heffernan and Blythe (n 64) 169.

While extended legal provisions for psychological assistance can go some way to improving the recovery of a traumatised survivor, they are only as good as the services responsible for providing this intervention. Significantly, a number of participants voiced their frustration over their clients' abilities to access the therapeutic services they were entitled to:

> I've found a real lack of support for those that are struggling with trauma, through the NHS, and appropriate counselling services so I think if there's a referral into a GP, they might refer into standard mental health services, but actually those aren't what someone needs, so there's quite a gap around appropriate trauma support.[73]

> Quite often it will take three or four months, by which time that trauma is over and that person feels brilliant again. It's quite useless. And PTSD isn't diagnosed.[74]

> What [the government] say is people should be able to access it through the NHS because it's an entitlement there, but as we all know, the NHS waiting lists for therapy are 6 months plus long.[75]

This again reflects discussions from Chapters 2 and 4, which revealed a disconnect between healthcare services and the voluntary sector. In fact, all aspects of the public sector that survivors may interact with seem to prioritise their own agendas before the needs of the survivor:

> When a person is giving evidence in a [Court] case, they're not entitled to any sort of counselling until that case is finished because it can affect their . . . it can be said that it affects their memories.[76]

It should be noted that the previous comment is factually incorrect. Practice guidance for therapists, as produced through the Home Office, Crown Prosecution Service and Department of Health over twenty years ago, clearly states that 'those involved in the prosecution of an alleged offender have no authority to prevent an adult vulnerable or intimidated witness from receiving therapy.'[77] The guidance does, however, state that prosecutors can offer advice as to the likely effect of therapy on witness evidence and make an assessment on how this may impact the trial itself. While the quote thus gives only

73 Rachel, London, UK, 11 May 2019.
74 Donna, Nottingham, UK, 10 May 2019.
75 Caroline, Nottingham, UK, 22 November 2019.
76 Becky, Sheffield, UK, 19 December 2018.
77 Action for Justice, *Provision of Therapy for Vulnerable or Intimidated Adult Witnesses Prior to a Criminal Trial Practice Guidance* (Home Office Communication Directorate 2002).

anecdotal evidence here, it raises questions as to how fine the line is between *advice* and *dissuasion* from Crown Prosecution Service representatives. Not all frontline support practitioners are therapists and are therefore unlikely to be familiar with the official guidance, while traumatised survivors are largely dependent on those practitioners for understanding their rights. The evidence here suggests that denial of survivors' rights to pre-trial therapy has frequently gone unchallenged. A greater examination of the criminal justice system is provided in the next chapter.

Meanwhile, Jenni's suggestion for improving therapeutic services was far reaching:

> So, it would be really interesting to see if there's a way to encourage people to be trauma-informed, not just around modern slavery but it would help survivors of sexual trauma, all kinds of abuse, torture, refugees and asylum seekers etc. So, is there a way to promote new mental health professionals to focus on trauma? Then there needs to be re-training options, so through the BACP or other accrediting organisations to push re-training on trauma and if it's possible for I know that people get. . . . UK has socialised healthcare but the support through the NHS is not good enough for survivors of specialised trauma.[78]

Where they have the resources to employ their own in-house therapists, third sector organisations can once again shoulder some of the responsibility for their clients' mental health needs. Caroline described this as 'supporting' the NRM contract where it is failing but admitted that her organisation now has its own growing waiting list for counselling as demand from service users is high. Practitioners from two services that did not currently offer direct psychological intervention also talked about the lack of external services that are available to survivors. Donna expressed a need for 'ready access . . . so that people can actually properly get over their experience and move forward'[79] and stated that the ideal psychological service would be provided within her own organisation, as this would eliminate the requirement to share information with external services. She also suggested that in-house therapeutic practitioners would be specialists in modern slavery aftercare and therefore be better able to address the complexity of the particular trauma that survivors experience. Although she stated that their organisation would be happy to bring in specialist external services 'if the funding was there,'[80] they had found that even identifying appropriate local services was a challenge.

Somewhat inevitably therefore, frontline practitioners – generally drawn to this line of work because of a genuine compassion – will often take on

78 Jenni, Manchester, UK, 13 August 2019.
79 Donna, Nottingham, UK, 10 May 2019.
80 Rachel, London, UK, 11 May 2019.

emotionally demanding supportive roles above and beyond their job description, as touched upon in Chapter 3. The support provided may even stretch their personal capacity, but given the choice between helping a client in need or leaving the problem to deteriorate, a caring support worker is likely to find the boundaries blurring: 'once they've been with you for six months there is more of a bond, and as a staff team you learn to care for these individuals so it's hard to step away from that, especially if there isn't an obvious progression or somebody else stepping in to take on that role.'[81] This brings the risk of vicarious trauma, a condition that affects individuals who are exposed second-hand to psychological harm through hearing about traumatic events. Vicarious trauma can occur even in experienced counsellors and psychotherapists, which is why the British Association for Counselling and Psychotherapy (BACP) guidelines recommend regular clinical supervision.[82]

Where a frontline practitioner is not employed specifically to provide psychological intervention, however, clinical supervision may not be offered through their organisation. Several practitioners explicitly identified this need, with Ayesha asking: 'What can we do to develop our staff teams in terms of resilience and dealing with trauma and vicarious trauma and also developing them as individuals . . . but then how does that impact the survivors?'[83] The implication here is that a balance needs to be struck in terms of keeping both workers and survivors safe but there does not appear to be any specific formal guidance for frontline practitioners in this field. Caroline described a policy that had been developed at her organisation, whereby all frontline staff are offered free counselling every month, alongside practical supervision. Whereas clinical supervision is designed to assist practitioners with the management of their client caseload, in these counselling sessions, workers are free to discuss whatever they wish and the counsellor notes are kept completely private. The initiative was described as 'just a safety net, I'm just trying to help look after the mental health of our caseworkers,'[84] but it was additionally noted that staff turnover was very low, which may be in part due to good morale and wellbeing within the organisation.

## 6.5 Conclusion

Almost all survivors of trafficking and slavery will experience symptoms of psychological trauma, many of which they are unlikely to recognise in the first few weeks and months after leaving captivity. Assimilating to new surroundings and new people, dealing with lawyers, law enforcement officers and medical

81 ibid.

82 British Association for Counselling and Psychotherapy, 'Supervision: A Guide for Practitioners and Supervisors' (*BACP*) <www.bacp.co.uk/membership/supervision//> accessed 8 July 2019.

83 Ayesha, Portsmouth, UK, 30 October 2018.

84 Caroline, Nottingham, UK, 22 November 2019.

practitioners, and simply coming to terms with a change of circumstances can mean that symptoms are often dormant until the individual is ready to deal with them. While European legal instruments and UK guidance state that therapeutic intervention is to be afforded to survivors, there is very little clarity on how this is to be achieved. This is pertinent in the case of NRM support as even a superficial examination of the evidence reveals the incompatibility of a ninety-day care package and six-month NHS mental health waiting lists. These issues serve to answer questions around limitations and barriers to success in the survivor support pathway. Lord McColl's Bill, if passed, would help to alleviate this by providing survivors with a full twelve months of statutory support. Nevertheless, this still does not acknowledge the fact that such a complex and deep-seated issue requires specialist, intensive intervention that is difficult for most to access. The call for more and better therapeutic services for survivors is evident in my own data and the devastating effects of untreated trauma sharply illustrate why these services are needed.

That said, there are clearly some strong areas of good practice: many frontline support organisations can and do create their own therapeutic provisions that do not require service users to face their trauma head-on. By viewing their service environment through a survivor-centred lens, some organisations have fostered a softer therapeutic approach that intertwines other elements of support, meaning that the process of recovery can be achieved gradually without individuals being re-traumatised. There is also scope for developing structured support groups that can be facilitated by existing practitioners. These are positive examples and will certainly go some way to help survivors in their move to independence, however, this once again shows how much the voluntary sector is taking on additional responsibilities in an already challenging situation. When independent charities, who are not in receipt of any government funding, consider paying for their own in-house therapist to ensure that their service users can access statutorily-mandated healthcare support, something is amiss in the system.

Meanwhile, despite the best intentions of these frontline support agencies, the potential for triggering and re-traumatising events are unfortunately unavoidable. Under the UK's criminal approach, the ultimate outcome of any modern slavery case is through the justice system; in the simplest terms, the perpetrator is convicted and punished and the survivor is thereby safe and free. Yet within that system, justice can only be achieved with assistance from the survivor, which means describing in detail exactly what has happened to them. This would qualify as a triggering event. The next chapter thus examines the criminal justice process as experienced by survivors of trafficking and slavery.

# 7 Criminal justice system

## 7.1 Introduction

Although much of this book has so far centred on frontline support, the focus of the UK's modern slavery approach is ultimately couched in the traditional criminal justice system. In 2000, the United Nations (UN) established the Convention against Transnational Organized Crime[1] with a supplementary Protocol to Prevent, Suppress and Punish Trafficking in Persons, Especially Women and Children (Palermo Protocol).[2] The Convention adopted a predominantly criminal justice model that has been cascaded down to domestic policies across the world.[3] Legal definitions of slavery 'emphasise the function or purpose of control for slaveholders and are therefore primarily framed from the perspective of the perpetrator,'[4] consequently ranking the prosecution of offenders over prevention and protection. The UK's approach to modern slavery likewise follows this model; the flagship Modern Slavery Act 2015 is a piece of criminal legislation that relies on the Gangmasters and Labour Abuse Authority, the National Crime Agency and the police to investigate, arrest and gather evidence for the Crown Prosecution Service to secure the conviction of modern slavery offenders.

This chapter begins by presenting an overview of the key organisations involved in the implementation of the MSA, identifying some positive early developments and barriers to success. Many of the barriers are connected to budgetary and resource deficits; however, there follows a discussion on more deep-seated criticisms of the traditional criminal justice approach as a

1 UNGA Convention against Transnational Organised Crime (adopted 15 November 2000, entered into force 29 September 2003) UN Doc. A/55/383.

2 UNGA Protocol to Prevent, Suppress and Punish Trafficking in Persons, especially Women and Children (adopted 15 November 2000, entered into force 25 December 2003) 2237 UNTS 319 (Palermo Protocol).

3 Idil Atak and James C Simeon, 'Human Trafficking: Mapping the Legal Boundaries of International Refugee Law and Criminal Justice' (2014) 12(5) *Journal of International Criminal Justice* 1019.

4 Andrea Nicholson and others, 'A Full Freedom: Contemporary Survivors' Definitions of Slavery' (2018) 18(4) *Human Rights Law Review* 689, 703.

DOI: 10.4324/9781032639895-7

means of combatting modern slavery and supporting survivors to recovery. This leads to analysis of the specific modern slavery legal framework pertaining to criminal justice, showing that much of the scope of the MSA is limited or ill used. Finally, some possible alternative means of empowering and supporting survivors throughout the criminal justice process are offered, alongside a consideration of the definition of 'justice' for survivors. This section of the book acknowledges the gravity of the offences of modern slavery and human trafficking and does not therefore propose a complete shift away from the justice system; instead, it aims to put forward additional and more flexible approaches that will enhance the survivor voice in the overall process.

## 7.2 Key organisations and actors

### *7.2.1 Law enforcement agencies*

Originally created in response to the deaths of 23 migrant cockle-pickers in Morecambe Bay in 2004,[5] the then-Gangmasters Licencing Authority (GLA) could investigate and prosecute organised trafficking rings but were limited to the agricultural sector and had the powers only to refuse or revoke licences for labour providers, with the option of a fine for non-compliance. Paul Broadbent, the first chief executive of the GLA, advised that these sanctions were inadequate deterrents – the fines were a mere fraction of the estimated profits accrued from labour exploitation.[6] Following a statutory review, which took place against the backdrop of pressure from lobbyists to widen its scope,[7] the Authority became the Gangmasters and Labour Abuse Authority in October 2016, one year after the enactment of the MSA. In light of exponentially rising National Referral Mechanism referral figures (as discussed in Chapter 2) and acknowledging the broad range of industries in which victims are enslaved, the government also extended the agency's remit. GLAA officers are now granted police-style powers to investigate trafficking and slavery across the entire labour market in the UK,[8] a move which was particularly welcomed by former IASC Kevin Hyland, who had been

5 Gangmasters Licencing Authority, *Gangmasters Licencing Authority Annual Report and Accounts 1 April 2015 to 31 March 2016* (Williams Lea Group on behalf of Her Majesty's Stationery Office 2016).

6 Ruth van Dyke, 'The UK's Response to Modern Slavery: Law, Policy and Politics' in Gary Craig and others (eds), *The Modern Slavery Agenda: Policy, Politics and Practice in the UK* (Policy Press 2019).

7 Gary Craig 'The UK's Modern Slavery Legislation: An Early Assessment of Progress' (2017) 5(2) *Social Inclusion* 16.

8 Gangmasters and Labour Abuse Authority, 'Transition to the GLAA' (*Gangmasters and Labour Abuse Authority)* <www.gla.gov.uk/whats-new/transition-to-the-glaa/> accessed 10 November 2017.

'calling for [it] since his appointment.'[9] The broader remit may have been welcomed by many more commentators were it not for the fact that GLAA resources have not been increased along with the responsibilities.[10] In 2016, the GLA operated with 75 staff for a catchment of 500,000 workers; a year later the GLAA was responsible for 31.5 million workers, with a staff count of just 125 .[11] However, post-Brexit changes to immigration rules for care workers have resulted in a 400% increase in allegations to the GLAA since late 2021, while its budget has been cut by over £1 million for the 2024/25 fiscal year.[12]

Meanwhile, the responsibilities of the NCA and the police, including Regional Organised Crime Units (ROCUs), focus on serious organised crime. They can thus investigate additional areas such as sex trafficking and criminal exploitation through drug cultivation/dealing; the latter has emerged as a particular risk for vulnerable young people and has led to the term 'County Lines,' which refers to 'gangs and organised criminal networks involved in exporting illegal drugs into one or more importing areas [within the UK], using dedicated mobile phone lines or other form of "deal line".'[13] However, these gangs often operate via complex business models and cross-border networks that sometimes even engage with legitimate companies through their supply chains.[14] The intricacy of organisation is frequently beyond the investigative capacity of law enforcement authorities,[15] meaning that many practices continue unabated and victims remain at the mercy of their traffickers. Although the NCA have established a Modern Slavery Human Trafficking Unit, capacity problems are compounded by the fact that police constabularies across the UK have suffered severe resource cuts over a decade of austerity.[16] Additionally, this depleted workforce is tasked with 'testing new legislation and some of the complexities around evidence gathering and working with very vulnerable victims.'[17] Since December 2016, the NCA is also required to

9 Kevin Hyland, *Independent Anti-Slavery Commissioner Annual Report 2015–16* (Williams Lea Group on behalf of Her Majesty's Stationery Office 2016).

10 Craig (n 7) 16.

11 Paul Broadbent, 'Risk – Response – Result' (Gangmasters and Labour Abuse Authority Annual Conference, Birmingham, October 2017).

12 Shanti Das, '"If You Want to Abuse Your #orkers, That's Fine": UK Modern Slavery Watchdog's Funding Cut' *The Guardian* (London, 30 March 2024) www.theguardian.com/world/2024/mar/30/uk-modern-slavery-watchdog-funding-cut accessed 5 April 2024.

13 National Crime Agency, 'County Lines' (*National Crime Agency*) <www.nationalcrimeagency.gov.uk/what-we-do/crime-threats/drug-trafficking/county-lines> accessed 15 July 2020.

14 van Dyke (n 6).

15 ibid.

16 Jodie Hargreaves and others, *Police Workforce, England and Wales, 30 September 2016 Statistical Bulletin 02/17* (Home Office 2017).

17 David, Birmingham, UK, 20 October 2018.

refer all NRM cases to the police,[18] meaning that law enforcement agencies are under yet more pressure as annual NRM figures continue to grow.

In response to Caroline Haughey's findings in the 2016 Modern Slavery Act Review, as explored in Section 2.4, Prime Minister Theresa May requested an inspection of all forty-three police forces in England and Wales with regard to their modern slavery investigations. The inspection report,[19] carried out by Her Majesty's Inspectorate of Constabulary, Fire and Rescue Services in 2017, identified problems with awareness and implementation of policy. It found that, despite strategically prioritising the countering of modern slavery, most police forces were not adequately carrying out their mandates at an operational level. Concerns were also raised about senior officers believing that modern slavery did not occur in their area or who 'openly expressed a reluctance to "turn over the stone" and proactively look for modern slavery and human trafficking offences, citing concerns about the potential level of demand.'[20] Diana confirmed the latter:

> Police forces are already stretched to their limit . . . they are naturally going to have to put their resources where they can. The problem with this subject matter is that if you lift the rock up from one place are you going to be able to manage what comes out from underneath it, in terms of resources and money and, as I alluded to before, whenever you do an investigation into this arena it's expensive. Because it's expensive in terms of manpower, it's expensive in terms of National Crime Agency tag teams, of interpreters, of support, giving immediate care.[21]

Nonetheless, the HMICFRS report indicated that the situation was improving and that plans to transform the police response to modern slavery were underway via the Police Transformation Programme. In response to the Haughey review, an £8.5 -million investment was provided to fund additional NCA staff, multi-agency working, training and specialist teams within the ROCUs.[22] There is some evidence that the Transformation Programme is enjoying success. Puja, a key stakeholder in the programme, agreed that there had been inconsistencies due to lack of knowledge and awareness at the time of the

18 Virginia Mantouvalou, 'The UK Modern Slavery Act 2015 Three Years on' (2018) 81(6) *Modern Law Review* 1017, 1025.

19 Her Majesty's Inspectorate of Constabulary, Fire and Rescue Services (HMICFRS), *Stolen Freedom: The Policing Response to Modern Slavery and Human Trafficking* (HMICFRS 2017).

20 ibid 10.

21 Diana, Bristol, UK, 22 February 2019.

22 Her Majesty's Inspectorate of Constabulary, Fire and Rescue Services (HMICFRS) (n 19).

HMICFRS report but felt that there had been significant improvements over the subsequent 12–18 months:

> I think that's thanks to the Transformation Programme as well, there's been a heck of a lot of work being done at grassroots level, within forces, working all the way up through the ranks, through operational, strategic leaders. I think, and that is reflected definitely in the amount of police operations that are being actively investigated. I don't think there's any force any more that can say 'we don't have a problem with it' and I think two years ago there may have been forces that could have said potentially 'it doesn't happen here.'[23]

Furthermore, although the aforementioned official reports depict a rather negative view of law enforcement in the UK, other sources demonstrate that many police officers are genuinely compassionate towards survivors and, despite resource and capacity issues, have offered support above and beyond their investigative responsibilities:

> We've had a few recently that have been referred by the police because they were in the NRM in another location, then they've moved to this area for whatever reason, and they didn't know about referring into us and the police are working as social workers then because the NRM has finished and the police are trying to look after them.[24]

What this does suggest, however, is that police resources are not always being used for their primary role as law enforcers. As noted in Chapter 4, the HMICFRS report found that many Constabularies have used their own funding to provide accommodation for survivors where local support services are unavailable. Again, this reflects the national disparities between regions as presented in Chapter 3 and shows how this patchy support landscape impacts the overall survivor pathway within the UK system.

### *7.2.2 Crown prosecution service and the courts*

CPS barristers do not meet with victims until the day they are due to provide witness evidence in court. The justification for this is that barristers 'must not rehearse, practise with or coach a witness in respect of their evidence'[25] in order to ensure unbiased testimony. From the victim's perspective, however,

23 Puja, Leeds, UK, 8 January 2019.
24 Caroline, Nottingham, UK, 22 November 2019.
25 Bar Standards Board, 'The BSB Handbook: Code of Conduct' rC9(4) (*Bar Standards Board*, 15 October 2019) <www.barstandardsboard.org.uk/the-bsb-handbook.html?part=&audience=&q=witness> accessed 15th January 2020.

their story – the worst event of their lives, and very often the most defining event of their lives – is reduced to a court listing in which they were reliant on the performance of a total stranger. They are no longer in control of their narrative. Indeed, most members of the public do not realise that it is the Crown who formally charge, believing that victims are the sole decision-makers on this issue. The CPS, however, must be satisfied that a case passes the Full Code Test,[26] a two-part test that informs the decision to formally charge. The *evidential stage* concerns the available information that they will need to present in court: is it admissible, reliable and credible? The second stage, *public interest*, is not just related to their perception of the danger a perpetrator may present to society but is also based on the CPS judgement as to how fair it will be to put the victim through the re-traumatising experience of testifying and whether the likelihood of a guilty verdict is enough to justify spending public funds on a trial and all the costs it incurs. The courts are then tasked with understanding and clarifying the MSA's provisions in order to secure justice, often through the witness testimony of a traumatised individual and complex or incomplete evidence.

Unfortunately, while NRM referrals and recorded crime figures grew, these increases were converted into successful prosecutions, leading to an exponentially diminishing conviction rate for offences committed under the MSA. Furthermore, as 'modern slavery' only became a distinct category in police crime recording in 2015, it is not possible to directly compare pre-MSA police data to more recent statistics.[27] Figure 7.1 therefore represents the number of victims entering the NRM process from the enactment of the Modern Slavery Act alongside criminal justice figures for the same period. These statistics were collated using official NRM data[28] and the most recent dataset from Office for National Statistics (ONS)[29] which includes numbers for police recorded crime, prosecutions and convictions across the UK. It should be noted that the monitoring and recording periods for each dataset are slightly different: the NCA released quarterly and annual publications for each calendar year between January and December,[30] whereas the ONS provides statistics from April to March of the following year. It should also be noted that the published ONS

26 Crown Prosecution Service, 'The Code for Crown Prosecutors' (*CPS*, 26 October 2018) <www.cps.gov.uk/publication/code-crown-prosecutors#section4> accessed 15th January 2020.

27 Caroline Haughey, *The Modern Slavery Act Review: One Year on* (Home Office 2016).

28 National Crime Agency, 'Publications' (*National Crime Agency*) <www.nationalcrimeagency.gov.uk/who-we-are/publications?limit=100&sort=title&direction=asc&search=national%20referral%20mechanism> accessed 8 June 2021.

29 Office for National Statistics, 'Modern Slavery in the UK: March 2020' (*Office for National Statistics*, 26 March 2020) <www.ons.gov.uk/peoplepopulationandcommunity/crimeandjustice/articles/modernslaveryintheuk/march2020> accessed 2 July 2020.

30 From 2019, the Home Office took over responsibility for the monitoring and publication of these statistics.

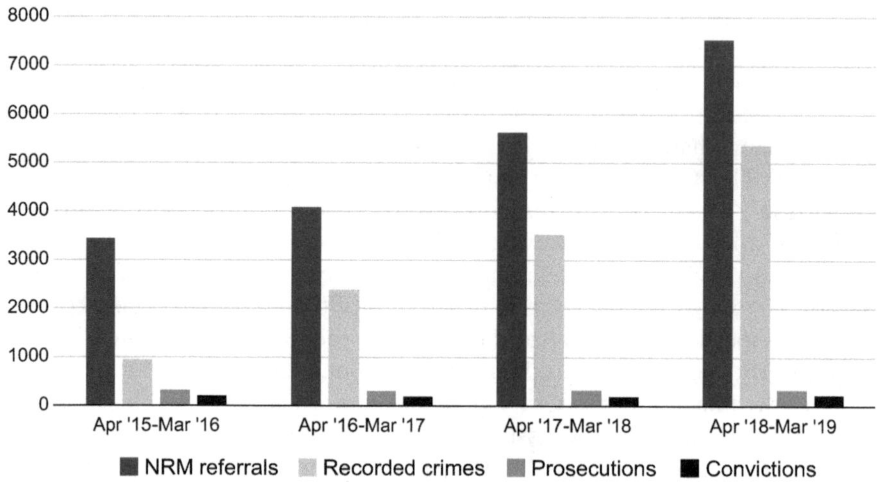


*Figure 7.1* NRM referrals and criminal justice figures

figures have not been updated since 2020, and this once again tells a story about the consistency (or lack thereof) of government published data.

As a proportion of NRM referrals, recorded crimes steadily grew from 27.5% in 2015–16 to 71% in 2018–19, although this can be attributed to the compulsory police referral from the NCA in late 2016. The ONS also cautioned that increases 'are more likely to reflect improvements in recording practices of police forces since the introduction of the Modern Slavery Act 2015.'[31] Prosecution and conviction figures, on the other hand, remained almost stationary during the same period; in relative terms, prosecutions dropped from an already low 9% of all NRM referrals to just 4%, while convictions fell from 6% of all NRM referrals in 2015–16 to just 3% in 2018–19. It is worth remarking that this mirrors Figures 2.1 and 2.2 in Chapter 2, which also showed a proportionate decrease in Conclusive Grounds decisions in comparison to the sharp rise in NRM referrals. The ONS figures show that, across all four periods, acquittals accounted for only 21% of all non-convictions on average,[32] while the largest proportion of non-conviction outcomes are due to a 'conflict of evidence or an essential legal element missing.'[33] Other reasons related to 'victim-related issues,' including 'retractions, non-attendance at trial or where the "evidence of the complainant does not support the case".'[34]

31 Office for National Statistics, 'Modern Slavery in the UK – Appendix Tables' (*Office for National Statistics*) <www.ons.gov.uk/peoplepopulationandcommunity/crimeandjustice/datasets/modernslaveryintheukappendixtables> accessed 8 June 2021, Table 21.

32 ibid.

33 ibid Table 27.

34 ibid.

Despite a minor spike in the 2016–17 period, victim-related issues appeared to be slowly decreasing. The prevalence of retractions and non-attendances fell from 3.4% of recorded crime figures in 2015–16 to 0.4% in 2018–19. While no obvious conclusion can be inferred from this data, the improvement in witness retention rates is worth further exploration as and when further figures are published.

Justice for survivors comes under further scrutiny when sentencing is taken into consideration. The MSA provides for a maximum custodial sentence of life imprisonment for those convicted, thereby signifying the seriousness of the offences. Between 2014 and 2016, however, the average prison sentence was approximately four years 'and has not changed significantly in recent years.'[35] Even in 'the UK's largest ever modern slavery prosecution'[36] in 2019, two defendants were sentenced to just six and three years imprisonment.[37] David stated that law enforcement officers 'have expressed frustration around some of the sentencing that's been passed down at the end of obviously very lengthy and complex investigations,'[38] revealing something of a disconnect between investigators and the courts. Police officers tend to be driven by the ethos of 'catching the bad guys' and perceive low conviction rates and short sentences as failures of the criminal justice process.[39]

It is not just the police who find fault with the system; in May 2016, a Public Accounts Committee report did not hold back on its condemnation. Its opening sentence, '[t]he criminal justice system is close to breaking point,'[40] set the tone for the rest of the document, which criticised the delays and inadequacies of the system, the lack of regard for victims' needs and the ruinous effect of repeated cuts to the overall CJS budget by the Ministry of Justice. The CPS, for instance, suffered a drastic loss of personnel even before the COVID pandemic, dropping from 8304 staff in 2010[41] to 5639 in 2016/17.[42] In a parliamentary debate on CPS funding in January 2017, Karl Turner MP raised this issue, voicing his concerns that the CPS was 'suffering a brain drain

35 Mantouvalou (n 18) 1017, 1026.
36 Attorney General's Office/Lucy Frazer QC MP, 'Solicitor General Welcomes Modern Slavery Conviction' (*UK Government*, 5 July 2019) <www.gov.uk/government/news/solicitor-general-welcomes-modern-slavery-conviction> accessed 9 August 2020.
37 *R v Brezinski* (Birmingham Crown Court, 5 July 2019).
38 David, Birmingham, UK, 20 October 2018.
39 Dale Ballucci and Keyanna Drakes, 'Beyond Convictions: Negotiating Procedural and Distributive Justice in Police Response to Sex Crimes Victims' (2021) 6(1) *Victims and Offenders* 81–98 <>https://doi.org/10.1080/15564886.2020.1766613>.
40 House of Commons Public Accounts Committee, 'Efficiency in the Criminal Justice System' (*UK Parliament*, 23 May 2016) <www.publications.parliament.uk/pa/cm201617/cmselect/cmpubacc/72/7202.htm> accessed 10 July 2020.
41 Crown Prosecution Service, *Annual Report and Accounts 2010–11* (The Stationery Office Limited on behalf of the Controller of Her Majesty's Stationery Office 2011).
42 Crown Prosecution Service, *Annual Report and Accounts 2016–17* (Williams Lea Group on behalf of the Controller of Her Majesty's Stationery Office 2017).

and haemorrhaging experienced in-house lawyers, who leave for independent practice, or simply take the money and run.'[43] Reports that the CPS are being encouraged to drop 'weak' rape cases to improve overall conviction rates[44] additionally do nothing to improve general public confidence in the CJS. Ultimately, this portrayal of an organisation running on empty does not suggest that it fit-for-purpose for a vulnerable survivor of long-term slavery and abuse. When that organisation depends on the investigative prowess of a national police force which, over the same period, lost nearly 20,000 officers – a fall of 13% – and sustained budget cuts of 20%, the window for error was opened even wider.[45] Even the much-lauded recruitment of 20,000 new police officers will do little to patch up the years of experience and knowledge that have been slashed from the service.

## 7.3 Criticisms of the criminal justice approach

While there is no doubt that the trafficking, enslavement and abuse of human beings should be treated as serious criminal offences, many commentators question the heavy reliance on a criminal justice approach. Targeting organised gangs, for example, diverts attention from more isolated victims such as those in domestic servitude or small, remote agricultural settings. Deeper criticisms unpack the entire model and examine the reality of the system as experienced by survivors themselves. As already stated, traditional policing places the emphasis on arrest, investigation and conviction,[46] following legislation and policies that are concentrated on the activities of the perpetrator rather than the needs of the victim.[47] At an event for professionals in the anti-modern slavery sector, for example, one police officer claimed that the nature of investigations was 'one size fits all.'[48] In other words, despite the complexity of the crime and vulnerability of the victims, the standard law enforcement approach is applied as equally to modern slavery offences as it is to vehicle theft.

Mirroring this standard policing approach, the CPS maintains the Full Code Test, relying on thresholds of sufficient evidence and public interest before making the decision to formally charge. The Home Office has

43 HC Deb, 11 January 2017, vol 619, col 148WH.

44 Alexandra Topping, 'Prosecutors Urged to Ditch "Weak" Rape Cases to Improve Figures' *The Guardian* (London, 24 September 2018) <www.theguardian.com/law/2018/sep/24/prosecutors-rape-cases-cps-crown-prosecution-service-conviction-rates?CMP=Share_iOSApp_Other> accessed 13 March 2020.

45 Hargreaves and others (n 16).

46 Ballucci and Drakes (n 39).

47 Nicholson and others (n 4) 689.

48 Combatting Human Trafficking and Modern Slavery: Developing a Stronger Multi-Agency Response for the Identification of and Support for Victims of Trafficking (Public Policy Exchange event, London, 14 September 2017).

conceded that the current approach to tackling modern slavery places a 'heavy reliance on victim testimony'[49] and that '[c]onsequently, there is a need to establish close working relationships with victims; a matter heavily dependent on the trafficked person trusting the State and feeling respected and safe.'[50] Fears of arrest, imprisonment, deportation or further abuse, even fear of the unknown, can all significantly limit the extent to which a survivor is prepared to discuss their experiences. This also highlights the difficulty of relying on a standardised system that attempts to systematically transpose survivor accounts onto 'legal notions of how experiences should be told, rather than how the survivor can tell her experience.'[51] In fact, Kevin Hyland, the former IASC, noted before the Work and Pensions Committee Victims of Modern Slavery inquiry that victims were 'looked at in a very clinical way to almost fit law enforcement requirements.'[52] To explore this paradigm, Jakobsen et al. conducted a study on police interviews with victims, acknowledging the fact that this is a process in which the need for information gathering is a priority.[53] They noted that the requirement to establish 'exactly what happened'[54] took precedence over the victim's personal narrative and potentially risked re-traumatising interviewees in the process. The research also examined how the police officers perceived their behaviour during these interviews. Some of the officers admitted that they felt sorry for the victims and often wanted to provide more support but believed that this would negatively impact the primary objective of gathering evidence. Many also stated that they were uncertain how to deal with traumatisation and therefore focused on the role they were qualified to carry out. Notably, this research took place in Norway, where criticism of the notion of 'victim' as 'witness' has already led to successive developments of victim's rights for over forty years.[55]

Even with more a more victim-centric approach, however, cases frequently fail because survivors have simply been unable to provide enough information for the CPS to proceed with a prosecution. Investigating agencies such as the police have admitted that early Achieving Best Evidence (ABE) interviews

49 'Modern Slavery Strategy 2014', cited in Amy Weatherburn, 'The Impact of the 2012 Domestic Workers in a Private Household Visa on Human Trafficking for Domestic Servitude' (2016) 30(3) *Journal of Immigration Asylum and Nationality Law* 204, 214.

50 Weatherburn (n 49) 204.

51 Paola Michelle Contreras and others, 'Psychotherapy in the Aftermath of Human Trafficking: Working through the Consequences of Psychological Coercion' (2017) 40(1–2) *Women and Therapy* 31, 43.

52 Kevin Hyland, *Oral Evidence, Victims of Modern Slavery*, HC 803 (11 January 2017) Q130.

53 Kristina Kepinska Jakobsen and others, 'Trauma-exposed Young Victims: Possibilities and Constraints for Providing Trauma Support within the Investigative Interview' (2017) 23(5) *Psychology, Crime & Law* 427.

54 ibid 427, 439.

55 ibid 427.

with victims are sometimes of virtually no use to the case. Ayesha encapsulated this problem:

> So 'I was picked up, taken to a forest, living in a house, big brother looked after me, when he told me to go I went' – those are the kind of stories you would be hearing and there is no questioning from my perspective truth or validity in that necessarily, but from a criminal justice point of view, there is nothing that would reach an evidential threshold that would allow you to act on any of that.[56]

Often, multiple interviews are undertaken before sufficient evidence can be attained.[57] Thus, the criminal justice process becomes delayed, for several years in some instances, before the witness feels able to disclose any valuable information about what happened to them.[58] As indicated previously, some survivors withdraw completely before justice can be accomplished.[59] A punitive approach also requires victims to give testimonies at a criminal trial, but fear of repercussions and the effects of trauma often mean that the victim is reluctant to face their trafficker in court.[60] *Brezinski*[61] established that one criminal gang had abused over 400 slavery victims before the police were finally alerted. Of those hundreds of victims, only 92 were formally identified, as the police believed that '350 more were used by the gang and either could not be traced, had left the country or were *too scared to give evidence*.'[62] As Ayesha stated, 'if we are over reliant on victim testimony we are never going to be in a position to prosecute a way out of this.'[63]

The effects of a system built on traditional, standardised approaches to criminal justice ultimately sideline the unintended consequences for survivors. Meanwhile, as discussed in Chapter 2, psychological trauma and difficulties in (re)integration are not formally prioritised in UK law and policy, and so the cycle continues. It is suggested that 'there is no political will to address structural factors, including legal structures, that create vulnerability to exploitation.'[64] Certainly, the emphasis on addressing the consequences

56 Ayesha, Portsmouth, UK, 30 October 2018.
57 Haughey (n 27) 11.
58 The Human Trafficking Foundation and others, *Supporting Adult Survivors of Slavery to Facilitate Recovery and Reintegration and Prevent Re-Exploitation* (Human Trafficking Foundation 2017) 9.
59 Haughey (n 27).
60 Stephanie Hepburn and Rita J Simon, 'Hidden in Plain Sight: Human Trafficking in the United States' (2010) 27(1) *Gender Issues* 26.
61 *R v Brezinski* (Birmingham Crown Court, 5 July 2019).
62 BBC News, 'UK Slavery Network Had "over 400 Victims"' *BBC News* (8 July 2019) <www.bbc.co.uk/news/uk-england-birmingham-48881327> accessed 8 July 2019 (italics added).
63 Ayesha, Portsmouth, UK, 30 October 2018.
64 Mantouvalou (n 18) 1017, 1018.

of modern slavery rather than the underlying causes[65] has come into sharp relief with the discovery of labour exploitation in Leicester garment factories.[66] While the legal nuances and issues surrounding the Leicester workers are explored more fully in Section 2.4, a critical discussion on the structural factors that lead to modern slavery are beyond the research aims of this book. Nonetheless, given that the current system is unlikely to drastically change soon, it is worth further examining the experience of survivors within the criminal justice system.

## 7.4 From victim to offender (part II)

Under the current criminal justice approach, it is fair to say that survivors are key to securing convictions of those who commit modern slavery offences. The primary challenge for law and policy makers is thus 'how to reach out to these individuals, so as to rescue them from abuse'[67] and create a safe and confidential environment for victims to recover. Early interactions with the police are particularly crucial trigger points as contact with law enforcement is usually the first survivor experience on a potentially long road to justice and recovery. If this experience is negative, it can compound their trauma[68] and cause distrust in the authorities, which ultimately reduces their willingness to co-operate with an investigation.[69] A positive engagement, on the other hand, can give rise to greater self-esteem[70] and therefore improve the survivor's overall rehabilitation. However, although law enforcement and survivor support provisions are separate and distinct entities in the anti-modern slavery system, engagement with criminal justice is 'often the gateway to services for survivors of trafficking.'[71] This could result in survivors feeling that they are participating in a trade exchange in order to access the support they need. In fact, multiple frontline support organisations have highlighted 'the pressure

65 Kate Roberts, 'Human Trafficking: Addressing the Symptom, Not the Cause' in Gary Craig and others (eds), *The Modern Slavery Agenda: Policy, Politics and Practice in the UK* (Policy Press 2019).

66 Sarah O'Connor, 'Dark Factories: Labour Exploitation in Britain's Garment Industry' *Financial Times* (London, 17 May 2018) <www.ft.com/content/e427327e-5892-11e8-b8b2-d6ceb45fa9d0> accessed 1 July 2020.

67 Virginia Mantouvalou, 'Modern Slavery: The UK Response' (2010) 39(4) *Industrial Law Journal* 425, 431.

68 Ballucci and Drakes (n 39).

69 ibid.

70 Bruce Winick, 'Therapeutic Jurisprudence and Victims of Crime. Victim Participation in Justice: A therapeutic Jurisprudence Perspective (Abstract)' (Forthcoming) <http://ssrn.com/abstract–1102350> accessed 30 June 2020.

71 Jordan J Steiner and others, 'Providing Services to Trafficking Survivors: Understanding Practices across the Globe' (2018) 15(2) *Journal of Evidence-Informed Social Work* 151, 155.

to help prosecute powerful perpetrators as part of criminal proceedings'[72] as a barrier to consenting to the NRM.

The parallels between modern slavery and other traumatic crimes, as indicated in Chapters 3 and 6, also carry relevance here. When a person's entire life is under the control of another, they are in a constant state of extreme fear[73] and the reality of abusive and exploitative relationships is often difficult to articulate for those who have survived them. Comparisons to the laws and defences concerning domestic abuse victims further highlight the similarities. Reflecting Biderman's theory of coercion, as outlined in Chapter 6, CPS guidance on coercive behaviour under the Serious Crime Act 2015 states:

> Controlling behaviour is a range of acts designed to make a person subordinate and/or dependent by isolating them from sources of support, exploiting their resources and capacities for personal gain, depriving them of the means needed for independence, resistance and escape and regulating their everyday behaviour [including] threats, humiliation and intimidation or other abuse that is used to harm, punish, or frighten their victim.[74]

In fact, just as the dynamics of exploitative and abusive relationships bear striking resemblances to each other, so too do the post-trauma actions and beliefs of their victims. As discussed in Section 6.3, where a survival strategy like traumatic bonding[75] has developed, victims may actually think of their trafficker as a boyfriend (in the case of sexual slavery),[76] an employer or a friend. One of the Rooneys' victims, during a recorded interview with the police, claimed that the family had given him the best years of his life.[77] These perceptions not only skew the belief that their trafficker is a criminal, but significantly diminishes the belief that they themselves are victims. Sustained coercive control means that victims can perceive themselves as being responsible for any decisions or actions they make, not realising that 'because of the various tactics often employed by traffickers such as deception and oath-taking, even adults are beguiled to fall victim to the traffickers.'[78] The feeling that one's own bad choices have simply produced bad results, combined with the shame attached

72 Maya Esslemont, *Supported or Deported? Understanding the Deportation and Detention Data Held on Human Trafficking and Slavery'* (After Exploitation 2019) 4.

73 Mantouvalou (n 67) 425.

74 'CPS Guidance on Controlling or Coercive Behaviour', cited in Susan SM Edwards, 'Coercion and Compulsion – Re-imagining Crimes and Defences' (2016) 12 *Criminal Law Review* 876.

75 Edwards (n 74) 876.

76 Alexandra C Duncan and Dana DeHart, 'Provider Perspectives on Sex Trafficking: Victim Pathways, Service Needs, & Blurred Boundaries' (2019) 14(4) *Victims & Offenders* 510.

77 Janice Sutherland, 'The Modern British Slave Trade' [Television Broadcast] (Documentary, Channel 4 January 2017).

78 Nlerum S Okugbule, 'Combating the "New Slavery" in Nigeria: An Appraisal of Legal and Policy Responses to Human Trafficking' (2013) 57(1) *Journal of African Law* 57, 75.

to those experiences, can create a psychological block to categorising oneself as a victim at all. Several frontline practitioners reinforce this, for instance:

> Foreign people who have been trafficked often don't speak English and they've got a fear of authorities and getting them to actually accept that they are actually victims can be quite a hard task in its own right.[79]

> We classify people as victims and . . . it leads you to the CJS but you might have someone saying 'but I'm not a victim' and does that undermine those processes or is it just indicative of the fact that a traumatised person, when you understand their background, may not see themselves as a victim but under our legal system, does that mean they're not?[80]

The resulting internalised identity of many survivors can create a multitude of challenges for both the criminal justice system and its support service partnerships,

> including whether trafficked persons perceived their own situation as exploitative, maintaining continued attachment to traffickers, being prepared to receive services, and feeling generally safe navigating the social and physical world. Other challenges were imposed by external structures based on perceived victim/offender status of the trafficked person, including logistical challenges in housing, programming, and connection to justice and service systems.[81]

In other words, law enforcement agencies and other professionals may themselves experience difficulty in distinguishing 'offenders' from 'victims,' frequently leading to the misplacement and incorrect treatment of traumatised individuals.[82]

Mistrust or fear of law officials may stem from the fact that trafficked victims are often forced to commit crimes during the course of their abuse.[83] Article 8 of the EU Anti-Trafficking Directive provides that being 'compelled' to commit crime can be a defence for trafficking victims,[84] while article 26 of the

79 David, Birmingham, UK, 20 October 2018.

80 Ayesha, Portsmouth, UK, 30 October 2018.

81 Duncan and DeHart (n 76) 510, 523.

82 Women for Refugee Women have gone so far as to suggest that this is a deliberate mistake on the part of the UK government: Gemma Lousley and others, *"From One Hell to Another": The Detention of Chinese Women Who Have Been Trafficked to the UK* (Women for Refugee Women 2019).

83 Hilkka Becker, 'Victims of Human Trafficking in Ireland: Caught in a Legal Quagmire' (2010) 24 *IANL* 134.

84 Directive 2011/36/EU of the European Parliament and of the Council of Europe on preventing and combating trafficking in human beings and protecting its victims (replacing

Convention on Action against Trafficking in Human Beings[85] 'obliges Member States to "provide for the possibility of not imposing penalties on victims for their involvement in unlawful activities, to the extent that they have been compelled to do so".'[86] These have subsequently been incorporated into the Modern Slavery Act, which offers a statutory defence to this effect under section 45;[87] however, the majority of newly released victims are highly unlikely to be aware of these legal rights.

This is exacerbated when police are poorly trained to deal with the complexity of the issue, as highlighted in the Haughey report. Meanwhile, the shared characteristics of trafficking and criminal offences such as pimping enable law enforcement officials to pursue a more established pattern of investigation and prosecution[88] or even ignore sex work altogether on the perception that it is a 'victimless crime.'[89] Furthermore, limited resources often result in the police taking the least line of resistance: for example, upon the discovery of two trafficked Vietnamese boys at a cannabis farm, investigating officers had a choice between swiftly prosecuting the victims for drug cultivation, or investing more of the Constabulary's thinly stretched budget into a full investigation of human rights abuses. They opted for the former.[90] Kevin Hyland, prior to leaving the IASC post, condemned this approach,[91] but a 2019 independent report suggests that the practice has continued. The Jesuit Refugee Service has worked with survivors who were forced to work in cannabis farms and found that law enforcement authorities are frequently focusing on the crime rather than the individual.[92] Most of the twenty-six survivors they supported were arrested and convicted of drug-related offences; some disclosed the details of their trafficking but were not believed and, upon release from prison, were then moved to immigration detention. One case study indicated that the NRM provided no assistance as, although the survivor was given a reasonable grounds decision following his release from prison, he was detained

Council Framework Decision 2002/629/JHA) (5 April 2011).

85 Council of Europe Convention on Action Against Trafficking in Human Beings (adopted 16 May 2005, entered into force 1 February 2008) CETS 197.

86 Becker (n 83) 134, 138.

87 Modern Slavery Act 2015 s45; Steven Bird and Philippa Southwell, 'Does the New "Slavery" Defence Offer Victims of Trafficking Any Greater Protection?' (2015) 9 *Archbold Review* 7.

88 Atak and Simeon (n 3) 1019.

89 April Rieger, 'Missing the Mark: Why the Trafficking Victims Protection Act Fails to Protect Sex Trafficking Victims in the United States' (2007) 30 *Harvard Journal of Law & Gender* 231.

90 Thanos Maroukis, 'Keeping Up Appearances: The British Public Policy Response to the Trafficking of Domestic Workers in a Changing Regime of Social Protection' (2017) 15(2) *Journal of Immigrant & Refugee Studies* 155.

91 Daniel Silverstone and Claire Brickell, *Combating Modern Slavery Experienced by Vietnamese Nationals En Route to, and within, the UK* (Office of the Independent Anti-Slavery Commissioner 2017).

92 Jesuit Refugee Service, *Survivors of Trafficking in Immigration Detention* (JRS UK 2019).

for the entire forty-five days in immigration detention 'due to his criminal conviction.'[93] These findings go some way to explain the high numbers of survivors in immigration detention, as identified in Chapter 5, but they directly contradict the government's assertion that victims are only formally identified *after* they have been detained (see Section 5.3). Furthermore, the priority given to immigration control is not conducive to encouraging potential witnesses to provide evidence to the police or in court, as further highlighted in Section 5.4.

Where Section 45 has been invoked and relied upon in Court, the nascency of the legislation has led to interpretative challenges. *R v MK and R v Persida Gega (aka Anna Maione)*[94] concerned two individuals who had been convicted of possession of an identity document with improper intention and sought to rely on the statutory defence. The Court of Appeal was thus asked to decide whether the defendants bore the legal or persuasive burden of proof to support the defence. The Court ruled that the defendants only bore the evidential burden of demonstrating that they were victims of trafficking, while it was incumbent upon the prosecution to prove beyond reasonable doubt that the defendants were *not* victims of trafficking. In the event that the prosecution failed to prove this, the defendant would be required to further show:

(a) That she was compelled to commit the offence;
(b) That the compulsion was as a direct consequence of her being or having been a victim of slavery or relevant exploitation; and
(c) That a reasonable person in the same situation as her and having her relevant characteristics would have no realistic alternative to doing the act which constitutes the offence.[95]

Here, the traditional criminal justice model appears to depart entirely from the overall anti-modern slavery system. There is no mention throughout the ruling of the NRM, suggesting that the defendants were never referred into it. Had either of the defendants received a positive Conclusive Grounds decision, this could have been instrumental in their defence. However in 2021, *Brecani v R*[96] considered the very question as to whether NRM decisions are admissible as evidence in Court. In deliberating the 'expertise' of the individual who would give evidence in this instance, that is to say, the Competent Authority decision maker, the court stated that 'we do not consider that case workers in the Competent Authority are experts in human trafficking or modern slavery'[97]. As a decision of the court, this already bears some weight. When other

93 ibid 6.
94 [2018] EWCA Crim 667.
95 [2018] EWCA Crim 667 [11].
96 [2021] EWCA Crim 731.
97 [2021] EWCA Crim 731 [54].

criticisms of the NRM decision-making process, as discussed in Section 2.3, are taken into account, this raises a serious question as to the validity and effectiveness of the UK's modern slavery administrative process. It also highlights an underlying deficiency in the broader modern slavery approach. The fact that resources are poured into lengthy appeals processes rather than relying on the very mechanism that was designed to establish indicators of modern slavery suggests that key aspects of the system continue to operate in silos. This is neither efficient nor cost-effective and reinforces the divide between the criminal justice system and the needs of survivors.

Modern slavery as a crime also means that the nature of the work performed by victims is not recognised as legitimate employment. This creates yet another barrier to justice, reinforced by Lord Bates during the Modern Slavery Bill debate.[98] While all workers in the UK are entitled to protection under employment law, victims of modern slavery – consequently not employed under legal contracts – are ineligible to access employment tribunals. This 'doctrine of illegality' enables UK courts to 'refuse to hear employment claims where the work has been arranged or performed illegally.'[99] The doctrine also disproportionately affects undocumented migrant workers, as illustrated by *Hounga v Allen*.[100] Fourteen-year-old Hounga entered the UK on a visa acquired through false identity documents, which had been obtained by her employer. Hounga agreed to work as a live-in worker for £50 per month plus education. Her initial claim through the Employment Appeals Tribunal was ruled as unenforceable due to her immigration status, which rendered her employment contract illegal. Hounga then went to the Court of Appeal, claiming race discrimination for dismissal and arguing that 'her employers had taken advantage of her illegal status . . . to treat her less well than a hypothetical white British comparator.'[101] As a tort claim, the illegality of the contract was insignificant; however, while the court expressed sympathy for Hounga, the illegality defence succeeded in defeating her appeal. Finally, the Supreme Court upheld the appeal, with Lord Wilson finding that the illegality defence could ultimately compromise the integrity of the legal system, as it could 'engender a belief that [employers] could even discriminate against such employees with impunity.'[102]

Although the outcome for Hounga ultimately went in her favour, her case and many others epitomise the 'otherness' experienced by survivors and shines a light on the legal difficulties they face even after they have left captivity.

98 Lord Bates, HL Deb 23 February 2015, vol 759, col 1464.

99 Ismail Idowu Salih, 'Viewing Domestic Workers Problems through a Human Rights Lens' (2015) 34(7) *Equality, Diversity and Inclusion: An International Journal* 622, 625.

100 *Hounga v Allen* [2014] UKSC 47.

101 Cliodhna Murphy, 'Enforcing Employment Standards for Undocumented Domestic Workers in the UK and Ireland: Rethinking Illegality in Zones of Invisibility' (2015) 29(4) *Immigration, Asylum and Nationality Law* 349, 360.

102 [2014] UKSC 47 [44].

## 7.5 Alternatives routes to justice

For survivors who are so traumatised they are unable to provide a chronological, detailed narrative in a timely manner, or for those survivors who simply feel unable to recognise the offences committed against them, is traditional criminal justice even the appropriate path to justice? In 2002, the UN High Commissioner for Human Rights addressed this issue, publishing a principles and guidelines document that acknowledged the human rights abuses inherent in the crimes of trafficking and slavery.[103] As well as confirming the need for states to protect and support victims, the document laid out how law enforcement agencies could incorporate a human rights approach in their interactions with victims.

One of the ways this could be amended is through a change in how evidence is collected during the investigation. This appears, *prima facie*, to be an obvious solution and 'looking at the networks, the organised crime gangs, the links between accountants and finances and cars and business ownership, land ownership, house ownership'[104] would of course produce a tapestry of hard evidence that would considerably reduce the pressure on witnesses. In reality, however, investigating crimes of this nature, especially where organised and sometimes international gangs are involved, costs a huge amount of time and resources.[105] David provided a typical example:

> But the one that kicked all this off in [county], for example, that started in 2012 or 13. We've only just brought some of those perpetrators to court very recently, I think we're just awaiting the sentencing so that just shows how long it can take to actually gather the evidence.[106]

Even the more victim-centric elements of support and care within the criminal justice process may not necessarily be suitable for those exiting modern slavery:

> Would a victim of modern slavery, would it be appropriate for them to access, for example, a SARC[107] suite? Or would it be appropriate for a victim of modern slavery to access Victim Support? Is that . . . would we have those discussions if it was appropriate, what would it look like? It would look different across all the victim services, and I think what

103 Office of the High Commissioner for Human Rights, 'Recommended Principles and Guidelines on Human Rights and Human Trafficking' (OHCHR 2002) presented to the Economic and Social Council as an addendum to the report of the United Nations High Commissioner for Human Rights (E/2002/68/Add.1).

104 Ayesha, Portsmouth, UK, 30 October 2018.

105 Puja, Leeds, UK, 8 January 2019; Diana, Bristol, UK, 22 February 2019.

106 David, Birmingham, UK, 20 October 2018.

107 Sexual Assault Referral Centre. SARCs offer free medical and forensic services throughout the UK to people who have recently been raped or sexually assaulted, as well as practical and emotional support.

> I've found in my line of work is that it's understood that survivors and victims of modern slavery do require a bespoke level of support.[108]

However, an even more subtle shift in priorities may be all that is needed in some cases. A further finding in the Jakobsen study suggested that officers deferred emotional responsibilities to other professionals who had the skills and qualifications to provide this type of support. In some respects, this reflects the importance of multi-partnership working, allowing those with designated specialised roles to undertake their own duties, freeing up other agencies to carry out theirs. There is also a value to facilitating holistic survivor support in improving CJS outcomes. Caroline, from an independent organisation, presented a vignette regarding one survivor who had originally been given a negative Conclusive Grounds decision. The organisation supported the survivor in appealing the decision, which was successful. Caroline continued:

> Because she was believed, first by us and then by the competent authority, she said 'Now that everybody does believe me I am happy to talk to the police' so she started talking to the police, who did an ABE interview, which lasted quite a while, they took the evidence back to their base. When they took it back to their base, they looked at their system and realised they had loads of evidence on the person she had named.[109]

What this shows is the importance of appropriate support prior to giving police evidence, rather than offering support as a condition of engagement with the authorities. This also links to the cost-effective concept of improving evidence gathering through better communication between partners. Again, this seems to be a patent observation, but multi-agency communication is vital to success, and is discussed at length in Section 4.4. In fact, in those areas where structured multi-agency networks have been established, participants were very positive about the cohesive nature of the relationships:

> I think from a policing perspective, the police officers and the people working in that unit would be the first to say that they can only do so much as the law enforcement side of it, and working with [charity], local authorities, other third sector voluntary organisations is absolutely key if we are to be successful.[110]

> The investigators and outreach workers identify people in the local area and then we've got a joint project with the police, where that intelligence

108 Puja, Leeds, UK, 8 January 2019.
109 Caroline, Nottingham, UK, 22 November 2019.
110 David, Birmingham, UK, 20 October 2018.

> is passed on directly to the police and then rescues, you know raids, and such like occur and [my organisation] are usually one of the parties that help, so they've got very good relationship with the police.[111]

Many of these networks are chaired by representatives from the police, and several police and crime commissioners have been very active in co-ordinating these efforts. This demonstrates the level of commitment across law enforcement where the resources exist to do so. While both statutory and voluntary sector participants expressed their desire for clearer communication between one another, the emphasis erred towards collaboration and mutual understanding of their individual roles:

> Supporting victims of modern slavery is extremely complex and the delivery of consistent advocacy on the frontline to make sure that victims are engaged with services so they don't drop off that cliff edge of support that's so often spoken about, or falling through the gaps or disengaging or going missing, disengaging with not just services but police investigations, managing victim support when they're witnesses and victims in a prosecution case, so I think a greater understanding of the complexities around victim support, that still needs to be a conversation about that still needs to be maintained and developed further.[112]

> It's really important for third sector to understand the role of policing and the complexities of investigating modern slavery crime.[113]

> It's giving that organisation the confidence to know that that intelligence needs to go somewhere, and that we will be the conduit for that intelligence and we would share that with their agreement, anonymised intelligence to the . . . because if you've got somebody and they've given you details: 'Joseph met me in a bus stop in Calnes, he passed me over to Alex who met me at Dover docks' 'What's his surname?' and he gave you a surname, you've got names of somebody who is a contact in Lithuania, you've also got the name of somebody who's met them at Dover docks. That is vital information for any investigating authority to be able to do something with.[114]

111 Donna, Nottingham, UK, 10 May 2019.
112 Puja, Leeds, UK, 8 January 2019.
113 ibid.
114 Diana, Bristol, UK, 22 February 2019.

Furthermore, the need for non-statutory adherence to boundaries and supporting the work of criminal justice professionals was clear:

> That is when you've identified or you think that something's not quite right, we would advise as an agency you stop, you don't investigate any further, you leave that to the authorities, to the agencies that have been given the remit to investigate. You manage the evidence so that should there be any subsequent judicial process, you've got that to give to that investigating authority but moreover, once you've identified a victim you have a very clear pathway and next steps process within your business or your larger organisation that will tell you exactly what to do with that person.[115]

This reiteration of understanding each other's distinct and specialised roles within the system also points to the negative impacts of poor communication between agencies. Diana additionally noted that where some support providers were privy to information that could help build a prosecution case, they were not always recording or passing the information on to the relevant authorities. The issue of confidentiality is of course paramount, but greater connections will help to reduce this problem. Further stressing the need for a more holistic, multi-partnership approach, Puja stated 'I think it's got to be understood that policing is not the answer to tackling modern slavery. We're not going to arrest our way out of this.'[116] The themes of communication and multi-partnership working here reflect the discussion in Section 4.4, which demonstrates the need for a cohesive approach across all stakeholder agencies. The requirements of such a complex issue cannot be managed by one organisation alone.

The role of the advocate is once again a potentially key factor in this area of survivor support (see also Chapter 4). The Stern Review noted that independent sexual violence advisers, as single-point advocates for victims of rape,

> represent continuity for complainants as they progress through the criminal justice process. In some cases this is critical to keeping their confidence and ensuring they do not withdraw. One police unit told us that without the long-term care and support provided by ISVAs, maintaining a victim throughout the whole criminal process, which takes between six and twelve months, would be 'incredibly difficult'. Of course, this is also a task the police are not resourced to do.[117]

115 ibid.

116 Puja, Leeds, UK, 8 January 2019.

117 Baroness Vivien Stern, *The Stern Review: A Report by Baroness Vivien Stern CBE of an Independent Review into How Rape Complaints Are Handled by Public Authorities in England and Wales* (Government Equalities Office and Home Office 2010) 104.

Even under more resource-affluent conditions, police officers are not necessarily able to dedicate the time and emotional effort required to fully support a survivor. In the UK, independent domestic violence advisors and ISVAs are currently employed to provide emotional and practical support for survivors of abuse. These roles also offer an element of advocacy for survivors; in this context, the term arose from the feminist foundations of organisations such as Women's Aid and Rape Crisis, whereby 'principles and practices based on ideologies of collaboration and empowerment'[118] were developed. In 2015 the Thames Valley Police and Crime Commissioner piloted the support role of independent trauma advisors (ITAs) to 'offer immediate crisis intervention and emotional support to victims of exploitation, and help integrate victims of trafficking and human exploitation into further services as required.'[119] ITAs also provided operational support to police officers in activities relating to modern slavery and trafficking investigations. At the end of the two-year pilot, a cost-benefit analysis found that 'taking a very conservative estimate . . . it is estimated that for every pound spent on the service £3.35 could be saved from the public purse.'[120] The project continued and, mirroring the Stern Review, early evidence suggested that ITA support increased the likelihood of victim disclosure, improving intelligence for the police.[121]

Addressing other aspects of survivor interaction is also important. Traditional theories of traumatised and vulnerable individuals have engendered a paternalistic criminal justice system that frequently views victims as incapable of making their own decisions.[122] However, victim inclusion in criminal justice increases the likelihood of recovery by providing them with a voice.[123] Procedural justice is often couched in terms that relate to offenders, but it is possible to apply its values to survivors in the criminal justice system. The key principles are:

- treating people with respect and dignity
- making unbiased decisions and interpreting and applying rules consistently and transparently

118 Oona Brooks and Michele Burman, 'Reporting Rape: Victim Perspectives on Advocacy Support in the Criminal Justice Process' (2016) *Criminology and Criminal Justice* 4 <>https://doi.org/10.1177/1748895816667996>.

119 Anthony Stansfeld, 'Support Service for Victims of Slavery and Exploitation to Continue' (*Police and Crime Commissioner for Thames Valley*) <www.thamesvalley-pcc.gov.uk/news-and-events/thamesvalley-pcc-news/2015/04/support-service-for-victims-of-slavery-and-exploitation-to-continue/> accessed 10 June 2021.

120 Thames Valley Police and Crime Commissioner, *Modern Slavery and Exploitation: Evaluation of a New Model for Identifying and Supporting Victims* (Office of the Police and Crime Commissioner 2017) 4.

121 Stansfeld (n 119).

122 Linda G Mills, 'The Justice of Recovery: How the State Can Heal the Violence of Crime' (2006) 57(3) *Hastings Law Review* 457.

123 ibid.

- giving people a voice and hearing their concerns and experiences
- showing and encouraging trust by being sincere, caring and authentic, and trying to do what is right for everyone[124]

Procedural justice gives survivors the opportunity to 'meaningfully participate in the investigation process,'[125] which in turn offers some catharsis. This links to findings from research into procedural fairness in the courtroom;[126] the evidence here indicates that individuals with experience of trauma are especially likely to benefit from a procedural fairness approach. As a group that is at greater risk of triggering from 'disrespectful court staff or feelings of hopelessness over case outcomes,'[127] survivor participation and understanding of the criminal justice process can help to reduce anxiety and re-trauma. Fundamentally, introducing this type of approach would bring the criminal justice system more in line with other aspects of the modern slavery support system, where the emphasis is on trauma-informed services and survivor empowerment (see Chapters 4, 6 and 8).

Restorative justice could also be worthy of consideration. The process aims to involve both the victim and the offender and thereby restore the pre-crime status quo.[128] It is acknowledged, however, that for traumatic crimes, complete restoration is often impossible.[129] Instead, restorative justice proponents seek 'holistic healing rather than the traditional justice system – one that is amenable to empathy, creativity, and long-term solutions.'[130] As with procedural justice, part of this approach enables the victim to be actively involved with the process, building empowerment through allowing victims to define their own version of justice.[131] Restorative justice conferences, in which the victim and offender undertake something of a truth and reconciliation process, have been shown to reduce victim anger, fears of re-victimisation and emotional distress.[132] Of course, this is a not a panacea for modern slavery, and bringing perpetrators and survivors face-to-face will not always be an option. Certainly for those survivors who live in abject fear of repercussions, the potential for

124 Her Majesty's Prison and Probation Service, 'Guidance: Procedural Justice' (*UK Government*, 17 June 2019) <www.gov.uk/guidance/procedural-justice> accessed 15 July 2020.

125 Ballucci and Drakes (n 39) 3.

126 Phil Bowen, *Improving Communication in Court: Evidence and Practice Briefing* (Centre for Justice Innovation 2020).

127 ibid 2.

128 Lori Carroll, 'Restoring the Weak and the Victimized' (2016) 1 *International Society for Therapeutic Jurisprudence* 119.

129 Laurie Kohn, 'What's So Funny About Peace, Love, and Understanding? Restorative Justice as a New Paradigm for Domestic Violence Intervention' (2010) 40(2) *Seton Hall Law Review* 517.

130 ibid 517, 532.

131 John Braithwaite, 'Restorative Justice: Assessing Optimistic and Pessimistic Accounts' (1999) 25 *Crime and Justice* 1.

132 Carroll (n 128) 119.

triggering re-trauma could bring more harm than good. Where it is possible, however, the emphasis on offender accountability rather than punishment has yielded positive results: Braithwaite's study of restorative justice programmes outcomes across a range of jurisprudence shows that the large majority ( 87% on average) of reparation and compensation agreements are completed.[133]

Independent research with the IASC further presses the need to move away from the entrenched CJS model:

> UK anti-slavery policy and funding to date has principally focused on enforcement-related responses and a number of our survey responses and interviews indicated a need for activity and strategy to move 'beyond enforcement'. As one government interviewee put it, 'if we only ever say it's about prosecuting cases we will have lost our way.'[134]

Furthermore, the traditional criminal justice process, while it can be part of the recovery process as a means of validating their experience, is not necessarily paramount to survivors. Several practitioners acknowledge the fact that survivors of modern slavery often express little interest in seeing their perpetrators punished. While this may have some roots in a reluctance to view themselves as victims, the concept of 'justice' carries different meanings for each individual. One participant described a survivor who had had some family heirlooms stolen from her during her time in domestic servitude. Following a police raid, the heirlooms were returned to her, and this alone was instrumental in her recovery.[135] Given that most survivors originally wanted to work for a better life for themselves and their families, a lot of them simply desire compensation: 'They will want the money that they should have earned.'[136] Compensation can 'empower them economically, support their societal reintegration, minimise their vulnerability to being re-trafficked and provide them with a sense of justice.'[137] To this effect, the Modern Slavery Act provides for the courts to make reparation orders for victims of slavery and trafficking offences.[138] Despite some law enforcement authorities' disappointment at the brevity of sentencing, there is growing positivity towards alternative means of justice:

> Some of the orders that have been attached are quite innovative and new and I certainly questioned our team here to what their views are around

133 Braithwaite (n 131) 1.

134 Office of the Independent Anti-Slavery Commissioner and University of Nottingham's Rights Lab, *Collaborating for Freedom: Anti-slavery Partnerships in the UK* (University of Nottingham and the Independent Anti-Slavery Commissioner 2017) 14.

135 Caroline, Nottingham, UK, 22 November 2019.

136 Diana, Bristol, UK, 22 February 2019.

137 Mantouvalou (n 18) 1017, 1033.

138 Modern Slavery Act 2015 s9.

> that and they seem to think they work quite well in restricting the further activities of some of the traffickers.[139]

Nonetheless, under the MSA, reparation orders 'must not exceed the amount the person is required to pay under the confiscation order.'[140] Even where modern slavery survivors have been eligible to claim recompense for lost earnings, frontline practitioners have found that 'it's quite time consuming to try and get money back.'[141] As well as the lack of audit trail, given the informal and illegitimate nature of the work performed, authorities in pursuit of perpetrator assets are dealing with a potentially complex financial network. In a 2016 Supreme Court case, Lady Hale reiterated this problem, and that of the 'doctrine of illegality,' stating that:

> Parliament may well wish to address its mind to whether the remedy provided by section 8 of the Modern Slavery Act 2015 is too restrictive in its scope and whether an employment tribunal should have jurisdiction to grant some recompense for the ill-treatment meted out to workers such as these, along with the other remedies which it does have power to grant.[142]

Lady Hale's comment also draws attention to the fact that the MSA fails to include provisions for civil remedies, which ignores the UK's obligations under the Council of Europe Convention on Action Against Trafficking in Human Beings[143] and the EU Trafficking Directive.[144] The latter requires that victims of human trafficking have access to the same compensation schemes as other victims of violent crime, which in this case would be the government's Criminal Injuries Compensation Authority (see Section 8.2). However, during the passing of the Modern Slavery Bill, Lord Bates presented the notion that prevailing civil remedies were sufficient for claiming damages from perpetrators, stating that Parliament had not identified a modern slavery scenario that would not involve at least one of the torts of intimidation, harassment, assault, unlawful imprisonment, negligence and breach of duty.[145] The problem with this is that survivors will then potentially walk away from one court experience only to grapple with the prospect of initiating another. The evidence strongly

139 David, Birmingham, UK, 20 October 2018.
140 Modern Slavery Act 2015 s9(4).
141 Diana, Bristol, UK, 22 February 2019.
142 Taiwo v Olaigbe and Onu v Akwiwu [2016] 1 WLR 2653 [34].
143 Council of Europe Convention on Action Against Trafficking in Human Beings (adopted 16 May 2005, entered into force 1 February 2008) CETS 197.
144 Directive 2011/36/EU of the European Parliament and of the Council of Europe on preventing and combating trafficking in human beings and protecting its victims (replacing Council Framework Decision 2002/629/JHA) (5 April 2011).
145 HL Deb, 23 February 2015, vol 759, col 1464.

indicates that survivors struggle to fully move on while they are subject to ongoing legal issues, even at their own behest. On a practical level, the delay in receiving any amount of financial award could make the difference between requiring ongoing economic assistance and independent living. The ability to be self-sufficient is so fundamental to survivor recovery that incorporating this into a justice model could be key to the UK's efforts to combat modern slavery and human trafficking.

## 7.6 Conclusion

As a horrific abuse of human rights, it is right and proper that perpetrators of modern slavery and human trafficking be brought to justice for their crimes. However, in order for this to be achieved, the system as a whole needs to be appropriately funded and stakeholders within that system need to work together. As the CJS currently stands, key agencies are not afforded the necessary financial and human resources to enable them to carry out their roles and remits, indicating significant limitations and barriers to success in the overall system. In addition to budget cuts, lack of understanding and training has led to some law enforcement officers taking the path of least resistance rather than delve into lengthy and complex investigations. This is not to say that the will to help survivors is not there; however, against a backdrop of support deficits in some regions of the country, goodwill efforts by CJS actors eat into their capacity to investigate and enforce the law. Furthermore, this contributes to a tendency to adhere to long-standing criminal justice approaches which try to make victims fit the system rather than exploring the ways in which the system can adapt to the crime. This is clearly not always yielding positive results and again highlights the limitations of the current strategy.

There are some positives to be drawn from the preceding. Early efforts in this area have resulted in initiatives such as the Police Transformation Programme, which shows initial signs of success. Police and crime commissioners have also made strong progress, with the introduction of designated survivor advocates and multi-partnership working, both of which stand out as key positive themes across this book. The courts, however, do not show as much inclination to work with other stakeholders as part of a cohesive effort, although their concerns about the expertise of some key actors should not be dismissed. Other more innovative approaches, based on trauma-informed models, have demonstrated some extremely positive outcomes although there are no obvious moves from central government to implement these as part of a nationwide criminal justice measure in this area. This fragmented approach results in a lack of effectiveness at the 'business end' of the UK's modern slavery system, revealing a clear problem at a crucial period in the survivor pathway.

The point is, the UK's modern slavery approach does not have to operate in two completely separate spheres. Perpetrators can be apprehended in tandem with survivor empowerment; it is discussed elsewhere throughout the book how much value is placed on the way in which survivor recovery actually helps to bolster the criminal justice process. Meanwhile, the Conclusive Grounds decision-making process – particularly at its current glacial pace – is adding another layer of bureaucracy to the survivor pathway without bringing any apparent benefits to the justice system. It extends the wait for justice, for recovery, and for the opportunity to lead a life that does not involve the authorities in some way. Yet beyond the NRM and the criminal justice process, little is known about long-term survivor outcomes. In Chapters 2 and 4, there was a clear message that the 'reflection and recovery' period was not enough to provide survivors with the means to progress and move forward. What does happen to survivors after this time? The following chapter explores this topic and addresses the ongoing needs of survivors as they work towards independent living.

# 8 Long-term support

## 8.1 Introduction

The National Referral Mechanism is the UK's statutory system for identifying victims of human trafficking and modern slavery and is discussed in detail in Chapter 2. Those who consent to referral into the NRM are entitled to a package of support that includes accommodation and legal assistance. This is provided by a range of frontline services across the UK, almost exclusively within the voluntary sector (see Chapters 3 and 4), with individuals entitled to support during the 'reflection and recovery' period. During this time, the Single Competent Authority or Immigration Enforcement Competent Authority reviews the available evidence and makes a Conclusive Grounds decision as to whether the person is actually a victim of modern slavery. Regardless of this outcome, however, there is no statutory means of support for survivors beyond the NRM.[1] Long-term care is therefore offered at the discretion and capacity of the aforementioned organisations, meaning that individuals are involved in something of a postcode lottery when it comes to post-NRM support. The range of aftercare and long-term support that has been recommended for survivors upon exiting slavery includes:

- medical care
- education and vocational training
- drug and alcohol rehabilitation
- therapeutic intervention
- employment skills
- safe and secure accommodation
- financial stability
- social and familial equilibrium.[2]

1 Carole Murphy, *A Game of Chance? Long-term Support for Survivors of Modern Slavery* (Centre for the Study of Modern Slavery 2018).
2 Naomi M Twigg, 'Comprehensive Care Model for Sex Trafficking Survivors' (2017) 49(3) *Journal of Nursing Scholarship* 259.

DOI: 10.4324/9781032639895-8

These needs are not mutually exclusive, although accommodation and therapeutic intervention are two of the highest priorities to facilitate recovery throughout the process, with education and/or employment playing a large role in longer term rehabilitation. Counselling and psychological support have been discussed in detail in Chapter 6. This chapter therefore focuses on the overarching challenges to independent living and provides examples of good practice and evidence-based organisational policies, with more in-depth focus on accommodation, education and employment. Focusing on the potential for improving systems that would benefit survivor support pathways, this chapter also addresses the issue of aftercare monitoring and what is being done to develop understanding of long-term survivor outcomes. Finally, we turn to the survivor voice within frontline organisational policy and in government-level decision making and how this could contribute towards future best practice.

## 8.2 Long-term support and the transition to independence

In 2017, a collaborative report on strategies for long-term survivor support gave the following recommendations:

1. Multiagency involvement in decision making that should inform ongoing support;
2. A positive Conclusive Grounds decision must carry status;
3. Legal advice and representation must be offered early to all potential victims of trafficking or modern slavery;
4. Case workers should be available to each individual to provide support and advocacy following a positive Conclusive Grounds decision;
5. Safehouse accommodation and transition to independent accommodation should be more flexible and support provision reduced gradually according to need.[3]

Multi-agency partnerships and their role in survivor support are explored more fully in Section 4.4; however, a recommendation by the Centre for Social Justice[4] reinforced the importance of collaborative relationships in which each organisation is able to operate within their specialist remits for the best overarching support packages. Likewise, legal assistance is discussed in Chapter 5 and the issues around post-NRM accommodation are addressed subsequently in this chapter. It is the status conferred by a positive CG decision (or lack

3 Human Trafficking Foundation and others, *Supporting Adult Survivors of Slavery to Facilitate Recovery and Reintegration and Prevent Re-exploitation* ((Human Trafficking Foundation 2017).

4 Centre for Social Justice, *It Happens Here: Equipping the United Kingdom to Fight Modern Slavery* (Centre for Social Justice 2013).

thereof) that is especially relevant for the long-term welfare and wellbeing of survivors, as identified by one research participant:

> At the moment, it doesn't mean anything. It's just a piece of paper that says, 'Pat you on the back, well done, you're a victim of trafficking, off you go.'[5]

Fundamentally, while conferring proof of status as a modern slavery victim, a positive CG decision does not afford individuals any statutory right to legal assistance or accommodation and crucially does not entitle survivors to leave to remain[6] (see Chapters 2 and 5), which impacts negatively on their ability to find accommodation, access education and gain employment. The underlying element beyond all these practical considerations, however, is the lack of access to ongoing support. While the concept of an allocated, specialist advocate for survivors is promoted by almost all frontline stakeholders (see Sections 4.2 and 7.5), the sudden removal of key support workers can be extremely damaging.

The transition to independent living is a pivotal period for survivors. It signifies that the individual has developed the practical skills and emotional stability to provide for themselves and any dependants they may have. Nonetheless, it can present new challenges and concerns, meaning that appropriate, adaptive support needs to continue during this time.[7] Survivors often experience multiple complex issues that impact on their mental health, as explored in Chapter 6. These issues – post-trauma, drug and alcohol problems, vulnerability to abusive relationships – are not resolved within 90 days, and support providers are alert to the fact that transition to independence can increase vulnerability and risk. Isolated incidents can trigger post-trauma symptoms while ongoing immigration or criminal justice cases exacerbate stress and anxiety.[8] Many survivors have given little thought to future plans and goals, as their time in confinement will have restricted their freedom to contemplate their possible options.[9] Consequently, a multitude of unforeseen challenges can arise as survivors navigate independent life. Even minor decision-making is extremely difficult after years of being under the control of another;[10] commentators have referred to a 'cliff edge' upon leaving the NRM, as dealing with day-to-day situations like attending appointments and going shopping can suddenly feel overwhelming without the safety net of support.[11] Evidence presented to the Home Affairs Committee inquiry on Modern Slavery also

5 Caroline, Nottingham, UK, 22 November 2019.
6 Murphy (n 1).
7 ibid.
8 Christine Beddoe and others, *Life beyond the Safe House for Survivors of Modern Slavery in London* (Human Trafficking Foundation 2015).
9 Murphy (n 1).
10 ibid.
11 Beddoe (n 8).

flagged up the lack of trauma-informed support available in other frontline services, leaving survivors rudderless in the event of ongoing need:

> Once I left the Salvation Army, I was to have surgery for some of the injuries from the experiences, and in the hospital, with the doctors and the care received, there was nothing tailored for survivors. . . . The only thing I could do was contact the Salvation Army back and say that even though I was out of their system, could they help me. There were no services; it was only because they had stepped up to do that. There were no services you could contact, or if people haven't got the support of their families, someone to advocate on your behalf.[12]

With this in mind, many frontline organisations have designed their services to include post-NRM support:

> I don't really believe in doing NRM work without post-NRM work because the damage that it causes to do it and then not do something afterwards is quite severe, so morally, ethically, professionally, I am not ok with just providing that and then nothing else afterwards.[13]

The concern is that where support is offered only to be taken away suddenly, there is a risk of further traumatising a survivor. It also breaks down any trust that has been built between organisations and survivors. One organisation has amended their time-limited service delivery so that survivors are given an allocated amount of support hours rather than a period of days. Sometimes, this can simply be for low-key assistance like 'getting a bus for somebody and learning their way to work, travelling to different places and seeing what else is in the community, what else can they engage in?'[14] but where more intensive levels of support are required, so are the resources needed to fulfil them. This places pressure on organisations, some of whom are not funded for post-NRM support and rely on donations and other monies to provide this aftercare[15] (see Chapter 3). Where charities would have ordinarily looked to statutory social care as a means of assisting with the transition, cutbacks have made this increasingly difficult:

> Generally, at a time of austerity, local authorities are struggling across the board which means that we are, under the Care Act, adding another population that they are responsible for looking after at certain points,

12 Witness F, *Oral Evidence, Modern Slavery*, HC 1460 (6 November 2018) Q99.
13 Caroline, Nottingham, UK, 22 November 2019.
14 Rachel, London, UK, 11 May 2019.
15 Ruth van Dyke, 'The UK's Response to Modern Slavery: Law, Policy and Politics' in Gary Craig and others (eds), *The Modern Slavery Agenda: Policy, Politics and Practice in the UK* (Policy Press 2019).

> they haven't had any extra funding to do that. I completely understand their predicament, but we then are often left sitting with someone not really knowing what's going to happen and that then potentially damages the relationship that you've built up over the last however long, if that's the ending. Endings are always hard and when someone hasn't necessarily got something to go on to, it comes back full circle to how we provide jobs, and a safety net for people?[16]

Frontline practitioners, who enter this field of work because they want to care for people, do not feel comfortable with the idea of cutting off contact with a survivor in need:

> Once they've been with you for six months there is more of a bond, and as a staff team you learn to care for these individuals so it's hard to step away from that, especially if there isn't an obvious progression or somebody else stepping in to take on that role.[17]

The reference to six months in the previous quote is also pertinent, as despite the recommended CG decision-making time of forty-five days, an exponentially increasing number of survivors are waiting much longer (see Chapter 2). The current backlog of cases has resulted in survivors having their NRM period extended – often more than once – which prolongs their wait for a decision and the ability to move on. Furthermore, until this decision is reached the Home Office is unable to make a negative decision on asylum claims, creating a knock-on delay to the UK's asylum system.[18] The government has been repeatedly criticised for its slow reaction to these issues,[19] and the financial impact on service providers and, consequently, state funding, has been noted by Parliament.[20] More directly, the effect of these delays on survivors is devastating, increasing their anxiety and rendering them in a state of perpetual limbo. By guaranteeing consistent support provision in the aftermath of a decision, the fears engendered during this waiting period could at least be managed. Practitioners are adamant that long-term support is essential to recovery:

> I think victims, if they've got enough time to – post-NRM – if they've got twelve months to really concentrate on getting the support that they need, just to recover a little bit, then I think you've got a much higher chance of those support services that come in further down the line,

16 Ayesha, Portsmouth, UK, 30 October 2018.
17 Rachel, London, UK, 11 May 2019.
18 National Audit Office, *Home Office: Reducing Modern Slavery* (HC 2017–19 630).
19 ibid.
20 Committee of Public Accounts, *Reducing Modern Slavery* (HC 2017–19 886).

> of actually making a real long term difference, whereas at the moment, we're only dealing with the crises that emerge without necessarily . . . if someone's not in a place to receive that or to progress much from it, the stuff that hasn't been dealt with will always resurface.[21]

> One of our survivors was rescued in 2015, and has just gone into long term employment, and there's not many charities that will stay in for that length of time.[22]

A fundamental and consistent suggestion is the need for a single specialist worker, or advocate, for survivors. While this is discussed in more detail in Sections 4.2 and 7.5, many participants also believed that the key to reliable long-term support was maintaining stability through this same approach:

> I think there needs to be much more consistent advocacy from start to . . . I mean, I don't actually believe there's ever an end really to victim support, that the more holistic approach needs to be taken with victim support, I certainly believe that's . . . definitely a priority in terms of supporting survivors successfully.[23]

> One of the most important aspects of support and care is an advocate who would, in an ideal world, see you through from beginning to recovery or if there isn't going to be somebody who is going to see you through, there's going to be a cohesive handover because the trust issue is real and very difficult. So, that the advocate for me is the most important bit.[24]

Additionally, this consistency would be achieved with the security of survivors knowing that they had a place to live and a plan for their future:

> A longer-term solution could be a leave to remain in the UK and understanding all the support that would need to come with that as well. I think there is something around job provision, training provision, understanding truly what survivors need and how long it's going to take them to recover from what they've been through and that almost needs to have a starting point so that we can then design and develop services based around their needs rather than around a policy or convention or what we think is best and I think that's what is missing at the moment.[25]

21 Rachel, London, UK, 11 May 2019.
22 Donna, Nottingham, UK, 10 May 2019.
23 Puja, Leeds, UK, 8 January 2019.
24 Caroline, Nottingham, UK, 22 November 2019.
25 Ayesha, Portsmouth, UK, 30 October 2018.

Moving on refers not just to the practical aspects of living self-sufficiently, but also to the psychological transition from 'victim' to integrated member of society. Survivors do not necessarily wish to be recognised solely as someone who has experienced trauma[26] and rebuilding and redefining one's identity is a fundamental element of recovery, as examined in Chapter 6. Engaging with other services and activities can be instrumental in achieving this:

> Then we look at community and social isolation because a lot of people when they come to us don't have a lot of community or family, and then looking at hope in the future so is the person wanting to build a family, do they need to get hold of their children from another country? It might be looking at what aspirations they've got, what educational desires they've got, what do they want to do employment-wise?[27]

> Lots of the men and women go out and volunteer in places, that's something else we've got partnerships with agencies where people can volunteer. They don't turn up as an [organisation] survivor, they just turn up as 'Kate' or 'Sarah', and actually they can be themselves so it's just trying to remove that label so they can disclose it if they want to but it's not our job to do.[28]

In addition to personal identity, financial security is also a major factor in moving on. Ultimately, this would be achieved through permanent, legitimate employment (see Section 8.2.3) but survivors are also eligible for compensation in the UK. This can be via a Reparation Order if a case reaches trial (see Section 7.5), while the Criminal Injuries Compensation Authority processes claims regardless of whether prosecution has occurred or traffickers have been identified.[29] As part of the Ministry of Justice, CICA manages a specific government fund that grants compensatory awards for victims of violent crime, including trafficking.[30] Individuals need to make an application outlining the

26 Sue Lockyer, 'Beyond Inclusion: Survivor-Leader Voice in Anti-Human Trafficking Organizations' (2022) 8(2) *Journal of Human Trafficking* 135–156 <>https://doi.org/10.1080/23322705.2020.1756122>.

27 Caroline, Nottingham, UK, 22 November 2019.

28 Ayesha, Portsmouth, UK, 30 October 2018.

29 Criminal Injuries Compensation Authority, 'About Us' (*UK Government*) <www.gov.uk/government/organisations/criminal-injuries-compensation-authority/about> accessed 23 October 2020.

30 Ministry of Justice, 'The Criminal Injuries Compensation Scheme' (The Stationary Office 2012) <https://assets.publishing.service.gov.uk/government/uploads/system/uploads/attachment_data/file/808343/criminal-injuries-compensation-scheme-2012.pdf> 10 November 2020.

nature of their criminal injury and there is an eligibility requirement but for some, the pay-out can be lifechanging:

> Not every person can claim compensation, just because of the difficulties within the law and it often takes a year, two years, sometimes three to claim compensation, it's a long haul, but at the end of it, on average our clients who've received compensation usually receive about £16 – 17,000, but the highest we've seen someone receive was £47,000 and she used it to go to university.[31]

The experiences of the previously mentioned individuals, while positive in the long run, demonstrate yet more delays and waiting in the life of a survivor. The Home Affairs Committee enquiry on modern slavery heard from several witnesses who complained about the length of time it took for CICA to reach a decision on survivor claims. Furthermore, the Committee heard that when awards were finally granted, the amounts were 'an absolute insult.'[32] CICA's published statistics only distinguish claims by the type of injury received so, as is the case with many areas of government records in this field, there is no measurable data to identify and compare for modern slavery and trafficking victims. In the meantime, most survivors have to rely on benefits while they wait for authorities and other stakeholders to make decisions and organise documentation that will entitle them to work. Diana outlined the problems of navigating the system:

> Oftentimes their documentation has been either controlled or managed or taken away by somebody else. Or they haven't got their ID on them, so it depends on how good that charity is in getting new ID, how quick they are. Because sometimes they can go through that NRM system and some of those processes haven't been done yet. So it's that uniformity, so you need to have every single charity singing from exactly the same hymn sheet.[33]

Moreover, the benefits themselves do not stretch far. Individuals under the NRM can 'in some cases' receive an allowance of £65 per week,[34] although accommodation, food and other basics are provided as part of the support package. Post-NRM, however, survivors who are also claiming asylum are not

31 Caroline, Nottingham, UK, 22 November 2019.

32 Witness D, *Oral Evidence, Modern Slavery*, HC 1460 (6 November 2018) Q111.

33 Diana, Bristol, UK, 22 February 2019.

34 After Exploitation, *Analysis: Trafficking Decisions on Non-EU Nationals "Nearly Five Times More Likely" to Be Rejected Than British Claims* (After Exploitation 2020) <https://after-exploitation.files.wordpress.com/2020/04/after-exploitation-analysis-nrm-statistics-2020.pdf> accessed 29 October 2020.

entitled to work and are given only £49.18 per week,[35] a sum which hasn't changed in line with inflation. This amounts to 'less than a third of the weekly spend of the poorest 10% of British citizens,'[36] leaving survivors at risk of destitution, homelessness and ultimately, vulnerability to further exploitation. Hodkinson et al. assert that this is another example of structural systemic discrimination that compounds rather than alleviates the problem of trafficking and modern slavery, primarily amongst non-EU nationals.[37] As Chapter 5 highlights, the immigration status of survivors is often instrumental in delayed recovery.

### *8.2.1 Accommodation*

Chapter 4 acknowledges that secure and safe accommodation is one of the most crucial factors in recovery and is thus a major step towards independent living. Access to accommodation, however, is not straightforward. The immigration status of survivors is frequently a major obstacle, as prospective tenants are legally required to provide proof of their eligibility to live in the UK.[38] The government's Statutory Guidance on accommodation states that '[a]dult potential victims at risk of destitution are eligible for Emergency Accommodation,'[39] which therefore only applies to those who are still in the NRM and waiting for an CG decision. Many practitioners express their frustration with current policies and practices:

> I worked in homelessness for a long time so I've worked with the benefits system, the housing/homelessness system, legally how you have to go around eviction procedures, all of that sort of thing, and then when you come across the last year, the Home Office stuff, it just . . . it's you know . . . it's unbelievably complicated and stupid.[40]

> Housing, I mean, that's such a huge issue but we're seeing survivors who are struggling even once they have status, they're going through this

35 UK Government, 'Asylum Support' (*UK Government*) <www.gov.uk/asylum-support/what-youll-get> accessed 15 March 2024.

36 Stuart N Hodkinson and others, 'Fighting or Fuelling Forced Labour? The Modern Slavery Act 2015, Irregular Migrants and the Vulnerabilising Role of the UK's Hostile Environment' (2020) 00(0) *Critical Social Policy* 1, 8.

37 ibid 1.

38 Home Office/UK Visas and Immigration, 'Code of Practice on Illegal Immigrants and Private Rented Accommodation' (*UK Government*, updated 29 September 2020) <www.gov.uk/government/publications/right-to-rent-landlords-code-of-practice/code-of-practice-on-illegal-immigrants-and-private-rented-accommodation-for-tenancies-starting-on-or-after-1-february-2016#excluded-agreements> accessed 12 October 2020.

39 Home Office, *Modern Slavery Act 2015: Statutory Guidance for England and Wales* (Home Office 2020) 41.

40 Becky, Sheffield, UK, 19 December 2018.

very challenging process of looking for housing and not having enough to put a deposit down and then they'll be on a waitlist for council housing but having to leave their accommodation and not knowing if they're gonna become homeless between leaving the accommodation and council. So there's got to be a way to plug that gap, that the government provided safehouse or accommodation must allow people to stay until they are secured in a council house.[41]

Some policies demand that survivors' housing security gets pushed right to the wire before statutory authorities will step in:

Our services are really disjointed so our homelessness teams will only pick someone up at the point where they are evicted so rather than saying 'this person is going to be leaving in three days, can we please work out a plan?' they don't have the right to reside but they will need homeless accommodation, the response will be 'no come to us and sit in the foyer of the homeless services when they are actually homeless.'[42]

Housing shortages exacerbate the situation, especially in areas like London, where waiting lists are already overwhelmed.[43] Rachel also identified a gender division in housing provisions, stating that the lack of independent accommodation disadvantaged single men:

Whilst on paper they might not be a high priority case, the risk of them actually becoming homeless or in inadequate accommodation is really high and hugely increases the potential for re-trafficking, although they aren't classed as a vulnerable adult by that point, actually they've still got a lot of vulnerabilities, so I think a lack of suitable good quality ongoing independent accommodation as a progression out of supported accommodation, there's a real lack of that.[44]

Lord McColl's Modern Slavery (Victim Support) Bill,[45] if passed, would automatically afford survivors twelve months' leave to remain in the UK as well as providing accommodation for that period. While this effort is to be applauded, it does not ultimately resolve the longer term challenges for survivors:

So Lord McColl's bill, of giving every identified victim a year to remain, whilst in principle, great, in practice, if it's a year to remain but they've

41 Jenni, Manchester, UK, 13 August 2019.
42 Ayesha, Portsmouth, UK, 30 October 2018.
43 Beddoe (n 8).
44 Rachel, London, UK, 11 May 2019.
45 Modern Slavery (Victim Support) HL Bill (2019–21).

> still got no job or access to education and we've still got a housing crisis, actually what are they doing in that year other than prolonging the inevitable?[46]

The 'inevitable,' in this case, is removal to an immigration detention centre or deportation; alternatively, survivors who fall through the Home Office net will have nowhere to go at all:

> If I'm honest, most times it hasn't been a truly positive outcome. Yes, we've had successes in convictions at court, but as far as the victims are concerned, it's very, very patchy. So, I can only talk from my experience. I had a case with chicken catchers down in Kent in 2013. 2013 . . . and in 2018 some of them were still homeless. That's the reality.[47]

Chapter 3 showed that, in the modern slavery support sector, 50% of accommodation is offered by organisations who only provide services for NRM survivors, with a considerable proportion of frontline services unable to directly provide any form of housing. The previous quote thus reiterates the fact that while immediate needs can be met following intervention, there has been very little government attention given to post-NRM survivors. Nevertheless, a 2020 legal development may provide some hope.[48] The Anti Trafficking and Labour Exploitation Unit (ATLEU) applied for Judicial Review following the Home Secretary's decision to refuse reinstatement of NRM support for a survivor (P) who had previously received a positive CG decision and was applying for discretionary leave to remain. P had been evicted from his asylum accommodation and faced destitution, but the secretary of state argued that, as P had left the NRM a year before, he was not entitled to further statutory support. ATLEU's claim was successful and a Consent Order was issued to reinstate NRM support for P, including accommodation. The case confirmed that survivors with positive CG decisions who had previously left the NRM are 'entitled to request reinstatement of support where the need arises,'[49] including those who are awaiting decisions on their application for discretionary leave to remain. While this is a step in the right direction, it does still place the onus on survivors to reach out for further support.[50]

46 Ayesha, Portsmouth, UK, 30 October 2018.

47 Diana, Bristol, UK, 22 February 2019.

48 ATLEU, 'Confirmed Victim of Trafficking Entitled to Reinstatement of Support after Being Exited from NRM' (*ATLEU*, 9 June 2020) <https://atleu.org.uk/cases/2020/6/9/confirmed-victim-of-trafficking-entitled-to-reinstatement-of-support-after-being-exited-from-nrm> accessed 13 October 2020.

49 ibid.

50 Beddoe (n 8).

#### *8.2.2 Education and vocational training*

Education can provide a lifeline to survivors who, for personal or practical reasons, are not yet ready for employment but who wish to build their skills and knowledge. Survivors who were trafficked as children will have gaps in their basic education, while adults may not have been given educational opportunities in their home country, a factor which contributed to being trafficked in the first place. As adults, however, access to education in the UK can present its own challenges. Very few colleges can accommodate the complex needs of survivors or deliver the type of educational programme that would be beneficial to them. Northern College, based in South Yorkshire, is an institution that provides education for adult learners, many of whom are 'familiar with unemployment or part-time, low paid jobs.'[51] The college offers mainly short, intensive residential programmes, with the aim of supporting access to higher education or building confidence and skills, depending on the individual students' wishes. In 2018, Northern College piloted its Free Thinking course, a ten-week programme written specifically for survivors of modern slavery. The course includes a variety of topics, including history, geography, outdoor activities, and creative arts, and accommodates language differences through translation software and digital recording.

In fact, foreign survivors who wish to remain in the UK will often find that language is one of their biggest obstacles. A limited understanding of English creates barriers to accessing healthcare and therapy, finding work and forging connections and friendships that will enable them to live independently.[52] English language classes are thus a popular aspect of survivor pathways – when Northern College offered ESOL[53] as an optional extra to its Free Thinking course, 'everyone turned up didn't they, even when they didn't have to!'[54] Many frontline support organisations also provide English classes, either in-house or through partnering with local colleges. Linguistic education does not even have to be formal, and survivors themselves have expressed the value of play in learning:

> What they said was that they wanted more English games because we sometimes, we would just play stupid word games, said that when they arrive, that those would be a good idea, just play more stupid word games so it gets their head into the English environment.[55]

51 Northern College, 'About us' (*Northern College*) <www.northern.ac.uk/about-us/> accessed 23 October 2020.

52 Kathryn Aldridge-Morris, 'The Importance of ESOL for the Victims of Modern Slavery' (2017) 28(2) *Language Issues* 63.

53 English for speakers of other languages.

54 Becky, Sheffield, UK, 19 December 2018.

55 ibid.

While this research did not seek to identify meaningful educational tools, there is an implication to be drawn that incorporating brief games into other support sessions will potentially help survivors to develop their English skills outside the classroom environment. There is also evidence to suggest that easing survivors into learning in this way is less daunting than a formal classroom setting. Unseen, therefore, has created the Butterfly Programme, which takes place within their safehouses and provides tailored, informal learning that prepares survivors for external classes and entering employment. English lessons are integral to the programme, especially for men; this survivor group is keen to earn money and, without the language skills, is vulnerable to re-exploitation in manual labour where English is not necessarily required.[56] Initiatives like the Butterfly Programme additionally tie in with the concept of trauma-informed services by recognising survivor apprehensions and accommodating their needs in a safe environment (see Chapters 4 and 6 for further discussion).

Beyond learning English, survivors who have lost years of their lives in captivity may have a desire to fulfil other missed educational opportunities. Education 'gives people their lives back . . . it's about building their hope for the future, actually starting to make plans again, planning what you want to do next.'[57] However, while there is enthusiasm from both survivors and practitioners, the current UK system does not create accessible avenues to formal adult education. Generally, this is a matter of funding:

> One thing that I see as a barrier is that people aren't able to get their Level 3, so people are able to get Level 2 at colleges covered but they're being halted in getting their Level 3 because of the cost, so if there could be some way that either to defer the cost so people can work, so people can pay the costs, so we're having people who don't have the right to work, so they have to go to college, but then they have a stop so they can't retrain.[58]

Nonetheless, it is possible that some education providers do not actually understand what survivors may be entitled to, as observed by one participant:

> What we have found is that most of the students that have come onto the course are actually eligible for ESFA[59] funding because they're asy-

56 Kathryn Aldridge-Morris, 'The Importance of ESOL for the Victims of Modern Slavery' (2017) 28(2) *Language Issues* 63.

57 Becky, Sheffield, UK, 19 December 2018.

58 Jenni, Manchester, UK, 13 August 2019.

59 Education and Skills Funding Agency (Homepage) (UK Government) <www.gov.uk/government/organisations/education-and-skills-funding-agency> accessed 23 September 2020.

> lum seekers who've been here for longer than six months. Regardless of that, we still find that they're being turned away from other colleges.[60]

This misunderstanding may be the result of rules that do not take the unique status of survivors into account. Funding for adult learners is provided if the applicant is an asylum seeker or claiming benefits; many survivors do not claim asylum, however, opting instead for Discretionary Leave, which does not feature on enrolment applications.[61] Survivors who are also prohibited from working at this point are thus left in a 'no man's land' where they are unable to begin building a future. Northern College is exploring options for linking in with businesses who could provide sponsorship for survivor students, which could assist with some funding issues. £5000 would pay for one student to complete the college's ten-week Free Thinking course, but some companies are

> only interested in these students that have been through this sort of trafficking. They're not interested in those ones, you know, domestic servitude, they're not interested in the sexual exploitation, it's the ones that are their responsibility because they've been found in their factories, that I think is their slant.[62]

Even where education fees can be secured, the practical aspects of accessing colleges can present another obstacle. Survivors who have been placed in accommodation in small villages or where transport links are poor can struggle to attend their timetabled classes; childcare difficulties can also be an issue. Some frontline organisations have successfully negotiated with local colleges to ensure inclusivity:

> At one place it was very heavily attended by men and our clients found that really difficult, then there was another class that was being provided in another location and that was great for women, but not for women with children because there was no childcare, so it was difficult for them to attend, so the gap we found in the city was ESOL provision with childcare. So we partnered with an ESOL provider and we said we will provide volunteers to do childcare and we'll train them and do the DBS checks if you can do the ESOL lessons.[63]

60 Becky, Sheffield, UK, 19 December 2018.
61 Kathryn Aldridge-Morris, 'The Importance of ESOL for the Victims of Modern Slavery' (2017) 28(2) *Language Issues* 63.
62 Becky, Sheffield, UK, 19 December 2018.
63 Caroline, Nottingham, UK, 22 November 2019.

Limited personal funds also place restrictions on access to public transport,[64] and Northern College has again considered tapping into local business resources to alleviate these concerns:

> Stagecoach run the minibus that comes up here. I've approached them once already but that was before we had a bit of press attention so I think I might get back in touch with them and say you know, just give us a load of free bus passes so we can give these people access to come here.[65]

Partnerships between non-profit organisations and businesses are growing in number (see Chapter 3) and this creative approach to improving services and survivor experiences is certainly worth further investigation. These links also establish an additional layer of trust and consistency enabling survivors to access external services more comfortably:

> So it's following up essentially on corporate connections and education connections, and trying to make those pathways smoother so that there aren't as many barriers for clients.[66]

Given its success so far, the Free Thinking programme stakeholders are looking at rolling out the course across other similar institutions. Unfortunately, funding could be a barrier to expansion:

> I'm hoping to do a little bit of campaigning and lobbying for other FE colleges to start thinking about their social purpose rather than their budgets and I know that it's a big risk. For us, I know you can say yeah, somebody comes on a three-day course, their asylum status is unlikely to change during those three days. Somebody signs on a six-month college course, then there is more of a likelihood that their asylum seeker status will change and I think people are not willing to take that risk.[67]

Much of the previous evidence suggests that the UK's adult learning infrastructure has simply not considered those students who do not fit the understood 'norms.' It would appear that there is a great appetite for education amongst survivors but they are precluded from learning by details that could be remedied by amendments to application forms and a more flexible approach from education providers. As a bridge from intervention to independence, language skills and other qualifications are valuable assets for survivors in the next step towards legitimate work.

64 Beddoe (n 8).
65 Becky, Sheffield, UK, 19 December 2018.
66 Caroline, Nottingham, UK, 22 November 2019.
67 Becky, Sheffield, UK, 19 December 2018.

### *8.2.3 Employment and employability*

Under the NRM, survivors are not allowed to work and even after a positive CG decision, their immigration status may still be a barrier to finding a job, as highlighted in Chapter 5. Education can provide a routine and sense of fulfilment as survivors wait for a change in circumstance; three quarters of the students on Northern College's 2018 Free Thinking course didn't have the right to work.[68] However, this is not a long-term solution and, as has been pointed out, 'let's face it, most survivors came here to work.'[69] Even in the event that an individual has the necessary immigration status and the right to work, the desire for purpose and gainful employment can override more nuanced legalities:

> We have people who have the legal status to work and then turn up and see their caseworker and say, 'I've got a job, I'm really excited. I'm working in this nail place and they're paying me £20 for a day's work and it's really exciting' and you're like 'Oh, not legal! Not OK! Let's have a look at the contract. Have you got a contract? No.'[70]

This stage in the process can present a dilemma for support providers. Given that a central aim of any survivor-centric organisation is to empower and encourage independence, the notion of identifying suitable job roles for themselves or undertaking an interview alone would appear to be a natural step. On the one hand, it is beneficial for survivors to enter the workforce as themselves, rather than under the label of 'trafficking victim'; however, unless an employer is exceptionally patient and sympathetic, they may not appreciate the additional needs of a survivor-worker:

> They'll do their job, they'll go to work. . . . There is a motivation to work, it's not about not working. And they get the job and they do the job for six months and then they go and move on and then they hear a gunshot outside the house, or somebody threatens them in a way that's a trigger and they just have this sudden down spiral where their whole world falls apart.[71]

> I think that one of the challenges has been people who are exiting [organisation] who we know are really good workers, very reliable, very committed, but probably if they've got a mainstream interview, wouldn't

68 Becky, Sheffield, UK, 19 December 2018.
69 Donna, Nottingham, UK, 10 May 2019.
70 Caroline, Nottingham, UK, 22 November 2019.
71 Donna, Nottingham, UK, 10 May 2019.

get the job. So it's that route into mainstream employment has also been a challenge for us.[72]

At the moment the job opportunities are only available for people who are legally allowed to be here and for people who are ready for work. I think we can guess that for a quite a few survivors being ready for work after 45 days in an NRM it isn't going to happen, so what kind of systems are we willing to put into place?[73]

The very nature of business as a profit-making enterprise also creates something of a conflict:

A business has got to be motivated to do it. Employing a survivor can be a rocky road and they're actually running a business. So you've almost got to be so motivated that you don't mind if that head count costs you the same money as your full time equivalent.[74]

Moreover, the time in confinement plus an extended period of prevention from legally working will mean long gaps in the CV,[75] something which survivors may not wish to discuss in applications or interviews. Acknowledging these challenges, a small number of initiatives have been founded to help develop survivors' employability skills and support them through the transition from safehouse to independence. The Bright Future programme was devised by the Co-op and launched in March 2017 in partnership with City Hearts, an independent organisation that provides post-NRM support to survivors.[76] The scheme initially operated within the Co-op's own food businesses, however, collaboration with other partners has grown significantly in since its inception. As well as joining forces with other frontline anti-slavery organisations such as the Salvation Army, Unseen UK and Kalayaan,[77] Bright Future has established a group of 21 business partners who can support and expand on the scheme in their own workplaces.[78] By July 2018, Dixons Carphone Warehouse and The Body Shop had signed up to the programme,[79] with John Lewis announcing

72 Rachel, London, UK, 11 May 2019.
73 Ayesha, Portsmouth, UK, 30 October 2018.
74 Donna, Nottingham, UK, 10 May 2019.
75 Hodkinson and others (n 36) 1.
76 Alex Balch and others, *Bright Future: An Independent Review* (University of Liverpool 2019).
77 ibid.
78 City Hearts, 'Bright Future' (*City Hearts*) <https://cityhearts.global/bright-future> accessed 23 October 2020.
79 Co-op, 'Ten UK Firms Join Jobs Scheme for Victims of Modern Slavery' (*Co-op*, 7 July 2018) <www.co-operative.coop/media/news-releases/ten-uk-firms-join-jobs-scheme-for-victims-of-modern-slavery> accessed 23 October 2020.

its backing weeks later.[80] Through the scheme, survivors are given a four-week paid work placement followed by a guaranteed non-competitive interview that potentially leads to permanent employment with the partnership company.[81] Bright Future claims that it has so far enjoyed a 73% success rate, with one survivor a month securing a permanent paid role.[82] Early reviews of the programme suggest that outcomes are largely positive, with City Hearts and the Co-op acting on recommendations swiftly. For example, the expansion of business partners was a direct response to findings that the programme needed to broaden and increase the range of placements available to survivors.[83] Additionally, Bright Future now identifies appropriate job opportunities for individuals through a national matching system, which includes a digital database that can 'streamline and automate communications between business and charity partners.'[84] Nevertheless, the review found that securing a placement in the first place was not always straightforward. Several business partners stated that only around one in five referrals ended in placement, with the most common reasons for non-placement being:

- English not at required level
- Right to work documentation not ready
- Ongoing charity partner support not in place for commencement of placement
- Instability in personal circumstances
- Arranging the initial meeting – it can be hard to match schedules
- Suitability of job opportunities[85]

Location also seemed to be a problem, with the Midlands highlighted as an area with a high number of referrals but not enough available placements to accommodate them.[86] Interestingly, two practitioners raised the same issue:

> There just aren't that many opportunities in the Midlands through Bright Futures so we've not had any successful referrals through them yet. But I think it's a really good model, it just needs expanding, so more options. I think, in the Midlands, they've got a Co-op stores, but they need someone with really good English who can do all roles, whereas we've got people who would be amazing at stacking shelves

80 Kieran Guilbert, 'Top UK Retailer John Lewis Backs Job Scheme for Slavery Victims' (*Thomson Reuters Foundation*, 23 July 2018) <www.reuters.com/article/us-britain-slavery-employment-john-lewis-idUSKBN1KD02A> accessed 23 October 2020.
81 Co-op (n 79).
82 City Hearts (n 78).
83 Balch and others (n 76).
84 ibid 9.
85 ibid 12.
86 ibid.

and accepting deliveries but who wouldn't work on the tills and so if we could get a large supermarket involved, that would be amazing.[87]

*Interviewer:* Is there anything else that you would like to see more available or completely available?

*Donna:* More employers. More 'move on' employers. So they've got to here . . . they've bought into employing survivors and with different levels of success depending on the survivor but their understanding of the issues, so yeah, many more businesses. Widening the jobs available so that there's more warehouse work, there's more kitchen work, there's more those low-level skilled jobs that survivors can do without many language skills. Cleaning jobs, hotel cleaning. There's loads of hotel cleaning jobs! So here, the social enterprises lean towards those things rather than customer services, which is what you've got in Birmingham.[88]

This further reiterates the need for accurate skills matching as well as expanding the programme to support the existing skills and employability of post-NRM survivors. It also alludes to the need for flexibility from employers, for example, enabling a survivor with poor spoken English to undertake tasks that are not customer facing without requiring them to fulfil a standard person specification for the job role.

The Jericho Foundation, which is itself based in the Midlands, provides training and employment to a more diverse range of clients. Founded in 1993, it supports individuals who have experienced homelessness, mental ill health or addiction, and has more recently expanded to include survivors of modern slavery.[89] Jericho offers a more intensive support package alongside its overarching project, making it a distinctive programme in this field. Each care plan is tailored to individual needs, including assistance with English lessons and access to healthcare:

> Mental health support, that can be something that fluctuates a lot so we'll help with firstly a referral into a GP, but then encourage if we can see someone's mental health is fluctuating, just trying to encourage survivors to act – we'll go with them to a GP for example, or make the referrals into specialist services. Also trying to overcome the fear. I think one of the barriers is not always knowing what services are available, so even though it's free to go to a GP, it is free to call 999, all those simple things that we take for granted, I think a lot of people don't appreciate that, it's a lot of education from the start.[90]

87 Rachel, London, UK, 11 May 2019.
88 Donna, Nottingham, UK, 10 May 2019.
89 Jericho, Home page (*Jericho Foundation*) <www.jericho.org.uk/> accessed 23 October 2020.
90 Rachel, London, UK, 11 May 2019.

Of course, this uniqueness requires many referred survivors to relocate, and reflects an underlying concern of 're-trafficking' during recovery, as shown in Chapters 3 and 4.

Although permanent, paid employment is more likely to occur towards the latter end of survivor recovery, it can make an enormous difference in their overall wellbeing and self-esteem:

> There's one quote that always sticks with me, with a guy who'd just started work with us, who said 'I've worked in the UK before but never been paid. Now I even get paid holiday, I feel like a king'. So not only was he being paid but actually valued enough to have paid holiday, I think you can't underestimate the impact of that on somebody who has been in exploitation . . . I think a lot of survivors really value that, being in a workplace where they're valued as an individual and they can share a joke and a laugh with people and they can learn to feel safe somewhere.[91]

This has been particularly noted in male survivors, for whom a strong part of identity is traditionally based in their work.[92] Across the board, however, the security and esteem that paid employment engenders can ultimately result in greater results for the wider system:

> All these people really want to do is work. So we are working in partnership with large labour users and providers, big supermarkets to see if there is a possibility, and it's happening already in some of our cases, where victims have been identified but they are given work and accommodation on another site that belongs to this larger organisation. Therefore, the victim has got what they want: they continue to work, they are continuing to earn money, they are still under the framework of the NRM, but then they have the ability, because they are still working, nine times out of ten, they are more likely to give evidence in court.[93]

In other words, where frontline organisations from all sectors can come together to create a network of support for survivors, the long-term outcomes are more positive for everyone involved.

## 8.3 Long-term outcome monitoring

Currently, there is no centrally managed monitoring system for survivor outcomes. Support providers can and do stay in contact with some survivors who

91 ibid.

92 Kathryn Aldridge-Morris, 'The Importance of ESOL for the Victims of Modern Slavery' (2017) 28(2) *Language Issues* 63.

93 Diana, Bristol, UK, 22 February 2019.

have moved on, but this is inconsistent, and there is no statutory requirement to do so.[94] In 2015, the Human Trafficking Foundation (HTF) carried out a review of post-NRM life for survivors. It highlighted the fact that there was scant information on long-term outcomes for survivors, noting that the Home Office acknowledged 'that there is no obligation in the government contract to monitor the outcomes for people who have received support or to collect data to show how survivors are assisted, and by whom, when they leave safe houses.'[95] Two years later, the National Audit Office raised the same point in its report on government progress in reducing modern slavery in the UK,[96] while an independent mapping study examining regional multi-agency partnerships found that '[o]nly tiny numbers were exploring the use of output or outcome measures, looking at the immediate products of their work or the longer-term impacts.'[97] By 2019, during the Modern Slavery Act Independent Review, Frank Field MP expressed his disgust at the continued lack of commitment:

> It is appalling that we collect no data whatever on what happens to those who enter the national referral mechanism for safety – they are mainly women, but some are men – once that period of safety ends. Most of our forebears would have been scandalised if they had allowed an Act to continue with that lack of data collection.[98]

The absence of efficient monitoring is concerning, not only for the paucity of tangible metrics of success, but because we have no way of knowing whether individuals are later re-trafficked.[99] There is some evidence to show that some individuals, with nowhere else to go, return to their original traffickers only to end up back in the NRM,[100] but, in keeping with a familiar theme across this book, the government does not record this data.[101] Consequently, even if authorities intervene again, the opportunity is missed:

> But once again, we've still got this problem where we anecdotally understand that this is happening, but it's then never recorded. So where on

94 Beddoe (n 8).
95 ibid 3.
96 National Audit Office, *Home Office: Reducing Modern Slavery* (HC 2017–19 630).
97 Office of the Independent Anti-Slavery Commissioner and University of Nottingham's Rights Lab, *Collaborating for Freedom: Anti-slavery Partnerships in the UK* (University of Nottingham and the Independent Anti-Slavery Commissioner 2017) 18.
98 HC Deb 19 June 2019, vol 662, cols 127WH-128WH.
99 National Audit Office, *Home Office: Reducing Modern Slavery* (HC 2017–19 630).
100 Samantha Ferrell-Schweppenstedde, *Day 46: Is There Life after the Safe House for Survivors of Modern Slavery?* (Human Trafficking Foundation 2016).
101 Letter from Sarah Newton MP to Chair of Work and Pensions Committee (17 February 2017) <https://old.parliament.uk/documents/commons-committees/work-and-pensions/

> the NRM form is there a place where it records that this person was a victim of re-trafficking or this person has come out of the NRM prior to being identified? There isn't.[102]

However, one piece of research suggests that collecting follow-up data from survivors is costly in terms of both human resources and finances.[103] Drawing on the experiences of domestic abuse services, it also found that over longer periods of time, retention decreased, leaving an unrepresentative sample of respondents at the latter end of evaluations.[104] In 2013, two years before the HTF report, the Centre for Social Justice recommended the development of an outcome-based support model for aftercare providers, adding that providers should establish partnerships with other local organisations to 'facilitate a reintegration-focussed package of support.'[105] The concept of an outcome-based support model, particularly in alliance with other agencies, could offer survivors consistency of service across the UK as well as tailoring support to their individual needs. This reinforces the idea of collaborating with service users, encouraging survivors to define success on their own terms.[106] The development of long-term trusting relationships between survivors and the frontline organisations responsible for collating follow-up data would also enhance retention in the future.[107] As with many other aspects of survivor support, a framework for this type of ongoing partnership work already exists in the domestic abuse sector. Multi-agency risk assessment committees (MARACs) operate across the UK and comprise representatives from relevant local stakeholders including the police, social services, the NHS, Women's Aid and Rape Crisis, who confidentially discuss individual cases and work together to establish an appropriate care pathway and additional support links. The suggestion of a system based on the MARAC has been put forward by practitioners[108] and academics[109] but has so far not been converted into a statutory requirement.

Notably, there is a difference between *outputs* and *outcomes*.[110] While outputs can provide information on quantitative data, such as referral figures and engagement in service projects, outcomes are more reflective of wider goals

Letter-from-Sarah-Newton-MP-to-Chair-re-modern-slavery-session-17–2–2017.pdf> accessed 27 October 2020.

102 Diana, Bristol, UK, 22 February 2019.

103 Kathleen E Krieger and others, 'Evaluating Human Trafficking Service Programs: What Can Be Learned from Domestic Violence Service Program Evaluations' (2020) *Journal of Human Trafficking* <>https://doi.org/10.1080/23322705.2020.1784686>.

104 ibid.

105 Centre for Social Justice (n 4) 180.

106 Steiner and others (n 71) 151.

107 Krieger (n 103).

108 Beddoe (n 8).

109 Murphy (n 1).

110 Krieger (n 103).

and aims. As part of an agreed-upon ongoing support plan, they can outline anticipated survivor outcomes, meaning that successes can be evaluated at various points in service delivery.

## 8.4 Agency, influence and the survivor voice

Any research, particularly that which seeks to influence policy, should necessarily seek to establish the views, perspectives and experiences of those at the heart of the phenomenon. In the field of modern slavery support, however, survivor voices are notably lacking in both academic literature and policy evidence.[111] This has not gone unnoticed by practitioners either:

> I think the survivor voice is lacking period. I don't know if it is one aspect. But what is frustrating to me is that we take for granted and believe that it is normal and OK to have most people who work in the field not be the people who are most affected by the issue.[112]

*Interviewer:* How strongly do you feel that survivor's voices are heard at the moment?
*Ayesha:* I think the flippant answer would be not at all.[113]

At this relatively early stage after the enactment of the Modern Slavery Act, it is perhaps unsurprising that policy-makers are still evaluating and reforming support initiatives. Nonetheless, many researchers and academics have reached out to agencies with a view to inviting survivors to give their opinions, only to be refused. A dearth of survivor-led input means that the available information and data about modern slavery experiences can be unreliable;[114] this impacts decision-making and criminal intelligence by failing to identify the 'systemic issues and root causes which contribute to the crime.'[115] For instance, the earlier heavy focus on the sexual exploitation of women and girls eclipsed the fact that men and boys can also become victims of sexual slavery, or that labour exploitation occurs in a multitude of otherwise legitimate industries. An even more damaging outcome of this selectiveness is how it filters through to victims and survivors themselves:[116] if policy initiatives and media concern is directed towards females in sex trafficking, how can a forty-five-year-old male agricultural worker see himself as a victim of slavery? In fact, a significant issue for survivors of any trauma is how they define what has happened to them.

111 RL Curran and others, 'A Theory for Aftercare of Human Trafficking Survivors for Nursing Practice in Low Resource Settings' (2017) 35 *Applied Nursing Research* 82.
112 Jenni, Manchester, UK, 13 August 2019.
113 Ayesha, Portsmouth, UK, 30 October 2018.
114 Lockyer (n 26).
115 ibid 4.
116 Frontline practitioner, in conversation.

Modern slavery survivors, particularly those who have been trafficked from other countries, may be unacquainted with the terminology that is frequently used to describe their experiences.[117] Upon intervention from the authorities, many victims are more inclined to focus on their asylum or immigration needs rather than disclosing the details of their enslavement.[118] Legal terms referring to their immigration status or criminal justice case are also unlikely to be familiar to them, resulting in detention at an immigration centre or prosecution for crimes committed during the course of their exploitation (see Chapters 5 and 7). This places an emphasis on their 'otherness' as an offender in an unfamiliar country while reinforcing any internalised beliefs that they have been employees rather than abused slaves. Moreover, this disconnect feeds into how survivors define *themselves*:

> They are defined by everybody else apart from themselves. Lots of people don't even . . . I think they understand that what's happened to them is wrong but I'm not sure that they . . . the concept of trafficking and slavery is a really interesting one and often when I interview people they would say, when I ask the question before we even start just to make sure they understand why they are there and they often say 'My lawyer has told me that trafficking is . . .' so they understand what's happened to them isn't what they wanted but the language that we assign to them isn't always the language that they would assign to themselves.[119]

Consequently, the potential for survivors to collaborate in research and policy is eroded by the state's 'hostile environment,' in contradiction to its proclaimed victim-centred approach to modern slavery.[120]

Alternatively, survivors can be infantilised by those who intend to help them, reframing them as childlike and overly vulnerable.[121] For example, one participant from a faith-based organisation repeatedly referred to 'rescuing' people, which reflected the wider sentiments of the organisation itself. Although well-meaning, this type of saviour complex can reinforce the label of 'victim,'[122] which again establishes an identity that has been defined by others. Furthermore, by appointing themselves as protectors during the post-intervention period, some organisations risk the continued disempowerment of their

117 David M Doyle and others, '"I Felt Like She Owns Me": Exploitation and Uncertainty in the Lives of Labour Trafficking Victims in Ireland' (2019) 59 *British Journal of Criminology* 231.

118 ibid.

119 Ayesha, Portsmouth, UK, 30 October 2018.

120 Doyle and others (n 117) 231.

121 Alexandra C Duncan and Dana DeHart, 'Provider Perspectives on Sex Trafficking: Victim Pathways, Service Needs, & Blurred Boundaries' (2019) 14(4) *Victims & Offenders* 510.

122 Lockyer (n 26).

service users and 'it becomes a repetition of paternalistic behaviours.'[123] Some service providers are already aware of the risks of being too protective. Ayesha stated that an overriding principle of her organisation was 'not viewing oneself as "the rescuer" and the answer to everything,'[124] and most participants acknowledged that organisations cannot pre-empt every eventuality for individual survivors:

> For NGOs to say 'Well, we're really afraid to send a survivor to X, Y or Z city because they're gonna get triggered', you know, we live with getting triggered so for us its about preventing that so we would never stop programming for that, which doesn't mean we're not paying attention to that, so that's where I feel like the paternalism can come in, which is 'we know what's better for you.'[125]

> Yes, we are dealing with people who have been through horrific things but they have survived those horrific things and they are adults and they will still make interesting choices and we might not agree with those choices but just because they have been a victim of something they don't have free will and the right to be empowered.[126]

Where policy and organisational decisions are made in the best interests of survivors, but without survivor input, it can give rise to a sense of gatekeeping or lack of transparency. Research on domestic violence survivor support has explored how service users respond to the rules of sheltered accommodation. Regulations that either restrict individual autonomy, for instance, curfews or drug/medication policies, or place conditions on residency (mandatory services or contributing to chores) were found to be problematic for some survivors. Essentially, it was felt that disproportionate rules, especially where they were not fully explained or justified, were paternalistic and exhibited signs of coercive control.[127] In fact, where support workers do not feel compelled to 'hide behind' rules and regulations, it enables them to respond more proactively to survivors and thus engenders more individualised support pathways.[128] Higher levels of transparency also increase service users' understanding and appreciation of 'the extent to which the projects undertaken contribute to achieving

123 Jenni, Manchester, UK, 13 August 2019.

124 Ayesha, Portsmouth, UK, 30 October 2018.

125 Jenni, Manchester, UK, 13 August 2019.

126 Ayesha, Portsmouth, UK, 30 October 2018.

127 Shanti Joy Kulkarni and others, 'Successful Rules Reduction Implementation Process in Domestic Violence Shelters: From Vision to Practice' (2019) 64(2) *Social Work* 147.

128 ibid.

the mission of the organization.'[129] However, participants also acknowledged their own internal conflict as a result of encouraging autonomy in survivors:

> I usually say to [staff] one of the hardest things you will experience in support work of survivors of trafficking is that if you are genuinely going into it from an empowering perspective, then what you will do as a case-worker is returning control to people's lives. You have to be OK with people making their own decisions.[130]

> The hardest thing probably is when people start building that, they start pushing back. It's hard for the staff, but it's an indication that what they're doing is good because people are finding their voice and they are telling us what they want and it is a pain but it's brilliant because we are actually getting somewhere.[131]

Ultimately, service providers need to strike the balance between supporting survivors and alleviating the potential for unexpected triggers or challenges while steadily directing them towards independence:

*Jenni:* That's where paternalism comes in, NGOs think they have to make the decisions and why can't they be collaborative decisions?

*Interviewer:* So that it's a partnership, rather than practitioner-client?

*Jenni:* Yes, and that has to be individualised, and I know that practitioners feel their hands are tied because it's like 'If I let you do this, I have to let everyone else do this' and that seems to be not tailoring people's interventions. Sometimes that's true, where if I let someone stay out of the shelter until 1am I have to let everyone, there may be certain realms where that's necessary and certain realms where it's not really a good reason.[132]

Although greater survivor input is to be welcomed in decision-making, organisations still need to manage the balance between inclusion and exploitation.[133] Where survivors become the face of anti-slavery campaigns, for instance, there is a risk of re-traumatisation if individuals are required to repeatedly talk about

129 J David Cabedo and others, 'Improving and Measuring Transparency in NGOs: A Disclosure Index for Activities and Projects' (2018) 28 *Nonprofit Management and Leadership* 329, 338.
130 Caroline, Nottingham, UK, 22 November 2019.
131 Ayesha, Portsmouth, UK, 30 October 2018.
132 Jenni, Manchester, UK, 13 August 2019.
133 Nellie Peyton, 'Don't Treat Us Like Zoo Animals, Say Trafficking Survivors' (*Thomson Reuters Foundation*, 14 November 2018) <www.reuters.com/article/us-slavery-conference-survivors-idUSKCN1NJ28B> accessed 13 October 2020.

their experiences.[134] Survivors themselves will often report that while much attention is given to their testimonies, policy makers are less inclined to listen to their suggestions for developing and improving support services.[135] Charities and statutory agencies will also ask survivors to give up their time and knowledge for free, without considering the ramifications of their request. As experts, survivors of modern slavery deserve to be compensated for their valuable contributions towards the eradication of this crime.[136] Conversely, charities who are overwhelmed with requests for survivor input may opt to universally close off this avenue – they do not wish to re-traumatise their service users or exhaust them with a series of interviews and conversations with strangers.[137] However, this creates a barrier to survivors who do wish to share their narrative with the wider world. Ayesha stated that when politicians visited her organisation, the survivors they spoke with 'found it cathartic to talk to people and explain what is good and what isn't good about the system.'[138] At this relatively early point in modern slavery support, a structured and robust evaluation of services is vital but there is more than one way to capture the survivor voice. The Modern Slavery and Human Rights Policy and Evidence Centre was established with the aim of encouraging greater collaboration between frontline practitioners and researchers and discussion is underway to create a central database of those who wish to either contribute or request contributions for the furthering of knowledge in this area.[139] This simple solution will reduce the volume of cold calls to busy agencies and provide current and reliable data that can inform policy decisions. Organisations are also in the best position to gather information that can be useful for wider dissemination:

> There are different ways of hearing survivor voices, we have just done a big evaluation on our men's project and we asked all the staff and survivors to contribute but they didn't have to do an interview, they wrote things down and we recorded stuff so we've got the voice in there.[140]

Meanwhile, a project by the Rights Lab, undertaken over a five-year period, has collated over one thousand survivor narratives and made them available for free online.[141] The purpose of this database is to enable organisations to

134 Lockyer (n 26).
135 Rights Lab, *Nothing about Us, Without Us Survivor Involvement in Anti-slavery Policy Making: Guidance for Policy Makers* (University of Nottingham 2020).
136 ibid.
137 Observational data from interactions in the field.
138 Ayesha, Portsmouth, UK, 30 October 2018.
139 Colleagues at the Modern Slavery and Human Rights Policy and Evidence Centre, informal meeting.
140 Ayesha, Portsmouth, UK, 30 October 2018.
141 Antislavery Usable Past, 'Voices: Narratives by Survivors of Modern Slavery' (*Antislavery Usable Past)* <www.antislavery.ac.uk/solr-search?facet=collection:%22VOICES:+Narratives+by+Survivors+of+Modern+Slavery%22> accessed 14 October 2020.

'to understand forms of slavery, what survivors require in regard to their own welfare in the wake of enslavement, and how organisations can design interventions to better prevent slavery and support survivors.'[142]

Another reason for low levels of survivor input is due to overall changes in the voluntary sector, as examined in Chapter 3. Grassroots charities run by individuals with experience of their own cause continue to operate in the UK, but there is an increasing move towards professionalisation within the sector.[143] Domestic abuse organisations exemplify this phenomenon: Women's Aid was founded in the backdrop of second wave feminism in the 1970s by women who had left abusive relationships.[144] While the idea of survivor-led services remains central to the ethos of the organisation, salaried roles that demand skilled employees with 'significant proven experience and practical support to survivors of domestic violence,'[145] DBS checks and a comprehensive understanding of the legal system may prevent a survivor from even applying. It is essential that vulnerable individuals are supported by professional workers who can help them navigate through complex legal issues and appropriately manage their trauma, but the space between practitioners and survivors needs to be bridged. Survivor Alliance is the UK's first fully survivor-based organisation for people who have experienced trafficking and slavery. Founded by Minh Dang, a prominent figurehead of the survivor voice, the organisation aims to create 'leaders of the anti-slavery movement'[146] and is strongly focused on empowerment through developing skills and knowledge. While many survivors will wish to pursue employment that is far removed from their exploitative experiences, the move towards improving opportunities for inclusion in decision-making is promising.

It is also important to note that survivors are not a homogenous group with easily identifiable traits:[147]

> It's really, really hard when you are talking about individuals who have had such differing experiences, from different cultural backgrounds, nationalities and faith backgrounds, the survivor voice is something that

142 Rights Lab, *Voices: Ideas for Using Survivor Testimony in Antislavery Work* (University of Nottingham 2019).

143 Lockyer (n 26).

144 Women's Aid, 'Strength in Number and Unity: Over 40 Years of Tackling Domestic Abuse' (*Women's Aid*, 29 November 2015) <www.womensaid.org.uk/16-days-strength-in-number-and-unity-over-40-years-of-tackling-domestic-abuse/> accessed 7 October 2020.

145 Salford Women's Aid, 'IDVA Job Advert' (*Women's Aid*) <www.womensaid.org.uk/job/idva-10/> accessed 7 October 2020.

146 Survivor Alliance, 'Vision and Mission' (*Survivor Alliance*) <www.survivoralliance.org/about> accessed 7 October 2020.

147 Rights Lab (n 135).

> is really hard to capture, because for one it would be incredibly different to another.[148]

This is a significant factor in media representation and, consequently, public understanding of trafficking victims. Cultural stereotypes and beliefs relating to race, gender, and class influence wider depictions of modern slavery, with negative repercussions for survivors, whose experiences of exploitation are reduced to clichés or misrepresentations.[149] Often, survivors are labelled via the binary of 'either pitiful traumatised or amazing resilient,'[150] neither of which consider the complexities and individual characteristics of such a diverse demographic. This diminishment of identity also correlates with perspectives of the 'ideal victim,'[151] where social attitudes and beliefs are applied to victims of crime; thus a little old lady beaten and robbed by a drug dealer would usually be treated with the utmost sympathy, while a sex worker who has been raped by a punter could be judged more cynically by some quarters. Furthermore, 'ideal victims' garner more media and public attention. Walklate's study on victim narratives looked at the case of Rosie Batty, an Australian woman whose son was murdered, and examined the factors that amplified Ms Batty's voice over others. Walklate concluded that societal attitudes around the 'ideal victim' and the moral persuasion of the narrative contributed heavily towards the amount of notice a survivor's story received. Additionally, Ms Batty was a 'skilled communicator; sufficiently resilient to speak to the media the day after [her son's] death and to communicate her message in innumerable public forums over a period of months and years.'[152] Traumatised individuals with a limited grasp of English do not have this level of control over how and where their stories are told, whereas articulate survivors are more likely to hold an audience's gaze. Moderate levels of media and public attention create more demand, which culminates in a handful of regular, prominent voices in the field. Presenting one or two survivor narratives as representative of all modern slavery experiences can ultimately result in tokenism,[153] which 'privileges individual experience over aggregate data.'[154] This skews wider understanding of the subject and can lead to limited or inappropriate policy decisions.

148 Ayesha, Portsmouth, UK, 30 October 2018.
149 Steiner and others (n 71) 151, 165.
150 Jenni, Manchester, UK, 13 August 2019.
151 Nils Christie, 'The Ideal Victim' in Ezzat A Fattah (ed), *From Crime Policy to Victim Policy* (Tavistock 1986).
152 Sandra Walklate and others, 'Victim Stories and Victim Policy: Is There a Case for a Narrative Victimology?' (2019) 15(2) *Crime Media Culture* 199, 207.
153 Lockyer (n 26).
154 Walklate and others (n 152) 199, 211.

## 8.5 Conclusion

This chapter was primarily concerned with the support systems available to survivors in the long term, evaluating consistencies and disparities in service delivery and identifying areas of good practice and barriers to success. Although the Modern Slavery (Victim Support) Bill is making its slow but steady passage through Parliament, more and more survivors are still leaving the brief security of NRM-mandated services and finding themselves without a safety net. This not only places them at risk of destitution and vulnerability to re-trafficking, it can erode trust with the very system that was created to help them. Fundamentally, where structures are not in place to enable survivors to move on, this creates a 'revolving doors' system and any previous support and assistance is nullified. A repeated theme throughout this book is that of consistency: that is, for survivors to enjoy a support pathway that takes them from intervention to independence, there has to be enduring stability every step of the way. The evidence analysed in this chapter shows that most frontline support organisations fully endorse this approach and do their best to implement it. Unfortunately, it is external elements that create obstacles to consistency. The UK's education and employment systems are simply not designed to accommodate individuals who are legally entitled to live here but who remain undocumented. This problem is exacerbated by survivors' ongoing complex needs surrounding trauma and language barriers. It should be remembered, however, that immigration status, psychological wellbeing and communication skills are potentially temporary issues; with the right changes, there is no reason why this state of temporariness cannot be supported by bridges in the system which assist survivors in moving forward. The Bright Future scheme has achieved this with its access to employment programme and, through receptiveness to constructive criticism, has adapted accordingly and continues to develop in this way. Flexibility, therefore, is also key.

Where these gaps in long-term support have been identified on the ground, the data indicates that yet again, the voluntary sector is picking up the shortfall. In fact, when it comes to post-NRM support, the government appears to be largely absent from the picture. Chapter 4 highlighted the government's eagerness to move survivors on from the NRM as quickly as possible and there is little to suggest that they are concerned about them beyond this point. The distinct lack of statutory outcome and long-term monitoring means that we have no data on survivor welfare after they leave their safehouses, creating a vacuum that is underpinning the revolving doors system. There is no rationale to designing policies that focus all their efforts on the initial intervention if those efforts are eventually wasted. For this reason alone, it is in the government's best interests to listen to survivors.

However, while one of the aims of this book was to examine the survivor pathway through the UK's support systems, this has only been possible through the proxy of frontline practitioners and a limited amount of already-published data. Even though the data shows that support agencies are unhappy at the lack of survivor input in policy decisions, several of those agencies also act as gatekeepers to their service users, thereby reinforcing the problem. Some frontline organisations are doing an excellent job of promoting survivors as 'real people' and acknowledging their agency and identity, but the tendency of others to protect and make decisions on survivors' behalf prevents them from being heard. Ultimately, only survivors know what it is like to have these experiences, and only they can fully understand what works for them and choose how and when to provide that narrative.

# 9 Conclusion

This book aimed to examine the effectiveness of the UK's legislation and policies for the support of modern slavery survivors and drew on a range of sources to develop a broad and detailed picture of the modern slavery survivor support system in the UK. From this, five key findings have been identified, which are listed and discussed in the following. These findings, it is hoped, will contribute to frontline practice within the area of survivor support. Finally, I offer some recommendations based on my key research findings and indicate some potential avenues for further research and future policy decision-making.

## 9.1 Summary

Evaluation of the UK's legislation, policies and practices in supporting modern slavery survivors reveals that 'successes' and 'limitations' here are not mutually exclusive. Chapter 2 demonstrates that a strong impetus to tackle the issue of modern slavery over the past decade or so has led to wide public awareness and an investigative framework that is admired by counterparts abroad. As a result of this growth, the discovery and of trafficked individuals and victims of modern slavery has surpassed early expectations. Unfortunately, the numbers have also exceeded the anticipated capacity of key organisations, leading to exponentially increasing waiting lists in the National Referral Mechanism and pressure on frontline agencies to continue supporting survivors during these extended waiting periods. Chapters 4 and 8 reiterated the issue, and there are strong indications that the government currently relies heavily on the goodwill and fundraising efforts of independent organisations to cater for complex support needs beyond standard frameworks of service delivery. Chapter 3 additionally shows that this has evolved from a growing governmental tendency to contract to the lowest bidder, resulting in a shortfall of funding across the voluntary sector. The subsequent effects of this include diminishing specialist support services, a theme which was further picked up in Chapter 6, where therapeutic intervention for survivors was shown to be much-needed but difficult to access, particularly within the state-funded NHS. Chapter 2, along with Chapter 7, also showed the heavy emphasis on a criminal justice approach to modern slavery in the UK. Here, the UK system runs

DOI: 10.4324/9781032639895-9

into some serious limitations as the criminal justice process is operated primarily by state actors and state-funded organisations. While there is certainly an option to liaise with voluntary sector and other relevant stakeholders, the evidence suggests that it is only law enforcement officers such as the police and the Gangmasters and Labour Abuse Authority who are inclined to do so. This has created something of a binary system at the court levels, in which survivors become witnesses for the Crown rather than integral to their own justice. Finally, Chapter 5 presented findings that demonstrate how another key area of UK policy – immigration – has been targeted to the detriment of survivor support. Where survivor needs conflict with provisions across immigration legislation, the data strongly suggests that immigration enforcement is likely to be the default course of action.

The exploration of the support systems currently in place largely combined with an analysis of the landscape of the UK's support provider networks. Chapter 3 clearly demonstrated the polarity of urban and rural areas in this regard, with London, West Yorkshire and the West Midlands providing a higher and more diverse number of support services than regions such as East Anglia and Cumbria. Chapters 4 and 8 further illustrated pockets of well-connected support provisions, ranging from individual specialist services working in cohesion to multi-partnership, cross-sector networks headed by committed and enthusiastic leadership. However, this again tended to gravitate in urban areas rather than more isolated regions. One of the significant difficulties in developing a rich and detailed representation of survivor pathways is the lack of central monitoring. Chapter 2 demonstrates that there is very little political will to record or publish data that would help us to better understand the full picture. This lack of monitoring is even starker in the long term, as Chapter 8 discusses. Perhaps the most negative outcome of this is in relation to immigration, where Chapter 5 showed the impacts on survivors who have been misidentified as immigration offenders and removed from support altogether. Once again, this can re-traumatise vulnerable survivors and result in delays to their NRM claims or worse, detention and deportation.

In terms of areas of good practice, there is much to be hopeful about. There is clearly a strong commitment from individual frontline practitioners and their respective organisations to continually improve support for modern slavery survivors. Chapters 4 and 8, in particular, identified specific projects and organisational practices that have been demonstrated to yield positive outcomes. There is also motivation from some of these stakeholders to roll out their ideas across other parts of the UK, either in partnership with other local agencies or as part of training and development initiatives. Communication was also a clear theme, with the evidence showing that multi-partnership working brings positive outcomes for both support providers and survivors. Barriers to success are, somewhat unsurprisingly, based on resource limitations, as discussed in Chapters 3, 4 and 8. While the government may rely heavily on the voluntary sector to undertake the majority of survivor support, the voluntary sector itself requires some co-operation from the public sector, particularly health and social care. Where these resources are lacking and, to reiterate the theme of communication, where other professionals are unwilling to share information, the system becomes fragmented. This leads to delays for survivors, which can be re-traumatising. Further barriers exist within the criminal justice system when appropriate support is not provided to assist survivors through the justice process. A more collaborative approach between criminal justice professionals and frontline support providers can improve criminal intelligence and evidence gathering, which benefits the overall modern slavery system.

Finally, an investigation into ways of improving or providing alternative, beneficial means of support to survivors revealed diverse and creative approaches across each facet of the support pathway. Chapter 2 discussed the current Modern Slavery (Victim Support) Bill, which would provide a guaranteed twelve months of support, while Chapter 6 highlighted the specific therapeutic support provisions that this Bill would afford survivors. As outlined, Chapters 4 and 8 demonstrated the frontline commitment to continually build on current successes. Another key theme throughout was consistency, and there is broad support for individual specialist key workers who would provide support from intervention to recovery. It is perhaps in the area of criminal justice, in Chapter 7, that the most innovative changes might be made. A greater focus on witness inclusion and more survivor-centric approaches to 'justice' could not only benefit survivors, but the modern slavery system as a whole.

Overall, this book argues that the current modern slavery legal framework is too narrow in scope to fulfil its aims of crime prevention and survivor protection. While the UK government maintains a predominantly criminal justice approach, it is placing a heavy reliance on other, non-governmental organisations to fund and manage the support of survivors. This has led to a lack of clarity and consistency in survivor pathways across the UK, with poor or unavailable data on various facets of the process, particularly post-NRM outcomes. This book additionally shows that conflicting policy and legislative initiatives, primarily those concerning immigration enforcement, have resulted in shifting survivors from victim to offender status, negating any positive impact that support provisions may have delivered. There is a strong argument for more cohesive partnership working, with positive steps being made primarily by those at the frontline. While there are clear indications that creative and innovative approaches to survivor support are beneficial, this needs to be backed up by political will and greater financial input.

## 9.2 Key findings

1. *Survivors are faced with delays throughout the entire process*
   This begins with extensions in the NRM period, which lead to uncertainty and delays to recovery. Until an NRM decision is confirmed, the Home Office is also unable to make a decision on asylum claims. Beyond this, survivors frequently have to wait for appropriate accommodation, while waiting lists for therapeutic intervention will significantly prolong the rehabilitation

process. Where vulnerable survivors struggle to provide legally reliable evidence, criminal justice can also take a long time to achieve.

2. *The UK government is too swift to move potential victims and survivors on*
   The data clearly shows that the government seeks to remove survivors from statutory support as soon as possible. This is often via the 'cliff edge' at the end of the NRM process, however, there is no statutory support for post-NRM survivors and their immigration status frequently means they are unable to access avenues that would be instrumental in their long-term recovery, for example, independent accommodation, education and employment opportunities. More crucially, by redesignating some survivors as offenders of immigration laws or through criminal activity undertaken in captivity, individuals are removed from support systems altogether and are instead placed at risk of re-traumatisation in detention.
3. *The current support landscape is patchy and inconsistent*
   The concentration of support providers in London, West Yorkshire and the West Midlands, paired with limited accommodation, means that survivors are frequently transferred across the country in order to receive the support they need. This not only effectively 're-trafficks' them but potentially damages their own support networks and any modern slavery criminal investigation that is taking place. Where communication is poor between agencies, this leads to further inconsistencies and potential delays for survivors in recovery.
4. *There is a distinct fragmentation within the overall modern slavery system*
   The government has narrowly compartmentalised its role in the survivor pathway and although statutory funding to voluntary services has increased since the introduction of the Victim Care Contract, there is a heavy reliance on the goodwill of all relevant organisations to manage a growing and complex workload. Individual agencies are often required to undertake tasks that either detract from their core roles and responsibilities, as in the case of law enforcement, or conflict with their primary objectives such as immigration control.
5. *Greater emphasis is needed on providing specialist support for complex needs*
   Almost all survivors will be managing emotional and mental health issues relating to the trauma they have experienced in captivity, which may include coping strategies that have resulted in addiction. Their holistic needs are therefore complex and will only be exacerbated by uncertainty and repeated changes to their status.

## 9.3 Recommendations

Based on the key findings outlined previously, I propose the following recommendations for future policy and practice decisions:

- Every survivor is entitled to a consistent quality of care and support from each organisation they come into contact with. Standardised training should therefore be given as a minimum for all frontline practitioners. This should incorporate awareness training of each agency's roles and responsibilities to ensure that communication between partners is maintained appropriately. Consistency of support would be best achieved through a single specialist advocate (SSA), who would be a first port of call for all aspects of their support pathway.

- Resources should be more evenly distributed to allow survivors to build a community in the area they reside in. While prevalence of local and regional support should reflect the population in those areas, once a survivor has been removed from their trafficker, every effort should be made to provide a consistent and secure support pathway within the area the survivor is now living in. This will reduce instances of 'retrafficking' within the system and empower the survivor as they develop knowledge and understanding of their environment, with continued assistance from an SSA.
- All stakeholder organisations need to employ at the very least a trauma-informed approach. Where the core functions of the organisation mean that it is not possible for frontline staff to undertake emotional responsibility (for instance, police officers), partnerships should be developed with those agencies who can provide emotional and practical support that will help the survivor to navigate the process.
- Stronger partnerships will result in better, more consistent support pathways for survivors. While it is vital to adhere to confidentiality, all channels of communication should be kept open and transparent to appropriate parties, including the survivor. Survivors should be empowered to make decisions on their support pathways and their role as a witness for the justice system.
- This communication should also incorporate efficient recording and collation of data. Lack of transparency from the Home Office/government, particularly in relation to non-EU nationals who are potential victims and long-term outcomes for survivors, has contributed to the destitution and re-trafficking of too many individuals. Appropriate sharing of information will reduce instances of the detention of trafficking victims and maintain avenues of communication for survivors should they need support beyond the NRM.
- Survivors should be afforded a more safe and secure transition to independent living. Lord McColl's Bill would provide them with twelve months' discretionary leave and access to a range of support, however, this needs to result in viable options for survivors at the end of the year long period. This could involve a structured and mutually agreed-upon twelve-month tailored plan for individuals, which works towards preparing them for independent living.

## 9.4 Final thoughts

The UK's system for processing and supporting victims and survivors of modern slavery and human trafficking has gone through significant changes in a very short space of time. Those at the heart of it all have gone from being championed by a prime minister to being sidelined for more immediate concerns such as Brexit and COVID, before effectively being dismissed as collateral damage by an increasingly right-wing Conservative government bent on reducing immigration.

Time will tell whether an incoming Labour government will take up the mantle of this cause and reverse some of the more draconian immigration measures; they have certainly made noises to this effect. However, alongside this, it is crucial that they prioritise survivor support and review the current referral, identification and aftercare processes. Fundamentally, while a criminal justice model serves to reinforce the gravity of subjecting individuals to slavery, this approach cannot operate in silo if the UK is to successfully support survivors to recovery. The modern slavery legal framework requires a holistic, structural approach that incorporates the views and lived experiences of those it purports to serve.

# Index

[Note: numbers in **bold** indicate a table. Numbers in *italics* indicate a figure on the corresponding page.]

FSC
www.fsc.org
MIX
Papier | Fördert
gute Waldnutzung
FSC® C083411

Kolibri 360 GmbH
Ferdinand-Jühlke-Straße 7
99095 Erfurt, Deutschland
produktsicherheit@kolibri360.de